4°

Soviet and Chinese Influence in the Third World

RUBINSTEIN, Alvin Z., ed. **Soviet and Chinese influence in the Third World.** Praeger, 1975. 231p 74-11604. 17.50. ISBN 0-275-07640-8. C.I.P.

CHOICE   *OCT. '75*

Political Science

DK 274 :
R 89?

Originally presented at a conference in Philadelphia in 1973, the papers collected in this volume mark a refreshing departure from most Western writings on the subject. As Rubinstein observes, the tendency among Western scholars has been to study the issue only on the basis of Soviet or Chinese "inputs," assuming that Moscow and China could "bend weaker nations to their will," as was done by the colonial powers in the past. The approach here is to find out how and to what degree Peking and Moscow have been able to influence the behavior and policies of the Third World countries. Thus one may have to study not only the foreign policy but also the domestic politics of the Third World countries. The message of most of the essays — some of which deal with Soviet and Chinese influence in Africa or Latin America as a whole, while others represent case studies of such countries as India, Indonesia, and Egypt, or a movement like of the Palestinian guerrillas — is that the ability of the great powers to influence the behavior and policies of smaller nations is very limited. Scholars would do well to pay attention to the spirit of independence of the smaller nations and the realities of the present international system which often make it possible for them

edited by
Alvin Z. Rubinstein

The Praeger Special Studies program—utilizing the most modern and efficient book production techniques and a selective worldwide distribution network—makes available to the academic, government, and business communities significant, timely research in U.S. and international economic, social, and political development.

Soviet and Chinese Influence in the Third World

PRAEGER SPECIAL STUDIES IN INTERNATIONAL POLITICS AND GOVERNMENT

Praeger Publishers   New York   Washington   London

Library of Congress Cataloging in Publication Data

Rubinstein, Alvin Z
    Soviet and Chinese influence in the Third World.

    (Praeger special studies in international politics and
government)
    Includes index.
    1. Russia—Foreign relations—1953-   2. China—
Foreign relations—1949-   3. Underdeveloped areas—
Foreign relations. I. Title.
DK274.R8   327'.09172'4   74-11604
ISBN 0-275-09640-8

PRAEGER PUBLISHERS
111 Fourth Avenue, New York, N.Y. 10003, U.S.A.
5, Cromwell Place, London SW7 2JL, England

Published in the United States of America in 1975
by Praeger Publishers, Inc.

The shift of the Soviet Union in 1954-55 from a continental-based strategy to a global one made the USSR a major factor in the regional and international politics of the Third World. Under the expansionist-minded Nikita S. Khrushchev, the Soviet leadership moved with skill and verve to frustrate the U.S. strategy of military and political encirclement and to project Soviet influence into the newly independent Afro-Asian nations. It perceived historically unprecedented opportunities for penetrating these new nations, for exploiting residual regional animosities, and for offering aid and developmental alterna- tives to Third World countries. Stinting neither on economic assistance nor on weaponry, the Soviet Union embarked on an intensive, highly publicized, often imaginative courtship.

The People's Republic of China formally joined the international competition for influence among the Third World countries at the Bandung Conference of Afro-Asian nations in April 1955. For a time the Western powers feared that an orchestrated Sino-Soviet offensive would subvert, even communize, the young, vulnerable, impressionable new nations. However, by the early 1960s it was clear that the colossuses of communism were rivals, not allies; that each was often more con- cerned with parrying the moves of the other than with undermining the Western position. While periodic internal upheavals and limited resources kept Chinese efforts at influence-building minimal, they have not been without some effect, though often more to the detriment of the USSR than of the West.

As we look at Soviet and Chinese prospects in the Third World, we need to reassess their activities and achievements in order to establish what influence they have actually exercised as a consequence of their efforts. Contemporary Western scholarship has produced useful studies on Soviet and Chinese policies toward Asian, African, Middle Eastern, and Latin American countries. It has informed us of the diplo- matic, military, economic, and cultural efforts of Moscow and Peking; but generally speaking these studies have not illumined the extent to which the Communist powers have in fact succeeded in influencing the behavior of key Third World countries. We know the input of the Communist powers, but we are unable to agree on the consequent effects because of the absence of any accepted method or criteria to evaluate influence.

These essays have a twofold purpose: first, to provide up-to- date analyses of Soviet and Chinese influence in strategically important Third World countries and regions; and second, insofar as is possible, to base such analyses on explicitly formulated criteria of influence and on empirical data that are relevant for the evaluation of influence relationships. By seeking to operationalize the notion of influence, they hope to improve the way that foreign policy is studied.

This book is an outgrowth of a Conference on Soviet and Chinese Influence in the Third World that was held in Philadelphia on October 25 and 26, 1973, under the aegis of the University of Pennsylvania's Anspach Institute for Diplomacy and Foreign Affairs. It is a pleasure to acknowledge the support of the Director of the Anspach Institute, Professor Henry Wells, and the assistance of his secretary, Mrs. Yola Green, who helped greatly with the arrangements; the Jewish Community Relations Council of Philadelphia which made possible the participation of Professor Moshe Ma'oz of the Hebrew University; and the Barra Foundation and the National Science Foundation which enabled me, at an earlier stage, to explore the phenomenon of influence as a concept in foreign policy analysis. Thanks also to Dr. Herta Schopf, who compiled the index. Finally, I should like to express my appreciation to the authors and the discussants for their willingness to grapple with a knotty problem in a critical and constructive spirit.

Alvin Z. Rubinstein

CONTENTS

Soviet and Chinese Influence in the Third World

ASSESSING INFLUENCE
AS A PROBLEM IN
FOREIGN POLICY ANALYSIS
Alvin Z. Rubinstein

The Third World has become a major arena for great power rivalry. Its importance is due as much to the emergence of a multipolar international system as to the growing independence and self-assertiveness of key Third World countries. It is in the Third World that the United States, the Soviet Union, and the People's Republic of China wage their multifaceted struggle through proxies, with minimal risk of direct military confrontation.

In recent years the anxieties of the three superpowers have shown signs of easing, though nuclear and missile arsenals continue to burgeon despite the agreements on strategic weapons signed by the United States and the USSR at the Moscow Summit Conference of May 1972. The evident desire of each superpower to promote a limited detente with at least one of its rivals is the result of a timely convergence of factors: the pressure of domestic problems that could no longer be ignored, the mounting costs of introducing new weapons systems, Peking's dramatic decision to respond positively to U. S. overtures for improved relations, the growing complexity of maintaining alliance cohesion, the seeming irreversibility of the Sino-Soviet schism, and the international impact of rising powers such as Japan and the two Germanies on the strategic outlook of the superpowers.

Thus far in the 1970s the superpowers seem driven less by fear or adventurism and more by longer term considerations and sober appraisals of potential gains and losses than they were in the 1950s and most of the 1960s. A vintage year for calculated superpower behavior was 1972: President Nixon visited Peking in February and Moscow in May; the Soviet-West German Treaty of Friendship and Cooperation was ratified by Bonn in May; both Moscow and Peking acted with remarkable restraint in the face of Washington's expanded interdiction of North Vietnam in response to Hanoi's massive invasion of South Vietnam in the spring and summer; Moscow, reluctant to jeopardize its improved relations with the United States and Western Europe and not wanting another round of Arab-Israeli fighting, refused

repeated Egyptian requests for a major increase in offensive weaponry
and accepted the sharply diminished stature and presence that were
the immediate results of President Sadat's ouster of most Soviet military
personnel in July 1972. Though these encouraging developments are
not yet irreversible trends, they hopefully presage an era of pragmatic
diplomatic interaction among the superpowers.

Nonetheless, the Third World remains the tinderbox that could
consume superpower hopes for detente: it is there that the parameters
of superpower vested interests and ambitions are not sharply delineated,
and it is there that opportunities for dramatic political victories can
arise with startling suddenness. Still, in the United States one
increasingly hears the case made that the Third World countries, with
few exceptions, are of no importance, that they constitute a permanent
drain on scarce resources, and that their friendship would not improve
the American position in the strategic relationship with the Soviet
Union — and since this is the crucial relationship of the next decade or
two, why bother with the Third World at all. However, the United States'
flagging interest there in influence-building, expressed in the Nixon
Doctrine, should be adjudged temporary — a classic case of imperial
fatigue not anemia, a pruning of commitments not an uprooting of
globalist concerns.

Soviet and Chinese Penetration of the Third World

There is every reason to assume that the Soviet Union and
Communist China will, in contrast to the United States, pursue a
"forward strategy" in the Third World. The Soviets and Chinese, who
are bitter rivals there, are expanding commitments, courting prospective
clients, and competing for local and regional advantages. Soviet involvement in the Third World has been the most notable new feature of
Soviet international behavior since Stalin's death in 1953; more than
any single phenomenon it denotes Moscow's shift from a continental-
based strategy to a global one. During the 1954-74 period the Soviet
bloc expended upwards of 15 billion dollars in military and economic
assistance to key Third World countries. In the early 1960s Peking
embarked on what appeared to be a major effort to challenge Soviet
inroads, but it withdrew into almost total isolation during the hectic
period of the Cultural Revolution (1966-69) as domestic turmoil
eclipsed influence-building abroad. However, since 1970 China seems
determined to establish a selective presence for itself in the years
ahead in key areas, partly as an extension of its conflict with the
Soviet Union, partly to weaken the position of India in South Asia, and
partly to mobilize radical movements in support of its international
diplomacy.

What is incontrovertible is that Soviet and Chinese efforts in the
Third World are serious, that they are expanding, and that they are

important in the calculations of Western and non-Western governments. What remains very much a subject of considerable disagreement is the question, "What have these Soviet and Chinese efforts accomplished in promoting the aims of Soviet and Chinese foreign policy?" In other words, to what extent have the Soviet Union and the People's Republic of China been able to translate their largesse into actual political influence?

We have many useful studies on the different aspects of the Soviet courtship, and to a much lesser extent the Chinese courtship, of the Third World: diplomatic activities,[1] economic aid,[2] military assistance,[3] trade,[4] and cultural relations[5] have been described and analyzed; a number of case studies treat Soviet and Chinese policies toward specific developing countries or regions;[6] several studies analyze the Soviet relationship with developing countries within international organizations[7] and the connections between local Communist parties and Soviet foreign policy;[8] and some overviews of Soviet policy toward the Third World as a whole have linked Soviet global and regional concerns.[9] In addition, there is a voluminous periodical literature on these topics.[10]

These works provide us with a fund of indispensable information about what the USSR or China have done; but generally speaking they do not develop the concrete ways or instances in which the efforts of these Communist powers have enabled them to influence the actual behavior of a target country. We know their input, but we lack any accepted method of establishing output. Similarly, these studies frequently postulate Soviet and Chinese foreign policy aims and motivations, none of which can be proven or verified. It may well be, as Samuel Johnson suggested, that "intentions must be gathered from acts." However, if we are to raise the level of the art of studying Soviet and Chinese foreign policy and enhance the value of scholarly studies to potential consumers in government, we need to know more than the acts and the presumed intentions which gave rise to them; we need to know the actual effects of these acts upon the intended target. Instead of highly individualistic judgments about Soviet aims, for example, we need systematic analysis and accepted criteria for determining what the Soviet Union is accomplishing as a consequence of its diplomatic, economic, military, and cultural input.

The Quest for Influence

Foreign policy analysts in any great power face the problem of assessing the relative success of their country's expenditures of aid and diplomatic support in promoting the concrete goals formulated by their political leaders. A great power expending enormous sums does so in the expectation of receiving tangible advantages on matters of concern to it. However, judging by the American experience, neither money (aid) nor its deprivation necessarily brings influence or benefits when these are most desired. This has been dramatically evident on numerous occasions in the searing American involvement in Vietnam: for example, not even with its extensive support over a 10-year period was the U.S. government able to pressure South Vietnam's President Thieu to allow a token opposition candidate in the rigged presidential election of 1971. And one of the insights to be gleaned from "The Pentagon Papers" was the inability of the United States to exercise influence on Saigon by withholding aid; there was "an almost universal consensus among American officials that the Vietnamese were too sensitive for such pressures to work."[11] During the crisis in East Pakistan in the spring of 1971, when the flight to India of more than 8 million refugees and the slaughter of thousands of East Pakistanis at the hands of the repressive West Pakistani military were irrefutable facts, the Nixon Administration refused to condemn these developments publicly and continued to provide the Pakistan government with economic aid, futilely hoping that it would give the United States "leverage in persuading President Yahya Khan to seek a political accommodation in East Pakistan," and that it would keep Pakistan from becoming more dependent on Communist China for aid.[12] Secretary of State William P. Rogers pointed up the problem in a news conference on December 23, 1969, when he observed: "It is interesting to me that we have had a study of how many times we have been able to influence the policy of another government by withholding military aid, and we find that it has not been successful in any instance." It is reasonable to assume that Moscow and Peking encountered comparable frustrations in their attempts to extract influence from aid given to Third World countries.[13]

The relationship between country A and country B, though important for both, generally involves more uncertainties and dilemmas for A, whose interests are more extensive. As donor, A commits resources to B in expectation of some benefits —immediate or future —whose minimum is known only to A; hence the real reason (or reasons) for its behavior may not be discernible to B or to any rival of A (herein designated as C), whose analyses must necessarily rest on permutations of rational alternatives and not on the also important vagaries of internal politics and personalities. A's willingness to subsidize B derives from the calculations of A, that is, of the faction dominating the formulation of policy toward B, that it is obtaining ample recompense, defined variously in terms of advantages furthering A's strategic, diplomatic, political, economic, or cultural aims. The continuation of support, irrespective of any change in A's political leadership, suggests that the individual or group exercising control will find it is easier to sustain aid than to curtail or abandon it. A rule of thumb for understanding the behavior of great powers in the Third World is that, having once commenced an aid program, it is politically easier to continue giving than to stop giving. Moscow has found this out in its relations with Egypt and Cuba; the United States, with Vietnam.

A's policy toward B may be shaped by a combination of bureaucratic infighting and decisions relevant more to its internal governmental
politics than to any ideological compulsion to advance doctrine or
imperial ambitions.[14] The bureaucratic-politics model persuasively
cautions against interpreting A's behavior as reflecting "a single
coherent, consistent set of calculations about national security
interests";[15] or overlooking the domestic political forces involved in
A's behavior; or minimizing the ad hoc, transient considerations
shaping B's actions. Disagreements within A's decision-making
structure over whether to provide (more) aid to B are rarely resolved on
a cost-effectiveness basis. Rather, aid is continued as a consequence
of internal domestic political considerations or the lobbying effectiveness of a bureaucratic power group having a vested interest in the
particular aid program. For example, the Defense Department urged
Congress to continue the program of training foreign military officers
in the United States, even though it lacked the empirical data to sustain
the argument that officers trained in the United States were likely to
be promoted more rapidly than their fellow officers who had been
trained in Communist countries. The importance of bureaucratic politics,
the paucity of relevant supportive data, the absence of unambiguous
success criteria, and the multifaceted character of justifications for
continuing aid all complicate the task of making decisions concerning
support for Third World countries.

The problem of assessing influence would be important even if
the only parties involved were A and B. However, the introduction of a
third party, that is, another great power, adds a significant new
dimension. The problem of C's assessment of the relationship between
A and B and the extent of its reciprocity lies at the heart of foreign
policy analysis. Whether we are discussing Washington's assessment
of Soviet-Egyptian relations, Moscow's assessment of U.S.-Israeli
relations, or Cairo's assessment of U.S.-Israeli relations, the policy
of C toward A and B derives in part from C's perception of the A — B
relationship. The American involvement in Vietnam was, among other
things, an outgrowth of Washington's lack of understanding in the early
1960s of the nature of the Sino-Soviet dispute and Hanoi's relationship
with Moscow and Peking. Without in any way underestimating the
degree to which the American involvement in Vietnam was bureaucrat-
ically generated,[16] I would argue that the massive U.S. involvement
emerged from the Bay of Pigs fiasco of April 1961, when the White
House overreacted from excessive fear of the threat of Castro-type
revolutions sweeping Latin America and of the extent to which
Khrushchev's speech of January 6, 1961, on "wars of national-
liberation" signalled the start of a major Soviet effort to undermine
pro-Western governments in the Third World by Communist-inspired
revolutions. In seeking to repair his image domestically and to convince Soviet leaders that he could not be bullied, President Kennedy
found reinforcement for his policy in the assumption, widely accepted

in Washington circles, of a monolithic international communism, and this led him to see Saigon as being as vital to the United States as Berlin.

A few general propositions regarding C's range of behavior may be useful:

1. C's perception of the extent to which A exercises significant influence in B shapes its attitude toward A and B.

2. If key decision-makers in C are led to believe that A does not exercise significant influence in B, they will be more likely to resist the recommendations of those bureaucracies urging a vigorous response to A, and they will adopt a relatively aloof position regarding the A — B relationship.

3. In order to enhance their importance to C's political leadership, vested bureaucratic interests in C will continually seek to gain acceptance for their assessments of the A — B relationship.

4. In crisis situations, C's relations with A will not move toward confrontation or necessarily deteriorate as long as C does not attribute B's crisis-producing behavior to A.

5. In situations in which A cannot directly project its power over B, C's response to A's alleged exercise of influence may be a product more of C's domestic politics than of A's actual leverage.

Although we appear to be entering a period of superpower stalemate and restraint, there exists a generally implicit acceptance by the USSR and China (especially the former) of the importance of incrementalism, that is to say, the quest for local advantages in areas not directly threatening vital superpower security interests on the assumption that such advantages can eventually contribute to the erosion of the adversary's core area and established relationships. Thus, the view is widely held in influential Western circles that Moscow's expanded presence in the Middle East and the Mediterranean, coupled with the disruptive effects of detente, has sowed the seeds of an incipient nonalignment among the southern members of NATO as it had earlier among the non-Western members of CENTO — Turkey, Iran, and Pakistan.

The Nixon Administration's emphasis on superpower relationships and strategic weaponry, its disdain for the United Nations and multilateral diplomacy, its readiness to tolerate sharp congressional cuts in foreign aid appropriations without too much fuss, and its oft-stated intention to reduce direct American involvement in regional disputes, strengthen the view that it is far less anxious over most Soviet and Chinese activities in the Third World than preceding administrations. This policy of "benign neglect" does not pretend that the Soviet Union's activities in the Third World are of no concern to the United States; or that Moscow and Peking are uninterested in expanding their influence there; or, indeed, that they have not developed oases of influence in a few areas. It would be reversed quickly in the event of a threatening major Soviet or Chinese tactical advance. But by what policy criteria is a major advance measured? How do we decide that an advance is really an advance, and not just a fleeting movement "full of sound and fury, signifying nothing"? The problem of developing a more accurate and empirically sound basis for assessing Soviet and Chinese influence in the Third World is crucial for sound foreign policy analysis.

Conceptualizing Influence

Any attempt to refine the process by which we assess Soviet and Chinese influence in Third World countries must deal with three questions:

1. What are the instances in which A exercised influence over B? In other words, under which circumstances and on which specific issues have Moscow and Peking been able to translate largesse into influence?
2. Exactly what changes in the actual foreign policy or domestic behavior of the target country were produced by these examples of influence?
3. What assumptions, criteria, and data were salient for the analyst in answering the above two questions?

Crucial to any analysis of foreign policy, whether it be interpretation of past actions or speculation about future ones, are the assumptions of the analyst. However, these are rarely specified; they remain implicit in a line of analysis or advocacy. To make them explicit would be to expose to scrutiny and inevitable criticism not merely the assessment itself, but the salience of the data, the suitability of the methods, the rigor of the logic, and the sensitivity of the analyst to the intangibles of personality, culture, and values. This becomes particularly important when it is realized that assumptions in the realm of politics are not easily tested, that they depend upon a priori beliefs and preferences, and that they are peculiarly resistant to revision precisely for these reasons. In foreign policy analysis it is indisputably evident that facts do not speak for themselves. At best, they are organized and acted upon by well-intentioned men who seek, not unreasonably, to rely on evidence and analyses that conform to and buttress their own predilections. At worst, they are manipulated to help justify a line of policy already adopted. Underlying the choice, organization, and interpretation of facts are the analyst's assumptions. Since their accuracy is essential for sound policy evaluations, there is a continual need to ensure that they rest on perceptions of reality that are as undistorted as possible, on data which shed light on the question they are intended to illumine, on comparisons and analogies which are pertinent, and on analyses which avoid reading into what we see or discover, that which we prefer and expect. There is clearly no Rosetta stone for deciphering influence, but identifying the central assumptions underlying our approach to the problem is a necessary first step.

Every nation engages in influence -building — the process whereby a ruling elite seeks to strengthen its domestic power base and advance national aims — but there are various types of political systems and internation relationships, and these must be distinguished in discussing the process and manifestation of influence. In this study we are dealing with one type of influence relationship: that between a great power — specifically, the Soviet Union or Communist China (it could as well be the United States) — and a nonaligned, developing, non -European country. * Though this bilateral relationship is between two nations of unequal power, the exercise of influence is nonetheless complex and not at all a mere reflection of the differential in motivations and in power base, defined in economic, military, or technological terms. Indeed, in the present international system power has less obvious utility in nonwar situations than at any previous period of modern history.

A number of assumptions underlie the concept of influence as used in this study. First, to be useful operationally, the concept of influence should be used in as limited and specific a sense as possible, in the context of normal diplomatic transactions. We will strive to avoid using vague statements, such as "Soviet influence in Iraq is growing, " because they are extremely difficult to treat empirically or even to use analytically Too restrictive a definition, however, cannot always be maintained because the phenomenon we are studying is itself at one and the same time specific and multifaceted, narrowly descriptive and broadly suggestive, and a process and a product. This confusion is not avoided by using another term instead.[+]

––––––––––––––––––

*The other types of relationships in which there are attempts to exercise influence are: (1) the relationship between two countries within an alliance system; (2) the relationship between two countries each of which is the member of a different alliance system; (3) the relationship between two nonaligned countries; and (4) the relationship between one country or group of countries interacting with another country or group of countries within the framework of international organizations. Each of the typologies has its own distinctive features and operational characteristics.

[+] For example, Richard W. Cottam, Competitive Interference and Twentieth Century Diplomacy (Pittsburgh: University of Pittsburgh Press, 1967). Cottam uses the term "interference, " which he defines, in terms of a continuum running from slight to intense, as any "act by

Second, because of the multidimensionality of the concept, influence may more readily be inferred or identified than measured with any precision.

Third, the number of instances of influence that can be identified are few because the number of behavioral changes in B that can be attributed to A is limited.

Fourth, if A's influence is present to a significant degree, it will be evident in the domestic political system of B, namely, in B's attitudes, domestic behavior, and institutions. As in the case of the human organism, the political system will reveal foreign influences most readily at key terminals in the system.

Fifth, an intimate knowledge of B's domestic politics is crucial for a study of the foreign policy relationship between A and B because the influence relationship will be manifested concretely in the context of certain "issue areas" in B.[17] Thus the student of Soviet-Indian relations needs to know as much about Indian domestic politics as he does about Soviet foreign policy. A detailed knowledge of Soviet domestic politics would be essential if we were trying to establish the roots of A's policy toward B, and it might provide us with some way of establishing B's influence on A, but it is of little help in assessing A's influence in B.

Sixth, while all influence of one country in another compromises the other's sovereignty to some extent, and sometimes strengthens and sometimes weakens the power of the ruling group in the influenced country, there are limits beyond which foreign influence cannot push any country or its leaders. B's ruling group will not make concessions to A that might undermine its domestic political power, unless A is in a position to apply military power against B.

Seventh, the donor is affected by its courtship of the donee. There is not just feedback from B to A, but from C, D, E, F, as well, that will be affected by the A — B relationship.

Eighth, the relevant data for evaluating influence fall into five broad categories: (1) measures of perceptual and attitudinal change, (2) measures of direct interaction, that is, quantifiable and aggregate data, (3) measures of attributed influence, (4) case studies, and (5) idiosyncratic factors (these categories of data are discussed below).

Ninth, a universally applicable system for assessing influence is beyond reach, given the wide variations existing among nation-states. The best that can be expected is a working model that will have applicability to similar types of societies within a particular geographic and cultural area.

---

the government or citizen of one state designed to influence the internal developments of that state whether they be political, economic, or social" (p. 36). He uses the term "leverage" to describe "those means not involving direct action by which one government can exercise some influence over the policies of another government at any particular time" (p. 82).

Operational Criteria

Our aim in defining and identifying influence is understanding and explanation, not prediction: we want to know when influence clearly exists, how it can be assessed, even measured in relative terms, and what its principal indicators are. As a working definition, we may use the following: influence is manifested when A affects through non-military means, directly or indirectly, the behavior of B so that it redounds to the policy advantage of A. Definition immediately raises a semantic problem because the phenomenon of influence is both a process and a product. As defined here, influence is a process; on the other hand, what is in fact observed and assessed is the net result or outcome of influence, that is, the product. No wording can completely free us of this problem. However, our use of either of the two meanings should be sufficiently precise to make our intent clear throughout.

A country seeks to exercise influence in order to obtain specific short term advantages, though very often the motives and consequences of a successful influence attempt may have most significance for the influencer as part of his long-term objectives. Like breathing, influence becomes especially noticeable when pressure is applied or concern heightens. Influence may be considered to have a number of characteristics.

1. It is a relational concept involving "the transferal of a pattern (of preferences) from a source (the controlling actor) to a destination (the responding actor or system), in such a way that the outcome pattern corresponds to the original preference pattern."[18]

2. It is issue-specific and situation-specific: the duration of influence is restricted to the life of the issue or the situation within which it transpired, and when these change so does the influence relationship.

3. It tends to be an asymmetrical, mutual interaction process: there is no fixed pattern of achievement costs.

4. It is a short-lived phenomenon.

A number of corollaries are important, a few of which may be mentioned by way of illustration: the influence exercised is not without cost to A; it is multidimensional, manifesting itself in different institutional settings and with different magnitudes and degrees; it requires continual reinforcement, since the ambience essential to its crystallization is everchanging; finally, variations in influence patterns will occur depending on the salience of issues to A.

Since in the international system of the 1970s influence can no longer be automatically assumed to coincide with the usual measures of differentials in power, we are confronted with the major problem of determining when, in fact, influence has been exercised. Earlier, we posed the question, "What are the instances in which A exercised influence over B? In other words, under which circumstances and on which specific issues have Moscow and Peking been able to translate support into influence?" How do we as analysts know that A has actually exercised influence over B? What criteria are helpful in identifying alleged instances of influence? To this may be added, what were the factors bringing about changes in the relative influence exercised by A on particular issues at particular times?

A number of suggestions for ascertaining influence are tentatively offered for examination in the essays on Soviet and Chinese policy that follow. First, the most obvious but empirically least satisfying procedure for determining whether A exercises influence in B is to poll specialists and on-the-scene observers. While the Delphic method is the most commonly used, its shortcomings are serious: a reliance on impressionism, an often exaggerated attention to the status and power of the individual analyst to the detriment of critical examination of the analysis itself, and a neglect of the assumptions and criteria underlying the analysis.[19] In a situation where one analyst's assessment is considered as valid as another's (comparable experience and knowledge being assumed for both), the Delphic approach feeds inter-bureaucratic rivalry, diminishes the status of reports from the field, and puts a premium on personal persuasion and access rather than on cogent political analysis.

Second, we can try to identify and classify the concrete instances in which B modifies its position or behavior in a manner congenial to A. From the degree, frequency, and implications of such modifications, inferences can be made concerning A's influence. What often seems to be influence turns out instead to be joint interests of the two parties; there are in practice only a few issues of generally equal importance to A and to B on which B adjusts its preference to A's. In such a situation A exercises significant influence; its influence is of lesser significance when B adapts to A's preferences on issues that are of low salience to B. But through the extension of support, A may enable B to do what both he and B want, but which B would not do otherwise. If the outcome which B then affects turns out poorly, can the "unanticipated reaction" be attributable to A's behavior or to B's? For example, Egypt's defeat in June 1967 derived from its closing the Strait of Tiran and massing troops on Israel's border — actions which might not have been taken without tacit Soviet encouragement for Nasser's "brinksmanship." In this situation, the answer is unknowable.

The problem of distinguishing between important and less important issues can be knotty. One possible approach to determining the salience of issues to B is to examine the domestic dissonance within B's political system arising from the responses that are made to A's presumed preferences or from concessions that are widely regarded as favoring A. In a relatively open society like India, identification of

11

dissonance is not difficult: the debates in Parliament, the commentaries in the press, and the access to officials and interested parties in the private sector provide varied information adequate for obtaining a fix on influence and assessing A's impact on B. In an authoritarian and relatively closed society, expressions of dissonance would be more difficult to locate, but not impossible, especially for those who know B's political system well. The issues salient to A will be even more difficult to pinpoint, but from the domestic debate in B on relations with A, B's interaction with A, a knowledge of A's broader objectives in the region, and commentaries in A, we may glean something of A's preferences. But there is no gainsaying the paucity of authoritative data on this facet of the problem. Another promising method of identify-ing influence is the close examination (possibly even content analysis) of joint communiques, which are usually issued at the conclusion of high-level meetings between leaders of A and B. These communiques can illumine A's influence, B's concessions, and the difficulties existing between them.

Third, a sharp improvement in A's ability to carry out transactions in B, especially relative to C (A's rival) will suggest significant incre-ments in influence for A.

Fourth, any sharp and sustained increase in the quantity, quality, and variety of resources committed by A to B suggests that B either is, or is on the threshold of, acceding to some of A's important prefer-ences. The concessions made by B to A need not be in the same areas into which A's expanded input is channeled; a trade-off arrangement is more likely.

Fifth, a major change in A's security commitment to B strongly suggests an increase in influence. However, though A's commitment to come to the assistance of B in certain unspecified situations is generally more significant for B than A — our assumption being that neither the Soviet Union nor Communist China has a vital security interest in any nonaligned, non-Communist, Third World country — the final determination of who is influencer and who is influencee must await examination of the other criteria and of the overall context within which the commitment was made.

Sixth, influence may in theory also be inferred from a non-decision, which is a type of outcome, albeit one that is virtually impossible to study empirically given the political actors we have set out to evaluate. According to Peter Bachrach and Morton S. Baratz, decision-makers may be limited to "relatively noncontroversial matters" by virtue of opposition within the decision-making hierarchy itself.[20] They note: "To measure relative influence solely in terms of the ability to initiate and veto proposals is to ignore the possible exercise of influence or power in limiting the scope of initiation."[21] Essentially, a nondecision is a decision to prevent or thwart an issue from being decided upon either affirmatively or negatively. And, a decision entails, among other things, implementation — again, either positively or negatively. Thus, for example, applying their concept of nondecision to an issue relevant to our study, we see that although Nasser agreed during the post-1967 period with the Soviets and some reform-minded members of his government who urged drastic reform of the Arab Socialist Union (A. S. U.) (Egypt's only legal mass political organization) along activist and elitist lines comparable to the Soviet Communist Party, and although Nasser even announced these reforms to the Egyptian public in March 1968, nothing was done: Nasser and the dominant A.S.U. oligarchs buried in committee and in camera the authorization that would have implemented the reforms in meaningful fashion. Nondecisions are difficult to study because they presuppose considerable data on the process of conflict resolution within the decisional units, data that are not available for the countries studied here.

Finally, influence can be viewed within a strategic context, and not merely in terms of the tangible, short-term interactions discernible within the A — B relationship itself. The success or failure of A's influence-building may be evaluated in terms of consequences that are observable only in the broader context of A's desire to have B opt for policy outcomes which B prefers, but which are made possible only by A, which believes they will redound to its long-term advantage: in other words, A is influencing B to do what B would prefer to do, but could not do without A's resources. Influence gauged in terms of the broader consequences for the A — B relationship of A's rendering or not rendering support is clearly open to the criticism of being imprecise, highly judgmental, and liable to complicate rather than clarify our task. Yet it does fill an explanatory function that adds a dimension, however imperfect, to our analysis.

A donor providing aid may have a number of objectives in mind: the desire for immediate return may be important but not crucial. The Soviet Union has given enormous aid to Egypt since the June 1967 Arab-Israeli war. In the short run it acquired handsome strategic dividends: naval facilities at Alexandria, Mersa Matruh, and Port Said; the use of air fields for reconnoitering the U.S. Sixth Fleet; and an expanded presence in Egyptian life. These capital gains were sharply reduced after July 17, 1972, when President Sadat ousted most of the Soviet military personnel in Egypt. One might be tempted to argue that the Soviet Union made a poor investment. If the argument relates primarily to the immediate payoff from the aid, the case is quite convincing. But this would tend to overlook, or at least minimize, what may well have been the most important Soviet objective in promptly providing Egypt with generous assistance, military and economic: to keep Egypt from negotiating a settlement of the Arab-Israeli conflict lest this eliminate from the Middle East a festering problem which has helped the Soviet Union intrude itself into the politics of the region. Having used arms aid to foster Egypt's military dependence on the USSR, Moscow has to maintain its provisioning

13

function: the alternative is a sharply diminished role in Middle East politics. It has gotten so far into the arms business that one needs to raise a serious question about who is influencing whom.

In addition to identifying influence, we wish also to improve our ability to single out those conditions or developments which facilitate or foreshadow A's influence on B. Ideally we should strive to establish the causal links making for influence in the A — B relationship. To provide some conceptual guidelines for project participants and to focus our collective efforts on the principal types of data that hold promise for our enterprise, a number of hypotheses are offered. Since the dimensions of each influence relationship will vary from country to country, each contributor is free to use or reject hypotheses, or to introduce additional ones which he regards as germane. A few hypotheses have been eclectically selected to show some of the possibilities that exist for identifying the factors conducive to the exercise of influence. They are the outgrowth of experimental research and experience, and aim at encouraging new mixes of existing and traditionally used data, which, as currently used, seem to shed little light on actual influence relationships. These hypotheses are:

1. The more B utilizes A's assistance, the more A is apt to exercise influence.
    Rationale: Developing countries seldom utilize as much as 50 percent of the economic credits made available by the USSR. This suggests dissatisfaction, a disinclination to become too dependent on Soviet equipment, and a preference for Western technology. The effect is to limit Moscow's ability to use economic aid as a lever for political influence.
2. The more political the character of the aid, the less likely A is to be able to exercise political influence.
    Rationale: Showcase projects make headlines, but little else. There is evidence that hotels, sports stadiums, highways, and so forth, once built, do little to facilitate a more permanent Soviet presence.
3. The political uses of economic aid diminish over time.
    Rationale: The initial purpose of economic aid was to enable A to establish a presence in B, after which influence presumably could be developed. Increasingly, however, economic aid seems more the price the great power has to pay in order to counter a rival's presence in B, than an instrument for acquiring political influence.
4. The volume and overall percentage of B's foreign trade with A is less indicative of the character of an influence relationship than the terms of trade.
    Rationale: Trade flows do not illumine the political nature of a relationship. B may trade increasingly with A for a variety of reasons, none of which is apt to result in A exercising greater

influence. Indeed, the obverse may result, because of B's resentment at dependence unleavened by advantageous conces-sions.

5. The more trade between A and B expands in commodities which B produces as a result of A's assistance, the more likely A is to exercise influence.

   Rationale: Many developing countries, which have plants built by the Soviets in the public sector, find that Moscow is unwilling to accept the manufactures that are produced in them at economi-cally feasible prices. As a result, serious frictions develop. The experience of India is notable in this respect. "Red elephants" abound in the Third World to the detriment of Soviet prestige.

6. The treatment in B's media of visits by A's officials and missions reveals more about the A — B influence relationship than does the number of visits exchanged or the asymmetrical nature of the exchanges.

   Rationale: Communications flow theory notwithstanding, interac-tions assessed as aggregates tend to miss much of the ebb and flow that characterizes most influence relationships. Interactions must be scrutinized at the points and moments of actual contact.

The Data Problem

The problem of handling the data is awesome. The researcher naturally uses the data that are easily available or most abundant. These data, however, may not be pertinent to an assessment of influ-ence in the form in which they are usually compiled. For example, foreign aid and trade statistics are easy to come by, but they do not tell us much about influence. Data that would shed more light on the questions here under consideration are less available. Instead of analyzing aggregate data on aid and trade, we need to know into which ministries and sectors of the economy the aid is channeled, how it affects not the economy but the political position of the ruling elite, and how it facilitates A's ability to cultivate close personal connec-tions with the bureaucracies in B which are benefitting the most from A's aid: we need to trace the aid into the political system and see its relevance for B's domestic political conflicts and outcomes. This is assuredly a major undertaking. However, it must be begun if we are to advance the art of foreign policy analysis.

The available corpus of data may be organized into five cate-gories:[22] (1) measures of perceptual and attitudinal change, (2) meas-ures of direct interaction, (3) measures of attributed influence, (4) case studies, and (5) impressionistic and idiosyncratic commentary. Under-standably, the individual researcher cannot be expected to investigate with equal thoroughness all these categories, or even to use all of them and their subcategories. However, in trying to pinpoint the most relevant kinds of data to be used for influence studies, each contributor has been asked to identify the data which are most important for his analysis.

A few words on the basic components of each category may be useful. First, measures of perceptual and attitudinal change involve analysis (including content analysis) of joint communiques, editorials in key newspapers and journals, official speeches and statements, public opinion surveys, and radio broadcasts. Our basic assumptions in using these data are that significant changes of attitude (as expressed in one or more of the above subcategories) have policy relevance for the relationship between A and B, and that, used wisely, they can provide insights into the strengths and difficulties inhering in the rela-tionship. These measures are especially useful in studying authoritarian and relatively closed societies. The least useful for our purpose are public opinion polls, which measure A's prestige, not its influence; they tell us about the general image of A held by representative but unauthoritative groups in B who are ordinarily not in a position to know much about the A — B relationship. The most valuable measures are analyses over time of joint communiques and editorials in government-controlled newspapers.

Second, measures of direct interaction bring into play the entire range of quantitative and aggregate statistics, such as trade, aid, exchange of missions, and UN voting patterns. Heightened interaction is generally assumed to characterize an influence relationship, though the assumption is by no means uncontroverted. What can be counted does not always count. The salience of the data needs to be demon-strated. There is good reason to believe that the quality (the kinds of goods and services) of trade may be more useful in assessing influence than the quantity of trade flows. UN voting statistics remind one of what Prince Philip once said about statistics in general: "Statistics are like bikinis — what they reveal is interesting, but what they do not reveal is vital. " On most of the issues that come before the UN General Assembly, the statistics do not tell us, for example, whether India voted with the Soviet Union because of Soviet pressure, because it independently preferred the same outcome as the USSR, because it wanted to be on the winning side on a popular issue, or whether it was perhaps the Soviet Union which voted for the resolution out of a desire to align itself with India (and other nonaligned countries), and not the other way around. Furthermore, voting studies rarely seek to understand the political dynamics attending the alteration of the antecedent reso-lutions on which, after much bargaining, the final resolution is based. Economic aid, too, is no sure indication of influence. Looking at the United Nations, one observer concludes that most donor nations are indifferent in their allocation of foreign aid to "the roll-call voting behavior of developing nations [because] the types of foreign policy positions and behavior represented by UN roll calls may be largely irrelevant to the central concerns of decision-making elites dealing with foreign aid allocations. "[23] In the bilateral realm, we need to know where the aid goes, who benefits, and how A's officials try to benefit. We need to differentiate between aid that facilitates influence and aid that does not. To paraphrase George Orwell, "Some data are more equal than others."

Third, measures of attributed influence involve sampling the specialists. They rest on the assumption that the leading specialists will know the answer and that consensus on their part will mean an authoritative analysis. This procedure may be useful as a control on the analysis of an independent researcher, but it cannot be used as a substitute for the systematic assessment that underlies our efforts here; it merely begs the questions raised earlier. For no matter what the specialists say A's influence is in a particular country, the problem remains of having them identify and explain the assumptions, data, and criteria which determined their analyses.

Fourth, case studies offer an opportunity to study the extent to which influence is exercised on significant specific issues. By examining the preferred outcomes of A and B and the factors shaping the final outcome, we can dissect an influence relationship, the influence being inferred from the consequences of the final outcome. A series of case studies on different sectors of B's political system would help narrow the areas within which A's influence seems to count in B. For example, a research paper done at the University of Pennsylvania on the subject of Soviet economic aid to India during the 1955-68 period, the economic sectors into which it was channeled, and the relationship between its geographic distribution and the regional strength of the Communist Party of India concluded that economic aid is an unreliable indicator of influence.[24]

Fifth, impressionistic and idiosyncratic material should not be overlooked or underestimated out of a misplaced insistence upon so-called hard data. Numbers are no substitute for experience. Because of his immediate contact with events, a well-informed observer on the scene may know a great deal about the real nature of the constraints on A's ability to exercise influence. He may be in the best position to answer such important, suggestive questions as: What is the day-to-day relationship of Soviet officials with their counterparts in B's ministries? What is the relationship between the Soviet Ambassador and B's top leaders? What is the quality of private conversations and contacts between personnel of A and B? What kinds of local favors do A's officials obtain? Systematic examination of the other kinds of data and adherence to the other suggested procedures will serve as a check upon the views of the on-the-scene observer.

One of the thorniest problems is determining how to weight the data obtained in each category. How much importance should be assigned to economic data compared to perceptual data? Even more specifically, how important is trade flow data compared to economic aid, military aid compared to economic aid? Social science has no definitive answer to the problem.[25] At present, each analyst must arrange his own order of priorities, persuading his colleagues by the logical sequence, internal consistency, comprehensive purview, and commonsensical basis of his choice.

Extensive investigation of Soviet and Chinese influence in Third World countries may enable us to isolate relatively effective indicators of influence. These indicators are not direct measurements of Soviet or Chinese influence itself; they are measurements which are presumed to correlate significantly with such influence. Ideally, they should indicate the likelihood that influence is present. To develop indicators that relate only, or even predominantly, to influence is a major undertaking because of the paucity, even under the best of circumstances and data availability, of "pure" indicators, that is, those which reflect on the phenomenon being studied and not on other phenomena as well. Universal indicators are unlikely, given the geographic, political, economic, and cultural diversity of the countries of the Third World. However, tentative agreement on even a few would be a constructive achievement.

No science of assessing influence is within reach, but a conscious systematizing of assumptions, data, and criteria is. Greater precision is basic to tighter political analysis. Our aims in the essays that follow are to isolate and describe instances of Soviet and Chinese influence in Third World countries, to present analyses which rest on clearly identified assumptions, data, and criteria, and, to the extent possible, to suggest approaches and guidelines for operationalizing the concept of influence in foreign policy analysis.

Notes

1. H. Kapur, The Soviet Union and the Emerging Nations (London: Michael Joseph Ltd., 1972); W. Z. Laqueur, The Soviet Union and the Middle East (New York: Praeger Publishers, 1959), and The Struggle for the Middle East: The Soviet Union in the Mediterranean 1958-1968 (New York: Macmillan, 1969); B. D. Larkin, China and Africa 1949-1970 (Berkeley: University of California Press, 1971); G. Lenczowski, Soviet Advances in the Middle East (Washington, D. C.: American Enterprise Institute, 1972); K. London (ed.), New Nations in a Divided World (New York: Praeger Publishers, 1963); A. Ogunsanwo, China's Policy in Africa 1958-71 (London: Cambridge University Press, 1974); R. E. Poppino, International Communism in Latin America, 1917-1963 (New York: Free Press, 1964); O. Smolansky, The Soviet Union and the Arab East Under Khrushchev (Lewisburg, Penna.: Bucknell University Press, 1974); A. H. Syed, China and Pakistan: Diplomacy of an Entente Cordiale (Amherst: University of Massachusetts Press, 1974).

2. J. R. Carter, The Net Cost of Soviet Foreign Aid (New York: Praeger Publishers, 1971); A. D. Datar, India's Economic Relations with the USSR and Eastern Europe 1953-1969 (London: Cambridge University Press, 1972); P. J. Eldridge, The Politics of Foreign Aid in

India (New York: Schocken Books, 1970); M. D. Goldman, Soviet Foreign Aid (New York: Praeger Publishers, 1967); W. Klatt (ed.), The Chinese Model (Hong Kong: Hong Kong University Press, 1965); M. Kovner, The Challenge of Coexistence (Washington, D. C.: Public Affairs Press, 1961); K. Muller, The Foreign Aid Programs of the Soviet Bloc and Communist China: An Analysis (New York: Walker, 1969); L. Tansky, U. S. and U. S. S. R. Aid to Developing Countries (New York: Praeger Publishers, 1966); and R. S. Walters, American and Soviet Aid: A Comparative Analysis (Pittsburgh: University of Pittsburgh Press, 1970).

3. W. Joshua and S. P. Gilbert, Arms for the Third World: Soviet Military Aid Diplomacy (Baltimore: The Johns Hopkins Press, 1969); and Uri Ra'anan, The USSR Arms the Third World (Cambridge: M. I. T. Press, 1969).

4. R. E. Ebel, Communist Trade in Oil and Gas (New York: Praeger Publishers, 1970); A. Nove and D. Donnelly, Trade with Communist Countries (New York: Macmillan Co., 1961); F. Pryor, The Communist Foreign Trade System (Cambridge: M. I. T. Press, 1963); C. A. Sawyer, Communist Trade with Developing Countries: 1955-1965 (New York: Praeger Publishers, 1966); and B. R. Stokke, Soviet and East Europe Trade and Aid in Africa (New York: Praeger Publishers, 1967).

5. F. C. Barghoorn, The Soviet Cultural Offensive (Princeton: Princeton University Press, 1960), and Soviet Foreign Propaganda (Princeton: Princeton University Press, 1964); and P. Sager, Moscow's Hand in India (Berne: Swiss Eastern Institute, 1966).

6. M. Confino and S. Shamir (eds.), The U. S. S. R. and The Middle East (New York: John Wiley and Sons, 1973); W. R. Duncan (ed.), Soviet Policy in Developing Countries (Waltham, Mass.: Ginn-Blaisdell, 1970); D. B. Jackson, Castro, The Kremlin and Communism in Latin America (Baltimore: The Johns Hopkins Press, 1969); R. E. Kanet (ed.), The Soviet Union and the Developing Nations (Baltimore: The Johns Hopkins Press, 1974); C. Lee, Communist China's Policy Toward Laos: A Case Study 1954-67 (Kansas City: University of Kansas Press, 1970); G. Lenczowski, Russia and the West in Iran, 1918-1948 (Ithaca: Cornell University Press, 1949); A. Stein, India and the Soviet Union: The Nehru Era (Chicago: University of Chicago Press, 1969); and A. Suarez, Cuba: Castroism and Communism 1959-1966 (Cambridge: M. I. T. Press, 1967).

7. W. E. Butler, The Soviet Union and the Law of the Sea (Baltimore: The Johns Hopkins Press, 1971); A. Dallin, The Soviet Union at the United Nations (New York: Praeger Publishers, 1962); H. K. Jacobson, The USSR and the UN's Economic and Social Activities (Notre Dame: University of Notre Dame Press, 1963); B. A. Ramundo, Peaceful Coexistence: International Law in the Building of Communism (Baltimore: The Johns Hopkins Press, 1967); A. Z. Rubinstein, The Soviets in International Organizations: Changing Policy Toward

Developing Countries, 1953-1963 (Princeton: Princeton University Press, 1964); and A. Z. Rubinstein and G. Ginsburgs (eds.), Soviet and American Policies in the United Nations: A Twenty-Five Year Perspective (New York: New York University Press, 1971).

8. A. D. Barnett (ed.), Communist Strategies in Asia (New York: Praeger Publishers, 1963); W. Eagleton, Jr., The Kurdish Republic of 1946 (New York: Oxford University Press, 1963); V. M. Fic, Peaceful Transition to Communism in India: Strategy of the Communist Party (Bombay: Nachiketa, 1969); D. Hindley, The Communist Party of Indonesia 1951-1963 (Berkeley: University of California Press, 1964); J. H. Kautsky, Moscow and the Communist Party of India (New York: John Wiley and Sons, 1956); W. Z. Laqueur (ed.), Nationalism and Communism in the Middle East (New York: Praeger Publishers, 1956); G. Overstreet and M. Windmiller, Communism in India (Berkeley: University of California Press, 1959); S. W. Simon, The Broken Triangle: Peking, Djakarta and the PKI (Baltimore: The Johns Hopkins Press, 1969); J. Van der Kroef, Communism in Malaysia and Singapore (The Hague: Martinus Nijotf, 1968); A. Yodfat, Arab Politics in the Soviet Mirror (New York: John Wiley and Sons, 1973); and S. Zabin, The Communist Movement in Iran (Berkeley: University of California Press, 1966).

9. Z. K. Brzezinski (ed.), Africa and the Communist World (Stanford: Stanford University Press, 1963); H. D. Cohn, Soviet Policy Toward Black Africa: The Focus on National Integration (New York: Praeger Publishers, 1972); B. S. Gupta, The Fulcrum of Asia: Relations Among China, India, Pakistan and the USSR (New York: Pegasus, 1970); C. Johnson, Communist China and Latin America 1959-1967 (New York: Columbia University Press, 1970); G. Jukes, The Soviet Union in Asia (Berkeley: University of California Press, 1973); R. Legvold, Soviet Policy in West Africa (Cambridge: Harvard University Press, 1970); or C. B. McLane, Soviet Strategies in Southeast Asia (Princeton: Princeton University Press, 1966); and E. Taborsky, Communist Penetration of the Third World (New York: Robert Speller and Sons, 1973).

10. Among the key journals are: Mizan, The Third World, Asian Affairs, Survey, Problems of Communism, The Middle East Journal, Orbis, Foreign Affairs, World Politics, International Affairs, The China Quarterly, and Foreign Policy.

11. The New York Times, September 26, 1971.

12. The New York Times, June 29, 1971.

13. For a discussion of some of the problems involved in analyzing the links between aid and influence see David A. Baldwin, "Foreign Aid, Intervention, and Influence," World Politics, vol. 21, no. 3 (April 1969), 425-447. Baldwin deals with the constraints on the donor; he does not raise the issue of the ways in which the donee's behavior is affected by the value of the aid to his internal power base, and he overestimates the donor's capacity to bring about changes in the behavior of the donee.

20

For a seldom used but highly suggestive approach, which treats foreign aid as an "opportunity cost" designed to maintain the existing elite and political infrastructure, see especially Warren F. Ilchman, "A Political Economy of Foreign Aid: The Case of India," Asian Survey, vol. 7, no. 10 (October 1967), 676-688.

14. Graham T. Allison and Morton H. Halperin, "Bureaucratic Politics: A Paradigm and Some Policy Implications," World Politics, vol. 24, Supplement (Spring 1972), 60, 70.

15. Ibid., 53.

16. For example, see Chester L. Cooper, The Lost Crusade: America in Vietnam (New York: Dodd, Mead and Co., 1970); and Robert Shaplen, The Lost Revolution, rev. ed. (New York: Harper and Row, 1966).

17. See James N. Rosenau, "Pre-Theories and Theories of Foreign Policy," in R. Barry Farrell (ed.), Approaches to Comparative and International Politics (Evanston, Ill.: Northwestern University Press, 1966), pp. 60-92.

18. Jack Henry Nagel, "The Descriptive Analysis of Power," unpublished doctoral dissertation, Yale University, 1972, p. 56. Nagel uses the terms "power" and "influence" interchangeably. His own definition of power, which he describes in terms of preferences among variables rather than of overt behavior of individuals or groups, is not operationalized in a way that has utility for students of foreign policy. However, he does provide a lucid assessment of the problems entailed in measuring and evaluating power (that is, influence).

19. See Alvin Z. Rubinstein, "U.S. Specialists' Perceptions of Soviet Policy Toward the Third World," Canadian-American Slavic Studies, vol. 6, no. 1 (Spring 1972), 93-107.

20. Peter Bachrach and Morton S. Baratz, Power and Poverty: Theory and Practice (New York: Oxford University Press, 1970), p. 8.

21. Ibid., p. 15.

22. The categories of data presented here owe much to the seminal essay on measuring influence written by James G. March, "An Introduction to the Theory and Measurement of Influence," American Political Science Review, vol. 49, no. 2 (June 1955), 431-451.

23. Eugene R. Wittkopf, "Foreign Aid and United Nations Votes: A Comparative Study," American Political Science Review, vol. 67, no. 3 (September 1973), 885.

24. Robert Flaten, "International Influence: Economic Aid as One Measure of Soviet Influence in India," unpublished seminar paper (University of Pennsylvania, 1970).

25. To facilitate comparative analysis across national boundaries, the proposal has been made to pair indicators that are shown valid for one country with different but equivalent indicators in another country. Thus far, few attempts have been made to develop such measures of equivalence, and these have been limited to the field of comparative politics, not foreign policy analysis. See Adam Przeworski and Henry

Teune, The Logic of Comparative Social Inquiry (New York: John Wiley and Sons, 1970).

2

SOVIET INFLUENCE IN INDIA:
A SEARCH FOR THE SPOILS
THAT GO WITH VICTORY
William J. Barnds

The concept of influence, while as widely and as frequently used as any term in the vocabulary of international relations by analysts and practitioners alike, is frequently referred to by both groups without an awareness of the complexities involved in understanding or utilizing it. Statesmen and diplomats, who are habitually attempting to influence other governments, know that they succeed on some occasions and fail on others. They are also aware that the results of their efforts are often diffuse and indeterminate. Lacking time, inclination, and institutional memory, government leaders and the organizations they head spend relatively little effort appraising the impact of most of their major policies in any systematic manner, and one must admit that the difficulties of making useful evaluations are enough to discourage all but the most valiant.[1] Moreover, many otherwise valuable scholarly works in the field of international relations treat the subject of influence only in a peripheral or tangential manner, although there are a few excellent studies available.[2]

It is simple to make an initial clarification of this murky concept by setting forth a definition and applying it rigorously. However, it is generally difficult to locate examples of influence being used on specific occasions (proving that influence rather than coincidence or some other factor was involved) and to measure the extent of such influence. But difficult as such a task is, it is nothing compared to moving from particular instances to the higher ground of solid generalizations and ultimately a theory of influence in international relations.

One approach would be to set forth Soviet interests and goals in India, the priorities assigned to different aims at different times, and the degree of success their policies have had over the years. Such an evaluation of their achievements would provide a measure of Soviet influence. However, two problems are involved in this approach. First, it is extremely difficult to describe Soviet goals —and especially their priorities when forced to choose —with any great confidence. Second, Moscow achieved some of its goals because Soviet and Indian interests were similar rather than because Moscow influenced New Delhi. Despite these difficulties, such matters as Soviet goals cannot be ignored; but in an attempt to avoid generalities and focus on specific examples, a different method has been followed.

The general analytical and evidential difficulties do not disappear even after one has decided to adopt a case study approach in view of the magnitude of the subject of Soviet influence in India and the space limitations of this paper. Is it more fruitful to conduct a broad (but shallow) survey, or should one probe deeply into a few narrowly restricted areas? The former approach makes it possible to examine more examples and, if successful, to provide more insights, but it risks leaving assumptions and criteria being deficient in analytical rigor and factual proof. The latter approach requires such detailed examination of each case — often necessitating interviews of people involved in the situation who are reluctant to discuss such politically sensitive matters — that there is no possibility of investigating enough instances to make meaningful generalizations possible. This chapter attempts to steer a course between these two approaches, recognizing that anyone attempting to stand on two stools may end up falling between them. The analysis will rely heavily upon an examination of a few cases or arrangements which could involve Soviet influence in India. These examples — and some thoughts about the basic nature of Indo-Soviet relations — will be used as the basis for some general propositions about Soviet influence in India. Hopefully, this will provide an incentive for more extensive research into the individual cases described — as well as other cases —which should then make it possible to refine the conclusions reached here.

The Concept of Influence

The meaning of influence used in this analysis is that set forth in Professor Rubinstein's chapter: "Influence is manifested when A affects through nonmilitary means, directly or indirectly, the behavior of B so that it redounds to the policy advantage of A."[3] As this definition suggests, it is often as important to state A that state B maintain a particular policy — such as membership in an alliance — as it is that B change a policy in a manner helpful to A. The support for India's border claims against China which was expressed in the Soviet journal Problemy Dalnego Vostoka (Problems of the Far East) — a support which had previously been withheld — may have been designed to make it more difficult for New Delhi to adopt a more flexible stance on this dispute in an effort to improve relations with Peking.[4]

A diplomat would find himself at home with this definition, since diplomacy is the art of letting someone else have your way. Under this definition, the Soviet invasion of Czechoslovakia, to take only one example, would not be considered a case of Soviet influence. However, we should recognize that both before and after the invasion the

Soviets attempted to influence events in Czechoslovakia in a non-coercive manner with varying degrees of failure and success. Similarly, we want to take care to exclude situations where B (India) took the same position as A (the USSR) because the Indian government, convinced that such a policy was in its own interests, intended to act in that manner irrespective of Soviet policy. Similar positions on colonial issues — although adopted for different reasons — or on the Anglo-French-Israeli attacks on Egypt in 1956 come to mind.

We do not, however, want to exclude examples where the Soviet Union's support of India enabled New Delhi to pursue a policy it regarded as in its own interests but would have been unable to follow if it had not received Soviet support. Nor should we fail to recognize that influence has been exercised successfully if India reacted more strongly — or was more reticent — because of Soviet efforts than it would have done in the absence of Soviet actions, although the problem of measuring the influence involved is especially difficult in such a case. For example, New Delhi's concern about setting a precedent that might be applied to Kashmir would have made it wary of supporting the call for elections under United Nations supervision in Hungary in 1956, but Soviet diplomatic efforts may have increased the strength of Indian opposition to this proposal.

A few comments about public attitudes concerning the exercise of influence are also in order. It is no exaggeration to say that influence is a dirty word — although less so than intervention — for most people in modern political debate. People in the former colonial territories regard it with intense distaste, seeing it as weakening if not undermining their newly won freedom. The term "Soviet influence" stirs particular worry or even fear in some Western circles, where it is seen as leading to — or even synonymous with — domination or subversion. We need to keep these attitudes — both of which are understandable — in mind lest we accept them uncritically and without awareness of what we are doing. No nation can be completely free from external influence, especially as interdependence increases in the modern world. But influence, even between stronger and weaker nations, is a two-way street. New Delhi influences Moscow as well as is influenced by it, if only because the USSR must sometimes modify its policies to gain Indian support as well as its existence; whatever decisions we reach about its importance and its implications should be conclusions rather than assumptions — and should not be uncritically projected as future trends.

Influence can be achieved by refraining from action as well as by initiating it. For example, the preference of the United States for private ownership of industrial facilities abroad is well known, and some Americans have argued — with some success — that the U.S. government should not make foreign aid available to construct state-owned industrial enterprises. Such a policy would hardly succeed everywhere, for other nations are often willing to provide such facilities — although sometimes the absence of U.S. assistance will change the terms involved. But in some cases the developing country may have little choice, and if it then turns to private foreign investors we have an example of foreign influence.[5]

Influence by A upon B can also grow out of a threat, or out of A's activities in country C. Soviet support of India has been consistent enough since 1955 so that New Delhi felt it could make its links with Moscow a central element of Indian foreign policy, but Soviet support has not been so firm that India could take it for granted. Thus one can argue that even the limited Soviet support extended to Pakistan (C) between 1965 and 1970 worried Indian leaders even more than it angered them, and that concern over the possibility of greater Soviet support for Pakistan led New Delhi to be especially careful in its dealings with Moscow.[*] Unfortunately, this type of influence is as difficult to measure as it is important to recognize.

The Setting

Let us begin our search for Soviet influence in India by reviewing a character from a literary classic well known to all. Not Diogenes, searching with his lantern for an honest man, but Rip Van Winkle sleeping peacefully for 20 years. Assume that Rip Van Winkle was, instead of an eighteenth-century New York countryman, a professor of international relations (specializing in Asian politics) who fell asleep in his study early in 1952. The Cold War was at its height, and dominated international life across the globe. New nations were being born in Asia as the colonial empires disintegrated in the wake of World War II, just as new nations had won independence in Eastern Europe when World War I undermined the Austro-Hungarian and Russian empires. Conflicts between Hindus and Muslims had led to the establishment of two hostile nations in the subcontinent when the British departed. The mass slaughters and migrations attendant upon partition, and the war between India and Pakistan over Kashmir, had weakened both nations. But despite the struggle for independence, India (as well as Pakistan) remained oriented to the West — membership in the Commonwealth, a parliamentary system of government, many British officials in the military services, and a pattern of trade almost entirely with the non-Communist world. A local communist insurrection in India had been firmly suppressed, and Nehru was being portrayed as a "lackey of the imperialists" by Soviet propaganda.

---

[*] There are arguments on the other side involving what was the most complicated period of Indo-Soviet relations. However, New Delhi's opposition to a number of Soviet moves in these years does not invalidate the basic contention, for New Delhi might have opposed Soviet policies even more than it did.

Upon awakening early in 1972 the professor would, when he surveyed Indo-Soviet relations, behold a vastly different scene. Although the United States had expended great effort and energy to limit the Soviet role and to increase its own influence in the Afro-Asian countries in general and India in particular, any objective observer would have rated Moscow as the clear victor in India. Indian trade with the USSR and Eastern Europe had increased over a hundredfold, and was over fifteen per cent of total Indian trade. The Soviet Union was the principal external source of Indian arms, having committed itself to supplying over $1.1 billion in military equipment. Soviet commitments of economic aid were nearly $1.6 billion, and Eastern Europe had added nearly $400 million. * Most important of all, Moscow and Delhi had the same antagonists — China and the United States. Soviet backing of India during the 1971 Bangladesh upheaval had enabled the latter to take military action that dismembered Pakistan and made India the preeminent power in the subcontinent over the loud but ineffective opposition of Peking and Washington. With Peking hostile and America alienated, the USSR was the only great power on whom India could rely. Their relationship had been formalized by a 20-year Treaty of Peace, Friendship and Cooperation which, while not a military alliance, imposed some obligations on both parties.

In such circumstances, the professor would have concluded that by historical standards, the Soviet Union should have acquired considerable influence and that it would not be difficult to discover instances of it in an open polity such as India's, although the intense pride and growing fascination with power so apparent among Indians would probably have led him to recognize that India remained determined to control its own destiny. He would have found support for his judgment in the views of Indian observers. One thoughtful Indian, while describing the Indo-Soviet coalition as one involving "competition and bargaining," referred to the "success of Soviet influence-building" as such that "Soviet influence is so predominant in the region that the United States no longer expects to match it. " While he did not make clear the criteria he used, he did cite Soviet backing as important for India's efforts to deal with its external enemies, and pointed out that Soviet support strengthens Mrs. Gandhi's leftist images and "enables her to win broader mass support. "[6]

The Indian government, of course, used no such language. While valuing its links with Moscow as a deterrent to China and, to a lesser degree, the United States, it took pains to portray its military victory in 1971 as due to India's military strength and just cause. Indian news

---

*Citing Eastern European aid and trade is not to be taken as implying that decisions on such matters are made in Moscow or redound to Moscow's direct benefit in its relations with India. However, Indians probably believe — correctly in my judgment — that Moscow has some influence over the Eastern European countries in such matters.

stories featured Indian-produced arms rather than Soviet-supplied equipment. Similarly, Indians sought to keep communal tensions in check by discreetly playing up the diverse backgrounds of the Indian leaders involved — a Brahmin prime minister, an untouchable defense minister, a Parsi chief of the army, a Sikh commanding officer in charge of the fighting units, and the Muslim soldiers that were fighting. And shortly after the war, Mrs. Gandhi attempted to convince the world — and perhaps warn Soviet leaders — that India would chart its own course when she told New York Times correspondent C. L. Sulzberger that "we are unable to display gratitude in any tangible sense for anything."[7] But strongly stated denials by national leaders that they are not subject to external influence is no proof that such influence does not exist, any more than extensive activities by a foreign power constitute proof that it does. Therefore an appraisal of several specific events in Indo-Soviet relations — mostly, but not entirely, since the mid-1960s — is in order.

The Tashkent Episode

The Soviet policy of firm support for India in the latter's disputes with Pakistan was a key factor in Moscow's effort to expand its role in South Asia after 1955. However, this policy began to be modified in 1964 as part of a general Soviet effort to broaden its ties in the Middle East and South Asia. The speeches of Soviet leaders during the visits of Indian President Radhakrishnan and Prime Minister Shastri in 1964 and 1965 made no mention of Soviet support for the Indian position on Kashmir, whereas Khrushchev and Bulganin had stressed such support during their 1955 visit to India.

Moscow continued and even expanded its economic and military assistance to India, but began to move to develop a closer relationship with Pakistan as well. Moscow was neutral during the Indo-Pakistani armed clash in the Rann of Kutch in April 1965. Pakistan's infiltration of guerrilla forces into Kashmir in August in an attempt to spark an uprising led step by step to the second Indo-Pakistani war. But Moscow, instead of blaming Pakistan for the war, simply proclaimed: "We would like Soviet-Pakistani relations, like our traditional friendship with India, to be a stabilizing factor in the situation in Asia and to contribute to the normalization of relations between India and Pakistan."[8]

Soviet leaders quickly recognized that neutrality would hardly be tenable if prolonged fighting steadily heightened passions in India and Pakistan. They also feared that China might enter the fray, posing choices they preferred not to face. Thus they worked in the United Nations for a cease-fire, arguing with the two parties that ascribing blame or attempting to settle the underlying dispute was inappropriate until the fighting stopped.

Premier Kosygin on September 4 offered Soviet good offices in an effort to find a means to halt the fighting and the offer was renewed on

September 19. Although both governments accepted the offer in principle, neither was eager to explore such an uncharted path, and negotiations remained centered on the UN proceedings. A cease-fire was finally agreed to on September 22. However, two months passed without any progress toward disengagement, and when the Soviet offer was repeated in November the leaders of the two countries accepted. Neither party was enthusiastic, as both governments had convinced their people they were winning the war. Pakistan was putting itself into the hands of the long-time friend of its enemy, although the desire to cement Soviet neutrality apparently weighed more heavily than the fear of antagonizing China. New Delhi's decision to attend stirred up considerable opposition within India, and Prime Minister Shastri assured Parliament he would not negotiate on the Kashmir issue. The irony of Ayub and Shastri proceeding to the USSR was caught by The Times (London) on January 3: "How strange and intolerable it would have seemed to Curzon that the affairs of the subcontinent he ruled should be taken to Tashkent to be settled under the patronage of a Russian."

Nor were the prospects for a successful Soviet intervention bright. Both Ayub and Shastri realized the importance of moving beyond the cease-fire to a settlement of at least some of the issues still outstanding, such as troop pullbacks, but inflamed public feeling in both countries left them with little room for maneuver. Both countries felt compelled to adhere to their respective approaches to Indo-Pakistani problems: India insisted on a no-war pact before taking up the issues in dispute, while Pakistan argued that a no-war pact without an agreement on Kashmir would amount to abandoning the issue. Yet in the end Ayub and Shastri reached a tenuous agreement, which, while it satisfied neither (and aroused strong opposition in both countries), was tolerable to both. The two sides agreed to return to the previous status quo as far as troop dispositions and borders were concerned. Pakistan's agreement to settle disputes peacefully in conformance with the UN Charter was a small concession on the no-war issue, and was matched by India's admission that a "dispute" existed over Kashmir.

The full story of what went on at Tashkent remains unknown.[9] However, there is general agreement among those who have studied this episode that Kosygin played an important part in making an agreement possible.[10] He met with Ayub and Shastri many times, and worked hard to create an atmosphere emphasizing new opportunities rather than old grievances. There is also general agreement that he acted with considerable finesse and skill, and went out of his way to maintain a low profile while still taking an active role. There is, however, considerable disagreement about how Kosygin was able to bring the two sides together. Some scholars stress that Kosygin put no pressure on the parties, but used only persuasion:

. . . the Soviet Prime Minister stuck to the letter and spirit of the offer of good offices. He did not make at any stage any proposals, or pressurize either of the leaders to accept the proposals of the other. All that the Soviet Prime Minister tried to do was to bring to bear on the two leaders his tremendous powers of persuasion to make them see each other's point of view in the interest of peace in the Indian subcontinent.[11]

Others argue that Kosygin must have used pressure as well as persuasion to secure Indian acceptance of an agreement to return to the previous status quo in view of India's stronger position, but they offer little in the way of evidence:

The Soviet determination to make the conference a success led Kosygin to undertake last-minute rescue operations. . . . It is not excluded that during these dramatic hours, the Soviet Prime Minister exercised considerable pressure on the two leaders; for one cannot otherwise rationally explain the agreement that was thereafter concluded between the two leaders.[12]

It is, of course, extremely difficult to draw a clear line between persuasion and pressure, especially when the latter is applied subtly and skillfully — not to mention in private. Kosygin clearly left Ayub and Shastri in no doubt that the Soviet Union wanted an agreement and both leaders — particularly after accepting his invitation to Tashkent — were reluctant to incur Soviet displeasure by being too rigid. Both countries wanted Soviet support on a variety of issues, but both were uncertain if they would have such support in the event the talks broke down. In short, Soviet efforts to improve relations with Pakistan worried India enough to induce some flexibility on its part, and Pakistan was hopeful enough of gaining a more forthcoming Soviet policy to lead it along a similar path. Moreover, Kosygin was helped by the disenchantment of both countries with the United States, which had cut off arms supplies to both, and thus taken itself out of the picture. Therefore the Soviet Union was in a position where its voice carried considerable weight, and while there were clear limitations on what it could get the parties to agree to, it was able to use its influence — whether one labels it "persuasion" or "pressure" — to bring about a settlement.

Soviet Arms to Pakistan

The Soviet leaders who had displaced Khrushchev were obviously pleased by their success at Tashkent, but they had few illusions that any of the fundamental causes of the Indo-Pakistani dispute had been altered. Despite many Soviet appeals over the next few years to observe the "Spirit of Tashkent," neither India nor Pakistan was willing to be flexible enough to make a full return to their pre-1965 relationship possible, much less a settlement of their basic differences. The Soviets moved cautiously in this atmosphere, but they refused to let Indo-Pakistani hostility deter them from attempting to strengthen their links to Pakistan.

Ayub was also wary, for he faced a delicate task. Essentially he wanted (1) continued American economic support (and at least a supply of spare parts for American military equipment), (2) Chinese military and diplomatic support, and (3) some combination of Soviet arms for Pakistan or reduced arms shipments to India sufficient to keep the balance of power in the subcontinent from turning decisively against Pakistan. As far as can be determined, Ayub had no success in limiting Soviet arms deliveries to India; Soviet leaders insisted this was strictly a bilateral issue between the Soviet Union and India. Despite Soviet concern over the trend of events within India and worry over India's continued dependence on the West, Moscow continued to provide extensive military and economic assistance to New Delhi. At the same time, Moscow wanted to induce Pakistan to remove the U.S. electronic intelligence facilities outside Peshawar, and to keep Pakistan from relying entirely on China for arms. Therefore the USSR slowly but steadily moved toward supplying arms to Pakistan. In 1966 the USSR provided a small number of jeeps and army trucks, and in 1967 a few helicopters were added to the list. The announcement on May 20, 1968, that the U.S. lease on the intelligence facilities would not be extended was an indication something more could be expected, and in July 1968 a Soviet-Pakistani arms agreement of undisclosed size was announced.

It had been obvious to Indians that an arms agreement was possible in view of the trend in Soviet policy, and New Delhi had tried to dissuade Moscow from such a move. Kosygin visited New Delhi briefly after his visit to Pakistan in April 1968, and India apparently thought it had convinced him not to provide arms to Pakistan. It is not clear whether this represented wishful thinking, a failure in communications, or Soviet uncertainty or dissembling, but that is not our primary concern.[13]

India's reaction was predictably unfavorable but uncharacteristically restrained. The Soviet decision was widely criticized in Parliament and in the press, and the right-wing Jan Sang organized a huge demonstration in New Delhi. However, the Indian government spoke in carefully measured terms. Mrs. Gandhi criticized the decision publicly, and told Parliament that the move would heighten tensions on the subcontinent and add to India's defense burden.[14] Yet the Indian government also exerted considerable effort to making sure that the Indian reaction did not get out of hand. She urged Indians to react to the Soviet move with "composure and dignity." More importantly, she insisted throughout the controversy that India's policy toward the USSR would not undergo any change, although New Delhi could not accept

Soviet arguments that by supplying arms to Pakistan Moscow would be able to exercise significant restraint over it.

Several points about this episode stand out. The Soviets moved with care as well as determination. Moscow made a particular effort to assure New Delhi that while the Soviet Union would not let India determine the character of Soviet-Pakistani relations, Moscow would continue to support India's military buildup and industrialization program. * When Mrs. Gandhi expressed her concern over the agreement to Kosygin, he assured her that "nothing would be done to undermine" Indo-Soviet friendship.[15] We do not know, of course, whether these pro forma assurances were accompanied by warnings that too strong an Indian reaction would endanger Soviet assistance for India. Perhaps Soviet diplomats found it unnecessary to be blunt on this matter. Nonetheless, it seems quite clear that the USSR had sufficient influence in India to mute that government's public reaction. In fact, Mrs. Gandhi had few options available. The United States and Britain were unwilling to meet India's arms requirements, and India was still faced with Chinese and Pakistani hostility. Thus a reluctant attempt to keep relations with Moscow on an even keel was deemed essential, and India's determination to prevent a rupture in these relations led it to be very circumspect in its criticism of the Soviet invasion of Czechoslovakia in August 1968.

Yet this episode must be put in perspective; for if New Delhi muted its direct criticism of Moscow's actions, it gave other signs of its disapproval. In August 1968 and again in January 1969 Mrs. Gandhi indicated that India was interested in discussions with Peking about Sino-Indian relations, and no mention was made of New Delhi's previous preconditions for such talks. While Peking did not respond, her moves were a sign to Moscow that India too could shift directions. Moreover, India in these years turned down a number of Soviet proposals, such as Kosygin's offer to mediate a dispute over the division of the waters of the Ganges River flowing from India to East Pakistan. And despite Soviet criticism of countries refusing to sign the Nuclear Non-Proliferation Treaty, India refused to alter its policy on a matter it believed might become central to its security.

Moscow and the Communist Party of India

One way for state A to influence the government of state B is to secure the support of a particular organization or group of people in country B and have them influence their government, either in terms of

---

* Soviet writers at this time were expressing concern over what they saw as a swing to the right within India and toward the West in foreign policy, but the Soviet government decided that any slackening of its support would only strengthen these tendencies. See William J. Barnds, "Moscow and South Asia," Problems of Communism, vol. 21, no. 3 (May-June 1972), esp. pp. 20-22.

its general orientation or on specific issues of particular importance to A. Yet such an approach has obvious drawbacks. It is indirect and thus likely to be less clearly focused than direct influence exerted by one government on another. The supporters of A in country B are only one of many contending groups there, and their support may alienate other groups — including the one in power — and thus reduce A's influence. Nonetheless, it may be useful at times; and in any case, the ideological foundations of the Soviet state and its inescapable relationship to the international communist movement bring such factors into play.

It has been amply demonstrated that the Soviet Union had influence amounting to near control over most communist parties around the world of the 1940s and 1950s. This was true as regards the Communist Party of India (CPI) — but only when Moscow chose it to exercise its authority, for poor guidance rather than too tight a control was the typical pattern. The CPI, like communist parties everywhere, switched its course after Nazi Germany attacked the Soviet Union in 1941. While the CPI's attempt to create a revolution by resort to violence in 1948-51 was not done in response to Soviet orders, the Zhdanov line enunciated in 1947 certainly encouraged such a course.[16] The CPI was nearly destroyed by its foolish resort to revolution, as New Delhi demonstrated its willingness to use whatever force was necessary to meet the communist challenge. Nonetheless, the CPI was unable to see where it had gone wrong, and a future leader of the party described its dependence on outside guidance in a disarmingly frank manner in a 1950 intraparty document:

> Everyone began to feel that somewhere things were wrong, but none could say it correctly and some would not say it — until the Cominform spoke. And the whole party felt relieved. Is it not good that we have a Cominform to tell us things and is it not good that we bow to the Cominform . . . ?[17]

Nehru's long-standing criticism of the CPI's subservience to Moscow made it clear to Soviet leaders that any attempt to work out a new relationship with India required either cutting the links between the USSR and the CPI or getting the CPI to adopt a less hostile position toward the Nehru government. Moscow adopted the second approach. Soviet authority was sufficient to move the CPI from its revolutionary path to a policy of "constitutional communism" in the mid-1950s, and to support Nehru's foreign and, to a lesser degree, domestic policies. This weakened the appeal of the CPI in the eyes of many of its cadres and members, although its more flexible approach enabled it to broaden its appeal to the Indian electorate. The CPI's shift probably was a small factor in New Delhi's willingness to move toward closer relations with Moscow, for the CPI's new course was taken to mean that Moscow was serious in its efforts to improve relations with the Indian government.

Soviet authority over the CPI had diminished greatly in the past 10 years, however, as a result of the party split in 1964 and the lack of a generally accepted center of authority for the international communist movement. (The more radical CPI [Marxist] was more attuned to the Chinese than to the Soviet approach on most issues, but was always independent of Peking.) Moscow's need for a foothold in the Indian communist movement altered its relationship with the CPI from one of control to one of bargaining, and its desire for a united communist movement as well as its fear that the Marxist CPI would drift closer to Peking led it to treat that party carefully. While the CPI is generally inclined to follow Soviet policy, Moscow can no longer count on its support. Thus the party was somewhat critical of the Soviet decision to supply arms to Pakistan in 1968, and the party's general secretary declared that "we are against any action that jeopardizes the security of our country."[18] But the party was unwilling to support any move to condemn the USSR, and backed Mrs. Gandhi's government when a censure motion was introduced by the opposition parties.

Despite the loosening of ties between Moscow and the CPI, there was considerable speculation that the party — and thus indirectly the USSR — would try to extract some concessions from Mrs. Gandhi when her move to the left in 1969 split the Congress Party and placed her government in a minority position. The CPI wanted to work with Mrs. Gandhi's New Congress in order to improve its own prospects as well as to influence the course she followed.

> The CPI . . . adopted the tactical line of a united front
> from above, and regarded the ruling Congress faction,
> after the Congress split, to be a progressive force eligible
> for the national democratic front. . . . Put another way,
> the CPI appeared to believe that it could influence India's
> national politics as a significant partner of the national
> democratic front. 19

Although the cooperation between the New Congress and the CPI gave the latter some bargaining power at times, there is widespread agreement among students of Indian politics that the CPI had very little success in influencing the policies of the Indian government in the late 1960s or early 1970s. There are several reasons for this. Even after the split, the New Congress had ten times as many seats in Parliament as the CPI, and the CPI was not the only possible source of support available to Mrs. Gandhi. Second, Indian politics are extremely complex, and similar ideological or policy orientations are often less important than a variety of other considerations.

A very loose pattern of alignments with ideological over-
tones emerged in late 1969 and early 1970, but many
natural members of a leftist or rightist front either moved
in the opposite direction or remained aloof from coalitions.
. . . The difficulty in achieving formal national alignments
reflected factional, regional and programmatic divisions
within most parties, particularly the two wings of Congress. . . .
The coalition-building maneuvers of both wings of
Congress were essentially pragmatic and nonideological.
Both factions tried to avoid coalitions with clear ideological identities. . . .
The New Congress drew early support from the
CPI, but kept relations at the level of ad hoc cooperation
in Parliament, state alliances in some areas in 1970 and
electoral adjustments in several states in the 1971 parliamentary elections. . . . Alliances are more easily forged
at the state level than at the Center where party-images
have more saliency. Moreover, ad hoc cooperation at the
national level does not require explicit agreement on
policies or symbols and a consequent alteration in images.
The question of a national alliance was related to the
struggle for legitimacy with the rival old Congress. An
alliance with the CPI would have given credence to the
opposition charge that the Prime Minister was pro-
Communist and might have resulted in defections to the
opposition group. 20

Finally, the period involved was a short one. Mrs. Gandhi's
dramatic victory in the 1971 national elections freed her from dependence on any other party at the national level, although the picture
remained more complicated at the state level despite her success in
most states in 1972. Some cooperation between the Congress and the
CPI is likely to be a feature of Indian politics, but such arrangements
will create frictions within both parties which will limit their effectiveness.
The long-term prospects of the communist movement in general
and the CPI in particular are far from clear, and will depend in part
upon whether or not Indian democracy retains its basic vitality. Despite
a promising environment, there are many obstacles facing the communists. Some are internal to each of the parties and to the movement as
a whole, and some are inherent in India's political culture. Moreover,
if any Indian communist party — even the Moscow-oriented CPI — were
to increase its strength to the point of being able to gain power in the
country, its policies would in all likelihood be increasingly directed
toward advancing its own interests rather than following any Soviet
line. (Such an attitude is probably a prerequisite for communist
growth, for the CPI has long suffered from its early failure to follow a

nationalist line or to work out a creative response to Indian conditions.)
The Soviet and Indian Communist parties occasionally issue a joint
statement critical of Indian conditions and policies, but Soviet actions
over the years have made it clear that its primary goal is good state-to-
state relations with the Indian government. Therefore Moscow's interest
in a communist "victory" in India is likely to be less than all-consuming,
especially as long as the Indian government is friendly toward the USSR.
In such circumstances, the CPI can hardly be considered as a reliable
or important instrument for the exercise of Soviet influence in India.

Trade as a Tool

Trade as an instrument of statecraft has often been regarded as a
peripheral matter by observers who have focused their attention on
dramatic arms agreements or commitments to construct modern industries
in poor nations. This is especially inappropriate in any long-range
appraisal of Indo-Soviet relations, for India's growing industrial
capacity — and its policy of encouraging import substitution — enables
it to produce a growing proportion of its military needs and capital
equipment. (Indeed, aid to Indian heavy industry is, as the Indians are
keenly aware, gradually reducing the country's dependence on external
sources of supply for capital goods and thus enhancing its freedom of
maneuver in one respect.) Therefore the provision of economic assistance
to major industries, while regarded as very important by Indians in the
short and intermediate term, is likely to decline in impact over the long
term. (Economic aid is discussed more fully in the following section.)
Trade generally involves a more enduring relationship, but one
whose impact is more diffuse and more difficult to measure. India's
trade with the Soviet Union and Eastern Europe increased more than
20-fold between 1955 and 1970, and has continued to expand since
then. The share of India's trade with these countries is over 15 percent
of its total trade. The USSR, which accounts for about 10 percent of
India's trade, has in recent years alternated with the U.K. as India's
second largest trading partner — after the United States.
The USSR and East Europe have provided a market for some
products that India could not sell in the noncommunist world; they have
purchased growing quantities of semifinished manufactured goods; and
their willingness to supply petroleum products has lessened Indian
dependence on Western-owned oil companies. This relationship has
not been without friction, for New Delhi has been annoyed at reports
that some of these countries have on occasion resold Indian products
in the West at discount prices, thereby cutting into India's direct
sales. Moreover, the Soviets have on occasion tried to drive hard
bargains, charging more and paying less than world market prices.[21]
New Delhi has probably felt compelled to accept terms it thought unfair
on some occasions, but there have been well-publicized Indian refusals
to purchase Soviet commercial airliners or to sell railway cars on Soviet
terms.

Nonetheless, Soviet willingness to become a major trading partner probably has been a net gain for India. Although direct evidence is lacking, it would seem reasonable to conclude that Moscow's readiness to trade has made New Delhi more receptive to Soviet requests for general cooperation than it would otherwise have been, for the Indian government has placed a high value on expanding trade with the USSR. The two countries have established a Joint Commission on Economic, Scientific, and Technical Cooperation. During 1972 there were reports that the two countries would coordinate their five-year plans, and some Indians saw membership in the Council on Mutual Economic Cooperation (Comecon) as the next logical development.[22] However, Mrs. Gandhi has denied having any intention to join Comecon.

Despite the importance of Indo-Soviet economic relations, there are few indications that Moscow has been able to use its trade to influence the general direction of Indian foreign policy. This reflects the basic fact that trade is a two-way street; the Soviet Union also benefits from an international division of labor. Its economy needs to import certain commodities not produced in the USSR, and Moscow finds it advantageous to import others rather than produce them. The USSR also needs foreign markets for some of its products, and in any case must export to pay for its imports. Since the dependency involved is mutual (although not necessarily equal) in a trading relationship, the opportunity for exercising any broad influence on matters outside the field of trade is limited.

One specific result of the growth of Indo-Soviet trade does warrant mention, however, and this concerns the steady increase in New Delhi's control of Indian foreign trade. The fact that Soviet and Eastern European trade is under direct government control probably made it easier for those in New Delhi who wanted their government to exercise control over foreign trade to move Indian policy in that direction.

Building Bokaro to Soviet Specifications

One of the central features of India's industrialization program has been its effort to develop a major steel industry. Three public-sector plants were built in the 1950s by the USSR, Germany, and the United Kingdom, and long-range Indian plans called for a fourth large public-sector facility at Bokaro. India wanted the United States — which led the world in the technology for producing the flat-rolled steel that Bokaro was to specialize in — to construct the plant, which would have demonstrated that even steel mills could partake of nonalignment. However, there were serious technical, economic, and political problems involved, including the half-billion dollars in foreign exchange needed for the first stage, and the insistence by American advisors that the project be built on a turnkey basis and be under American management for 10 years. With opposition to the project mounting in the U. S. Congress, India decided to withdraw its request for American aid and seek help elsewhere.

The Soviet Union responded in the spring of 1964 with an offer that pleased the Indians in several respects, including a provision for reducing the foreign exchange costs substantially by utilizing a larger proportion of Indian-produced equipment. Much of this was to come from the heavy machinery plant at Ranchi, built earlier with the help of the USSR and Czechoslovakia, which had found few markets for its products. However, New Delhi wanted to rely on Indian talent as much as possible for designing as well as building Bokaro, and had already contracted with the Indian firm Dastur and Company to provide these services. Moscow was unwilling to accept such an arrangement and insisted that if it were responsible for the construction it must be in control of the design. This created considerable public controversy in the press and Parliament in India, but the USSR remained adamant. New Delhi felt that in the absence of offers of collaboration from other countries it had no choice but to accept Soviet terms. Similarly, when Dastur and Company submitted a report on possible cost reductions in the Soviet plan for Bokaro, which included less reliance on Soviet technicians, Moscow again balked and insisted on what was essentially a turnkey operation. Once again, New Delhi acquiesced.

Padma Desai, in her careful study of the Bokaro project, points out:

> The analysis reveals that arranging for Bokaro's import requirements with aid-financing from any source would necessarily imply, as it did with the Soviet aid, that India would retain no initiative in bargaining for the crucial details of the arrangement. Given the aid-tying practices of donor countries, it was inevitable that the Soviet Union, which was treated as the lender of the last resort, would end up by tying supplies of equipment to consulting services and complete control over the management of its construction during the first phase. 23

However, she relates the Indian decision to faults and contradictions in Indian planning as well as to Soviet insistence, and concludes with a thought about the future:

> There are lessons from Bokaro also for the Soviet Union. There is no doubt that the continuous debate on Bokaro in India arose out of the phenomenon of an Indian consulting firm being gradually edged out of its predominant role as consultants and designers of the steel plant. The debate on this issue has remained animated and detrimental to the Soviet image in India; indeed, given the current climate of self-reliance, criticism of the Soviet Union cuts across party lines. . . . Indeed, unless the Soviet Union comes to grips with the fact of a vastly increased

technological self-reliance in India, the future of Indo-
Soviet economic collaboration is likely to be bleak and
the Bokaro episode more than a temporary lapse in Soviet
aid and diplomacy. 24

The Bokaro episode demonstrates a clear case of the successful
exercise of influence by the Soviet Union — successful, that is, in
terms of Moscow's specific short-term goals. Yet the events are hardly
surprising to any student of international economics or politics; for
whenever there is — or seems to be — only one supplier, he is likely to
be able, within broad limits, to impose his own terms. What is
interesting is that this relatively minor dispute caused more controversy
in India than any other project involving Soviet aid. For overshadowing
the controversy has been the widespread Indian appreciation for Soviet
assistance in developing a heavy industrial base, although from time to
time there have been complaints about particular developments involving
some of the projects.25 The $1.6 billion in Soviet aid commitments
extended from 1954 to 1971 on relatively easy terms (supplemented by
$382 million from Eastern Europe) has inevitably had an influence on
Indian economic policy.26 Soviet emphasis on aid for state-owned
projects has enabled the Indian government to move toward greater
control of the country's economy — something many Indian leaders
wanted to do in any case. Whether this trend, given the inefficiency
of many state-owned enterprises, has helped or harmed Indian development efforts is not at issue here. Although many Westerners have been
dismayed by this trend, India's economic system bears little resemblance
to Soviet-style socialism. Indeed, Soviet leaders have apparently been
disappointed at the modest pace of such developments. At the 24th
Congress of the Communist Party of the Soviet Union in 1971, Brezhnev
referred to such nations as Syria, Algeria, and Burma as oriented toward
socialism. India was only characterized as having experienced "progressive social changes."27
   Yet the Soviet Union faces two dilemmas involving its future
attitude toward economic assistance for India. The first of these concerns a major policy question: would continued or even increased aid
result in benefits commensurate with the cost now that American aid
has declined drastically?* Perhaps waning American competition makes
it safe for Moscow to be less forthcoming as well. Arguments on this
point probably have been going on in Moscow in recent years; but so
far there has been no evidence they have been resolved affirmatively,
as no new aid agreements have been announced. Until Moscow made

---

*It is not that the cost has been inordinately high, for deliveries
have been slow and repayments have partially offset outlays. (See
James R. Carter, The Net Cost of Soviet Foreign Aid [New York:
Praeger Publishers, 1971], pp. 39-41.) However, Soviet leaders have
found the benefits uncertain and difficult to measure.

a loan of 2 million tons of wheat in 1973, repayments for past aid exceeded the flow of new assistance for several years — a situation Indian leaders can hardly approve of even if they seldom discuss it publicly.

Even if Soviet leaders do decide that the USSR would benefit by continuing its aid program — or would suffer if it failed to continue it — they are confronted with the dilemma over the type of aid to provide. Soviet aid has been overwhelmingly directed toward individual projects (usually large-scale ones), but India now has — thanks in part to Moscow's earlier efforts — the ability to produce much of the equipment for such projects. Its needs are for program rather than project assistance — raw materials, components, and so forth — which is a type of aid the USSR has been notably reluctant to provide. While program assistance can (if it is large enough) provide the donor with some influence over the donee's general economic policy, it also carries with it a greater responsibility for the success or failure of the recipient's record than Moscow has wanted to assume. (Its experience with Castro's Cuba illustrates the problems involved in such a relationship.)

The Military Dimension

The Indian military establishment has been one of the pillars of the nation since the day India achieved independence amidst the upheavals that accompanied partition. The military forces — chiefly the army — have had three separate but related tasks: (1) preserving order when violence occurred on a scale too large for the police to handle; (2) extending New Delhi's control over such areas as Junagadh, Hyderabad, Kashmir, and Goa; and (3) enabling New Delhi to deal with its hostile neighbors — first Pakistan, and then China — from a position of strength. The second task has been largely accomplished, unless one includes the continuing struggle with such tribal groups as Nagas under this heading, but the armed forces' responsibility to act as the ultimate guarantor of domestic order and to protect the national security remains.

The military establishment India inherited from the British proved adequate to meet its early challenges successfully, and it contained the potential for the expansion necessary to enable it to face the larger tasks that were to confront it after Pakistan secured a powerful ally and Sino-Indian relations shifted from friendship to animosity. But the armed forces inherited from British India were deficient in two respects. The first, and least important for our purposes, was that the reliance of British India on the Royal Navy and Royal Air Force left independent India with only embryonic air and naval forces. The second and more fundamental weakness was the lack of defense production facilities capable of turning out anything but the most basic items of military equipment.

New Delhi has attempted to deal with this problem in two ways — by importing military equipment to meet its short-term needs, and by building up its defense industries so that it would eventually be self-sufficient in terms of arms. While it has made considerable progress in expanding the capabilities of its defense industries — especially in the past 10 years — it has encountered two handicaps which have made the shift toward self-sufficiency slower and more difficult than might have been expected 25 years ago. First, the Indian government has felt forced to expand the country's armed forces far beyond the size it originally thought would be necessary. Second, the technological spiral has not only shortened the useful life of certain types of arms but has made it more difficult to establish defense production facilities that are able to produce whatever types of arms are "modern" at a given time.

Indian policy has gone through several phases in its attempts to fill the elusive gap between its production capabilities and its perceived needs. After the United States began arming Pakistan in 1954, India, whose foreign exchange position was still strong, continued to buy its arms from the West (chiefly Britain and France). This policy became both untenable and undesirable by the early 1960s. India's economic development efforts had resulted in a sharp drain in its foreign exchange reserves; and New Delhi, now embroiled with China as well as Pakistan, needed not only much larger quantities of arms but also wanted Soviet and American political support on its struggle with Peking. One obvious way of meeting its arms needs while demonstrating great power support was to secure military assistance from both Moscow and Washington, even though this required the abandonment of Nehru's earlier insistence that India would not accept arms aid. Since the United States and the USSR were at odds with China, both were willing. Thus New Delhi was successful in its efforts, and was able to argue that Soviet and American willingness to assist India was a vindication of its nonalignment policy.

To say that New Delhi was successful does not mean that the process was smooth. The United States (and the United Kingdom, which also provided military aid after 1962) tailored the quantities and types of equipment to what they hoped Pakistan could tolerate, and the USSR moved cautiously as long as it had any hope of keeping its own quarrel with China within bounds. Indeed, during the brief but traumatic Sino-Indian border war of 1962, Moscow pulled back from its earlier support of India; but this proved to be only a temporary deviation from the long-run Soviet policy of increased support of India.

What was not temporary was the major change in American policy that grew out of the 1965 Indo-Pakistani war, for the United States cut off arms aid to both countries. (Although the United States later sold small quantities of arms to Pakistan — and even smaller quantities to India — the modest amounts involved indicated that neither country could look to the United States as a major source of military equipment.) In retrospect it is also clear that even before the United States ended its military aid in 1965, New Delhi had turned to the Soviet Union as its major supplier; and by the end of 1971, Moscow had agreed to supply \$1.1 billion in arms to India.[28] And the United States rapprochement with Peking made it doubly clear that India would be dependent on the USSR for nearly all of its arms imports for the fore-seeable future.

This dependency, involving as it does India's national security vis-a-vis two hostile neighbors (who are cooperating with each other), would seem to offer the Soviet Union its greatest opportunity to exercise substantial influence on India. A detailed examination of all the records (if they were available) would very likely show examples of Soviet influence on particular matters, such as the types and terms of equipment, training, arrangements, and the construction of defense protection facilities. But there are no Soviet military bases in India, although Soviet naval ships bunker in Indian ports. Indian government officials have repeatedly denied that there are or will be any Soviet naval bases in India, and Soviet naval activity in the Indian Ocean has remained quite modest in recent years.[29] If we look at the larger picture in terms of Moscow's influence on the direction of India's foreign policy it is difficult to see the Soviet hand behind New Delhi's position on any basic issues. New Delhi has backed Soviet policies wherever it feels they do not conflict with India's basic interests, and has refrained from opposing Soviet policies in most instances — or has opposed them with notable restraint. (While New Delhi has not demonstrated nearly as much restraint in its criticism of the United States, it has hardly been the most vociferous Afro-Asian critic of the United States.)

Collective Security and War

Two episodes warrant specific consideration: India's response to Brezhnev's 1969 collective security proposal, and Indo-Soviet relations during the Bangladesh upheaval. India did not respond to Brezhnev's 1969 proposal for a collective security system in Asia, or rather it responded by trying to influence Moscow to cast its proposal more toward Asian cooperation in general than toward collective security in a traditional military sense.[30]

New Delhi has held to its position, even though the Brezhnev proposal received heavy Soviet propaganda emphasis in 1972 and 1973 and was apparently a major issue in the Brezhnev-Gandhi discussions in New Delhi late in 1973. India, already involved in a treaty relationship with the USSR, sees few advantages and many potential drawbacks from any additional formal ties to Moscow outside the economic sphere. (India had responded affirmatively to Kosygin's 1968 proposal for economic cooperation between India, Pakistan, and Afghanistan — later Iran was included — but this was the type of activity India had always favored.) New Delhi's ability to fend off the Soviet Union on this issue is made easier by the vague and shifting nature of the Soviet proposal, which sometimes appears to be a scheme to contain China and at other times is represented as nothing more than a call for economic cooperation among Asian states. Even authoritative Soviet statements on Asian affairs do not dispel this confusion, which suggests that the Soviet leaders are basically casting about for some means of institutionalizing their presence in Asia. * Speculation that the Indo-Soviet treaty was to be the cornerstone of the Soviet collective security edifice has diminished since mid-1972, and some Soviet officials now claim these are to be two separate affairs. This suggests that Soviet officials — despite their propaganda about growing support for the proposal throughout Asia — are uncertain of its appeal and recognize the impossibility of using India as a proxy in Southeast Asia.

Although many aspects of Indo-Soviet diplomacy during 1971 remain obscure, the problem posed by the simultaneous occurrence of the Bangladesh upheaval and the Sino-American rapprochement prompted one Indian observer to comment:

> If India decides to refuse to accept subordination to China,
> it can only refuse it in association with the Soviet Union,
> the only country which in the first place has a symmetrical
> motivation with India, in the second place has the means
> to make its motives effective and yet needs, in the third
> place, as any power must in handling such a large fact as
> China, the support of other countries which share the
> motivation. This means that Mr. Nixon and Mr. Mao
> have conferred a community of interest upon the Soviet
> Union and India which they would have found it difficult
> to develop without this help. 31

While New Delhi stated that the Indo-Soviet treaty signed in August 1971 had been under discussion for two years — or roughly since the Brezhnev proposal — it is far from clear that this represented Indian acquiescence in a Soviet demand. It could be just the reverse, since India wanted a public demonstration of great-power support in the face of the Sino-American rapprochement as the Bangladesh crisis moved toward a climax. However, the most likely explanation is that both parties saw their interests served by such a treaty and acted accordingly. A bargaining relationship was involved during the Bangladesh

---

*Soviet writings on the subject do not do much to clarify the content of Soviet-style collective security, although they repeatedly assert that it must be based upon links between the socialist countries and the forces of national liberation. For an analysis, see Bhabani Sen Gupta, "Soviet Thinking on Asian Collective Security," The Institute for Defence Studies and Analyses Journal, vol. 5, no. 2 (October 1972), 173-195.

crisis, in which each country made an effort to accommodate the other on the points it regarded as essential, while striving to accommodate itself to its partner whenever it felt it could safely do so.

India probably saw such an agreement — and the sharp rise in Soviet arms shipments that followed — as serving several functions: It would solidify its ties with the USSR, and it was a useful warning to Pakistan — and China — that India would have a powerful friend if a new war came; it may have also felt that a dramatic move was required to jolt the United States and force it to reexamine its attempt to maintain some links with Pakistan. Moreover, India had been disappointed and angered that most Afro-Asian states supported the Pakistani government or remained silent, and this increased its feeling of isolation. Mrs. Gandhi, under heavy domestic pressure to recognize Bangladesh, may also have seen the Indo-Soviet treaty as a way of deflecting such pressures. New Delhi emphasized that it had not compromised its policy of nonalignment and remained free to follow its own dictates.

The Soviet Union probably saw the agreement as formalizing the links it had developed with India without committing it to any more specific course of action than the logic of its position already did. Moscow may also have hoped that the agreement would enable it to exercise restraint on New Delhi more effectively if that became necessary, for a principal Soviet concern seemed to be to prevent a new war. The Soviet Union's long-term geopolitical interests in West Pakistan were greater than its interests in East Pakistan. Thus it appeared dubious about any recognition of Bangladesh, and its publicly expressed hopes of a settlement acceptable to the "entire people" of Pakistan were not well-received in India. (The efforts of Soviet leaders to satisfy other Afro-Asian nations — most of whom opposed the division of Pakistan — that the USSR did not favor secessionist movements was another factor that limited Soviet support of India for many months.) But once the die was cast and India's stepped-up military pressure on East Pakistan led to the third Indo-Pakistani war, Moscow found itself with little choice but to stand firmly behind India. Whatever implicit and explicit obligations New Delhi accepted in signing the treaty, and however much its tactics and the timing of its moves were conditioned by its concern for Soviet support, it was able to utilize the treaty for its own ends.[32] Ironically, Moscow's backing of India strengthened the latter's position in the subcontinent to an extent that made it less dependent on Soviet support.

The Scope and Limits of Influence

Limitations of space and investigative resources have made it impossible to analyze and evaluate all the methods involved in the Soviet effort to influence the Indian government. (Nor has any effort been made to appraise Soviet attempts to influence Indian society generally; for if New Delhi's influence on its own society is still very limited, Moscow's must be even less.) Neither the impact of Soviet aid and trade on particular bureaucracies within the Indian government (including the military establishment) nor the effect of Soviet training programs in India or the USSR has been examined. Are such groups sig- nificantly more cooperative in their dealings with the Soviets than other Indians as a result of their greater contacts? One may doubt it if the American experience is any guide — and Moscow's unhappy experiences with some foreign students is well known — but the matter warrants careful study. Nor have polls concerning Indian attitudes toward foreign countries been evaluated; for while such attitudes influence the climate in which New Delhi operates, it is difficult to draw specific conclusions about particular Indian policies from such data. Soviet cultural and propaganda efforts to portray the USSR as a friend of India have been reasonably successful, but it has been actual Soviet support of New Delhi rather than Moscow's propaganda that accounts for this success. On the other hand, Soviet ideology has had a very limited impact on the thinking of Indian intellectuals and policy makers despite the incorpora- tion of a few Marxist concepts into the Indian political vocabulary.[33]

One other topic that has not been considered warrants examination, and that is the matter of linkages.[34] Has the Soviet Union tried — and has it succeeded — in gaining a military output from an economic input? I would set forth the hypothesis that economic aid yields economic dividends and politico-military support yields gains in the same area. However, this needs to be tested to determine whether there are enough exceptions to destroy the general thesis.

Yet even a careful appraisal of the issues left unexplored would be unlikely to change the general conclusions that emerge from this study.[35] The first of these is that Soviet influence in India has grown over the past 20 years to the point of being of some importance. At a minimum, Soviet officials receive a hearing, and their views are care- fully considered when New Delhi makes the decisions. The second is that Soviet influence is not the key determinant in Indian decisions. Having ruled out these extremes, we are left with the harder task of describing in some brief manner the extent of Moscow's influence. My own judgment is that it is quite modest — and is likely to remain so. This is not to say that it is of no consequence. Moscow's role at Tashkent was of considerable importance, and New Delhi's support for many Soviet foreign policy moves — and its retraint in criticizing those it disagrees with — are valued by Soviet officials. New Delhi's relative silence about Soviet naval activity in the Indian Ocean is a case in point. Yet these reflect the normal flow of world politics rather than a pattern which threatens the autonomy of Indian decision-making. *

---

*Ironically, one of the most dramatic descriptions of Soviet influence was obtained by James Reston in interviews with Prime Minis- ter Shastri and other Indian officials, when they told him that India

One might ascribe greater influence to Moscow if it had had a greater impact on Indian domestic politics — perhaps persuading New Delhi to work closely with the CPI, or to include local communists in the national government. A more dramatic sign of Soviet influence would have been the establishment of Soviet naval bases in India — or guaranteed access to Indian bases. Looking to the future, Moscow's ability to keep India from normalizing relations with China would signify more substantial Soviet influence.

It is also important to note that the major impact of Soviet efforts in India has been to enable New Delhi to pursue more effectively policies it wanted to follow in any case. Soviet economic activities strengthened those forces in the Indian government who favored greater state control of the economy. Soviet military aid and political support substantially enhanced Indian military strength and international stature, and enabled it to maintain firm positions in its disputes with Pakistan and China. It is, of course, impossible to say whether India would have been forced to be much more flexible in dealing with its two major neighbors if it had not received such extensive Soviet support. Nor is it clear whether the Soviet leaders expected their support for India to bring them substantially greater influence there, or whether they have been generally satisfied with what they have been able to achieve in India.

Nonetheless, it is worth analyzing the reasons Moscow has not been able to gain greater influence in India. Some of them are both simple and obvious. Moscow's investments, while large in absolute terms, have been quite small compared to the total resources available to New Delhi. A billion dollars in arms over a 10-year period must be related to an Indian defense budget of some $2 billion a year. The $1.6 billion in economic aid commitments — much of it still not disbursed — must be related to the much larger sums India has received from the West and to the even larger amounts spent on economic development from its own resources. Such comparisons cannot be made in any mechanical fashion, of course, for some of the items supplied — modern aircraft and heavy industrial equipment — have been unavailable from other sources, or at least in the quantities or on the terms involved. Even so, they must be viewed in relation to the totality of India's needs.

Even more important than any quantitative appraisal of Indian needs and Soviet assistance is an understanding of the political context of Indo-Soviet relations. India's size and intense nationalism need no elaboration; India sees itself as a major power in its own right, and has been determined to appear as well as be independent of external

---

"was not prepared to take any action that would jeopardize its increasingly close relations with Moscow." The New York Times, December 17, 1965. However, it should be kept in mind that they were speaking only a few months after the United States had withdrawn all military aid during the 1965 war with Pakistan. Moreover, the evidence indicates that India has opposed Moscow on numerous occasions.

influence to the maximum degree possible. Moreover, there is a wide-spread awareness in India that world politics is a shifting and uncertain business, and that while Soviet and Indian interests have generally coincided in the past, they may not do so in the future. Mrs. Gandhi's expressed concern about the superpowers' embarking on a spheres-of-interest policy comes to mind here.

Equally important has been the fact that Moscow has had to com-pete with other countries — especially the United States — for India's favor. Indeed, it is clear that the existence of a competitor, potential as well as actual, almost automatically serves to limit the ability of A to influence B, although this is not something that can be measured with any precision or spelled out in any ratio. Nor is it possible to weigh the balance of influence as regards external powers, especially when their influence is of quite different kinds. Soviet influence grows out of military and diplomatic support, while the West predominates in the economic, cultural, and educational areas. (There were 11,000 Indian students in the United States in 1973, compared to 350 in the USSR.)

Moreover, India's need for Soviet support cannot be considered in isolation from Moscow's need for Indian cooperation. If the USSR is to maintain the coveted status of a superpower, it must have a strong position in the lands to its south from the eastern Mediterranean through the Indian subcontinent. And if the Soviet Union is to partici-pate effectively in the Asian balance of power in order to contain China, it needs the cooperation of India. These Soviet goals have two effects on its attitude and policy. In the first place, they lead Moscow to value stability in India as well as in the subcontinent generally; radical upheavals hold little attraction in view of their uncertain outcomes. Similarly, the Soviet need for a position in a few scattered countries, which it won in the 1950s by backing such nations as India in their disputes with their neighbors, is no longer a fully adequate basis for policy. Thus since the mid-1960s Moscow has attempted to ameliorate Indo-Pakistani disputes whenever that seemed possible, and has worked to establish a position in Pakistan — although when forced to choose (as it was in 1971), its ties with India retain top priority.

There is nothing dramatic or original in these propositions — that it is easier (and cheaper) for A to sustain B's preferred course of action than to alter it; that influence is more difficult for A to exercise when it is in a competitive rather than a monopolistic position; and that the potential for influence is reduced to the extent that A's dependence on B approaches B's dependence on A. Nonetheless, they are important points in two aspects: (1) they extend beyond Indo-Soviet relations, and can be applied to international relations generally, and (2) they demonstrate that the conventional wisdom is sometimes wise as well as conventional, and that it retains some of its validity in an era of rapid change.

Notes

1. For an illustration of some of the problems involved, see Warren F. Ilchman, "A Political Economy of Foreign Aid: The Case of India," Asian Survey, vol. 7, no. 10 (October 1967), 667-688.

2. Two useful works on this subject are K. J. Holsti, International Politics: A Framework for Analysis, Chap. 7 (Englewood Cliffs, New Jersey: Prentice Hall, 1967); and J. David Singer, "Inter-Nation Influence: A Formal Model," in James Rosenau (ed.), International Politics and Foreign Policy: A Reader in Research and Theory (New York: The Free Press, 1969), pp. 380-391.

3. See Chapter 1 of this volume.

4. G. V. Matveyev, "Peking's Political Machinations on the Hindustan Peninsula," Problemy Dalnego Vostoka, no. 4 (1972); in The Current Digest of the Soviet Press, vol. 25, no. 11 (April 11, 1973), p. 4.

5. For a discussion of this point, see David A. Baldwin, "Foreign Aid, Intervention, and Influence," World Politics, vol. 21, no. 3 (April 1969), 425-447 (esp. pp. 429-432).

6. Bhabani Sen Gupta, "The New Balance of Power in South Asia," Pacific Community, vol. 3, no. 4 (July 1972), 698-713.

7. The New York Times, February 17, 1972.

8. Pravda, August 24, 1965, in The Current Digest of the Soviet Press, vol. 17, no. 34 (September 15, 1965), 15-16.

9. Both Ayub Khan in his autobiography, Friends Not Masters (Lahore: Oxford University Press, 1967), and Z. A. Bhutto in his book, The Myth of Independence (Lahore: Oxford University Press, 1969), stop their accounts before the time of Tashkent.

10. Bhabani Sen Gupta, The Fulcrum of Asia: Relations Among China, India, Pakistan and the U. S. S. R. (New York: Pegasus, 1970), pp. 227-232; Arthur Stein, India and the Soviet Union (Chicago: University of Chicago Press, 1969), p. 264; J. A. Naik, Soviet Policy Toward India: From Stalin to Brezhnev (New Delhi: Vikas Publishers, 1970); Harish Kapur, The Soviet Union and the Developing Nations (London: Michael Joseph Ltd., 1972); M. S. Rajan, "The Tashkent Declaration: Retrospect and Prospect," International Studies, vol. 8, nos. 1-2 (July-October 1966), 8. Also see articles by correspondents at the scene in The Washington Post (January 9, 1966); The New York Times (January 11, 1966); and The Times (London, January 11, 1966).

11. M. S. Rajan, op. cit., p. 8.

12. Kapur, op. cit., p. 94. Also see Stein, op. cit., p. 280. Pakistani scholars speak less about Kosygin's role than do Indian scholars. While less enthusiastic than the Indians about the results of Tashkent, they generally agree Kosygin was impartial. See M. A. Chaudhuri, Pakistan and the Great Powers (Karachi: Council for Pakistani Studies, 1970), pp. 66-67; and Zubeida Hasan, "Soviet Arms Aid to Pakistan and India," Pakistan Horizon, vol. 21, no. 4 (4th

Quarter, 1968), 348.

13. See Sen Gupta, op. cit., p. 273; and Kapur, op. cit., p. 97.

14. The New York Times, July 23, 1968.

15. The Times of India, July 12, 1968.

16. Charles B. McLane, Soviet Strategies in Southeast Asia: An Exploration of Eastern Policy Under Lenin and Stalin (Princeton: Princeton University Press, 1966), pp. 351-360.

17. Cited in Gene D. Overstreet and Marshall Windmiller, Communism in India (Berkeley: University of California Press, 1959), p. 353.

18. The Times of India, July 11, 1968.

19. Bhabani Sen Gupta, Communism in Indian Politics (New York: Columbia University Press, 1972), p. 123.

20. Hampton Dewey, "Polarization and Consensus in Indian Party Politics," Asian Survey, vol. 12, no. 8 (August 1972), 703-704.

21. See James R. Carter, The Net Cost of Soviet Foreign Aid (New York: Praeger Publishers, 1971), pp. 39-41.

22. R. V. R. Chandrasekhara Rao, "Indo-Soviet Economic Relations," Asian Survey, vol. 13, no. 8 (August 1973), 793-801.

23. Padma Desai, The Bokaro Steel Plant: A Study of Soviet Economic Assistance (New York: American Elsevier, 1972), p. 86.

24. Ibid., p. 87.

25. See Marshall Goldman, Soviet Foreign Aid (New York: Praeger Publishers, 1967), pp. 97-100.

26. Bureau of Intelligence and Research, Department of State, Communist States and Developing Countries: Aid and Trade in 1971, RECS-3 (May 15, 1972), p. 4.

27. Twenty-Fourth Congress of the Communist Party of the Soviet Union, March 30-April 9, 1971, Documents (Moscow: Novosti Press), pp. 24-25.

28. Bureau of Intelligence and Research, Department of State, Communist States and Developing Countries: Aid and Trade in 1971, RECS-3 (May 15, 1972), p. 18.

29. Geoffrey Jukes, The Indian Ocean in Soviet Naval Policy, Adelphi Paper, no. 87 (London: The International Institute for Strategic Studies, May 1972).

30. See Ian Clark, "The Indian Subcontinent and Collective Security — Soviet Style," The Australian Outlook, vol. 26, no. 3 (December 1972), 315-325.

31. Pran Chopra, Before and After the Indo-Soviet Treaty (New Delhi: S. Chand & Co., 1971), p. 153.

32. For appraisals of the Indo-Soviet treaty and its consequences, see J. A. Naik, India, Russia, China and Bangladesh (New Delhi: S. Chand & Co., 1972); Ashok Kapur, "Indo-Soviet Treaty and the Emerging Asian Balance," Asian Survey, vol. 12, no. 6 (June 1972), 463-474; and Vijay Sen Budhraj, "Moscow and the Birth of Bangladesh," Asian Survey, vol. 13, no. 5 (May 1973), 482-495.

33. Stephen Clarkson, "Non-Impact of Soviet Writing on Indian Thinking and Policy," Economic and Political Weekly, April 14, 1973.

34. For a general discussion of this issue see Robert O. Keohane and Joseph S. Nye, Jr., "Power and Interdependence," Survival, vol. 15, no. 4 (July-August 1973), 158-165.

35. For two appraisals made several years ago, see Richard L. Siegel, Evaluating the Results of Foreign Policy: Soviet and American Efforts in India, The Social Science Foundation and Graduate School of International Affairs, University of Denver, vol. 6, no. 4 (1969); and Wayne Wilcox, The Expansion of Soviet Influence in South Asia and Its Implications for U. S. Policy (Santa Monica: Rand Corp., October 1971), R-939-ISA.

SOVIET AND CHINESE
INFLUENCE IN INDONESIA
Justus M. van der Kroef

In an effort to come to a more precise understanding of the idea of Soviet and Chinese influence in Indonesian affairs, and, hopefully, in order to be able to draw some broader methodological inferences from such a concept, the first two sections of the following essay will offer brief chronological analyses of Indonesia's relations with the USSR and People's China respectively, dating from the close of 1949, when the Indonesian Republic formally attained its national independence. Considerations of space, as well as the theme of this book, compel emphasis in these analyses on (1) those instances or alleged instances in which the policies of Moscow and Peking had, or are generally said to have had, an unusual impact on the Djakarta government and/or on the Indonesian political scene generally, and (2) on the reasons why such an unusual impact is believed to have existed at the time. Within the limits set, there can be no enumeration of all instances of the foreign Communist impact on Indonesia; but it is believed that the following pages do note the highlights. A concluding section of the paper will then attempt to focus on some theoretical implications and conclusions that may be drawn from a consideration of the Indonesian case.

Early Soviet-Indonesian Relations, 1945-49

Despite Soviet political support for the fledgling Indonesian Republic in its independence struggle against the Dutch from 1945 to 1949, a support particularly evident in the United Nations (which involved itself directly as a mediator in Indonesian events), and through Moscow-oriented media and organizations throughout the world, nevertheless the principal matrix of the earliest Soviet-Indonesian state relations was provided by the ill-planned and abortive coup attempt of a number of leaders of the Indonesian Communist Party (Partai Komunis Indonesia — PKI) in Madiun, East Java, in September

1948. Prior to this time the Soviet perception of the Indonesian independence struggle had passed from a UN-focused moderation to a much more militant line, which reflected the ascendance of the Soviets' uncompromising "two camp doctrine" in the autumn of 1947 and implied that Indonesian Communists needed to seize direction of the Indonesian revolution. This perception was spurred on by the Communist-sponsored Southeast Asian Youth Conference held in Calcutta, in February 1948.[1] The PKI's Madiun coup had been quickly suppressed by the forces loyal to President Sukarno and Premier Muhammed Hatta of the revolutionary Indonesian Republic, and, though not formally outlawed, the party's wings had been clipped severely. The failure of the PKI's "stab in the back," as its Indonesian enemies quickly branded the coup attempt, in turn had found its immediate corollary in Moscow's sharp new hostility toward the alleged "reactionary" Sukarno and the Indonesian government as a whole, even though the Russians continued to support the latter in the United Nations, and formally recognized the government when Indonesia at last officially attained her independence from the Dutch on December 27, 1949.

There can be little question that the new Indonesian Republic (apart from the shattered and disarrayed state of the PKI) entered formal independence with its Soviet relations in a deep freeze. Indeed, despite Soviet diplomatic recognition, embassies were not exchanged until 1954, reflecting defeat for another Soviet initiative. For during 1947-48, Suripno, a member of the PKI Central Committee, who had been travelling in Eastern Europe to win support for the cause of the revolutionary Indonesian Republic, had reached agreement with the Soviet Union on an exchange of consuls. But his efforts were, in effect, disavowed by his superiors in Indonesia. Notwithstanding a precipitate Pravda announcement on May 26, 1948, that a consular agreement with the Indonesian Republic had been initialed, and despite claims by the People's Democratic Front (Front Demokrasi Rakjet — FDR), the principal fulcrum of PKI united front pressures in the Republic at this time, that the consular exchange would bring vast supplies of Soviet aid to Indonesian revolutionaries, the Indonesian Republic government resisted, possibly because she feared loss of critically important American goodwill for its cause.[2] The subsequent abortive PKI coup attempt in Madiun seemed to underscore the desirability, if not the wisdom, on the part of Indonesian leaders of having turned aside the Soviet consular overtures.

Domestic Indonesian Changes

In any event, when Indonesia at last became free, Russian stock was very low indeed on Djakarta's diplomatic and political exchange. And it was destined to remain low for at least five or six years longer, even though in April 1950, largely on Soviet initiatives, and also via Dutch diplomats, tentative discussions had been begun again to establish formal Soviet-Indonesian diplomatic relations. The reason for the continuing coolness was, first, that from 1950 to 1952 Indonesian cabinets were dominated by the anti-Communist Masjumi (Muslim Federation) party (there were mass arrests of Communists and sympathizers in August 1951); and later, when cabinets led by the National Indonesian Party (Partai Nasional Indonesia — PNI) emerged, the issue of formal diplomatic ties with the Soviets became one of several, increasingly more severe, parliamentary crises. On April 9, 1953, despite Masjumi's opposition, the Indonesian parliament passed a resolution calling for the establishment of diplomatic relations with the USSR by the end of 1953. However, not until March 1954, and after yet another cabinet change, was an Indonesian embassy finally opened in Moscow.[3]

The events surrounding the exchange of embassies illustrated what has been in fact the principal factor in Soviet-Indonesian relations throughout the recent decades. It was not any particularly significant Russian policy pronouncement or tactical move that impelled first the Indonesian parliament to approve the establishment of an embassy and, later, the first cabinet of Premier Ali Sastroamijojo (1953-55) to implement it. Stalin's last years may or may not have witnessed inauguration of more flexible and opportunistic policies toward the Third World. But the dynamics of ambassadorial exchange with the Soviets were first and foremost the important changes that had been taking place in the Indonesian political economy and in the alignment of parties and emergent interest groups connected with these changes. A more nativistic, and to a degree more radical Indonesian nationalism was emerging, associated with indigenous business, professional, and military elites. These elites were chafing under Western-style parliamentary and constitutional procedures established at the time the country received its independence from the Dutch, under the dominance of foreign, particularly Dutch and Chinese (even if native born) corporate and entrepreneurial interests, and under a foreign policy that seemed too dependent on existing big power concerns and only minimally appeared to reflect the aspirations of the new nations.[4]

Diplomatic relations with the USSR could, under these conditions, almost be perceived as an aspect of a kind of second Indonesian Revolution, one that would presumably liberate Indonesians from the political processes, cultural habits, and economic practices, inherited from the colonial era and which had been preserved during these early years of independence in the context of the Dutch-Indonesian Union. Then, too, there were possible trade advantages, which might lessen the dependence of Indonesian exports on Western markets. And not least, there was the remarkable resurgence and rehabilitation of the PKI from the ignominy of the 1948 coup episode under a new youthful party leadership. D. N. Aidit, the new PKI chairman and principal theoretician, developed at this time an effective new party program which seemed in particular harmony with the aspirations of the restive "national bourgeoisie" of Indonesian entrepreneurs and professionals.[5] In the Indonesian parliamentary sphere, the tactical and ideological affinities between the PKI and the PNI (despite occasional sharp competition, as during the 1955 general elections), which were directed against the anti-Communist Masjumi, gave Communism a new respectability.

But these developments, particularly the new appeals of a more radical nativistic nationalism, also seriously began polarizing Indonesian political life. In November 1956, dissident anti-Communist and anti-Sukarno Indonesian Army commanders, eventually joined by leaders of Masjumi and the anti-PKI Socialist Party, began to seize power in various areas of Sumatra and Sulawesi (Celebes), eventually bringing the country to the brink of civil war. This polarization of Indonesian political life was undoubtedly a major asset to the PKI, which staunchly supported President Sukarno and his authoritarian "Guided Democracy" scheme promulgated in the later fifties to meet the deepening domestic crisis. But it also paved the way for an accelerating improvement in Soviet-Indonesian relations, hard on the heels of the reciprocal opening of embassies in 1954. Sukarno, pleased by the success of the 1955 Bandung conference of 29 African and Asian powers, meanwhile had increasingly come to like his role as a world leader. During more frequent, pompous, journeys abroad, from 1956 onward, as well as during crisis flash points at home, Sukarno began articulating a new, symbol-larded, radical, and anti-Western nativistic ideology that could not but be pleasing to Moscow.

Soviet and East European Trade and Aid

In September 1956, almost immediately after the first Soviet-Indonesian trade agreement had been concluded the previous month, Sukarno made his first visit to the Soviet capital. Although the Soviet-Indonesian communique (which denounced military pacts) and the Soviet credit grant of $100 million subsequently became ensnarled in partisan political controversy in Indonesia upon the President's return, this Moscow visit, and the May 1957 return visit to Indonesia by USSR President K. Voroshilov, marked the starting point of an entente which grew so steadily that within a few years one respected writer could comment: "Since Premier Khrushchev's 10-day visit in February 1960, Indonesia has become a major target of Soviet aid and influence and only massive Western efforts can now prevent its gradual incorporation into the Communist bloc."[6]

While with the advantage of hindsight few would agree that Indonesia was gradually drifting into the Communist orbit because of Soviet aid, there is no denying that from 1956 onward aid was truly massive. In 1958, for example, in an arms agreement with Poland and Czechoslovakia, who acted as intermediaries for the USSR, Indonesia received some $250 million in weapons (including 90 MIG-15 and MIG-17 jet fighters, as well as bombers and cargo planes,

submarines and other naval vessels); during the February 1960
Khrushchev visit to Djakarta, $250 million in Soviet economic aid was
granted. In January 1961, during the Moscow visit of the Indonesian
National Security Minister and Army Staff Chief, General A. H. Nasution,
a $400 million military credit was extended to the Indonesians. Along
with aid provided by other Communist countries and some smaller Soviet
credits, Indonesia had received more than $1.5 billion from the Commu-
nist bloc by the end of 1961, more than any other country at the time,
and exceeding even the estimated $1.3 billion which the People's
Republic of China had received from the USSR between 1949 and 1957.
On December 31, 1965, Indonesia's total foreign indebtedness to all
nations was estimated to amount to $2,538 million, of which $990
million was owed the Soviet Union, making the USSR Indonesia's
largest single creditor. A Soviet-Indonesian financial protocol, signed
in Moscow on November 22, 1966, fixed the total of Indonesia's debts
at $804 million, including $23 million in military debts; accumulated
interest on this indebtedness was set at an additional $127 million.[7]

The Indonesian "Momentum" Policy

What had the Soviet Union hoped to gain by this largesse
extended over such a relatively short period of time? An answer to this
question must first focus again on domestic Indonesian policies and
their projection outward in terms of the crisis over Irian Barat (West
New Guinea). On February 15, 1958, the chronic unrest in the
provinces beyond Java, evident since 1956, escalated into the
proclamation of a new "Revolutionary Government of the Indonesian
Republic" (Pemerintan Revolusioner Republik Indonesia — PRRI) in West
Sumatra, with which a number of dissident military commanders and
Masjumi and PSI politicians affiliated, as meanwhile parts of Sulawesi
(Celebes) also proclaimed their adhesion to the rebel cause. With the
support of most of the Army, which remained loyal to Sukarno (despite
the deep misgivings of senior officers), and of the PKI, PNI, and lesser
parties, the beleaguered Sukarno regime struck back, developing a so-
called momentum policy, in which a new national unity was to be forged
not only through a determined anti-PRRI military campaign, but also
through a "nation building" mass mobilization and indoctrination effort
in the context of Sukarno's "Guided Democracy" concept.[8] The framework of this new centripetal "momentum" policy was the so-called
Constitution of 1945 of the original revolutionary Indonesian Republic
which gives the President great powers. After Indonesia had obtained
its independence at the close of 1949, this Constitution had been
replaced. But now, backed by emergency powers, Sukarno unilaterally
reimposed the 1945 Constitution, solidifying his authority. The spirit
of a Rousseauist levee en masse, cultivated by new government-
sponsored organizations and expressed in new slogans and symbols
developed by Sukarno, presumably pointed the way to a future era of

national greatness and unity via the present thorny path of provincial rebellion and economic crisis.

As, in the course of 1959-60, Djakarta slowly reestablished its authority over the dissident provinces, the "momentum" tactic was in the following years reaccentuated and directed this time with increasing militancy on behalf of a campaign to acquire Dutch held West New Guinea. The one part of the former Dutch East Indian empire, Dutch-held West New Guinea (or Irian Barat, as Indonesians called it) which had not been transferred to Indonesian control when the Indonesian Republic formally obtained its freedom at the close of 1949, now became the new focal point of Sukarnoist tactics of forging national unity through mass mobilization in a perpetual crisis atmosphere. To be sure, Indonesia had begun pressing its claim to West New Guinea since 1950. But it was not until the 1960s that acquisition of the territory became an element of the "momentum" policy and its mass mobilization tactics. Through a highly charged, bellicose, international press and diplomatic campaign, which suggested that a Dutch-Indonesian war and a full-scale Indonesian invasion of West New Guinea (in order to "liberate" its inhabitants from alleged colonial oppression and brutality) were imminent, the Sukarno regime with the enthusiastic support of the PKI conveyed an image to the world of all-out determination, prepared to endure domestic economic chaos in order to attain its irredenta.[9] The Irian campaign was spectacularly successful, and thanks to very strong U.S. pressure on the Dutch, an agreement was reached on August 15, 1962, providing for the phased, but complete transfer within one year of the disputed territory to Indonesian control.

Soviet Arms for Indonesia

Indonesia's initial $100 million credit (obtained at the time of Sukarno's Moscow visit in September 1956) provided for some military purchases; and in the weeks before the proclamation of the PRRI in mid-February 1958, as relations between the Djakarta central government and the dissident provinces worsened, discussions for additional arms purchases were held in Prague. The outbreak of the PRRI rebellion greatly accelerated Soviet arms supplies: "Within days Soviet vessels were docking in Indonesian harbors, soon followed by a swelling flood of reports concerning the arrival and assembly of Soviet-made planes at Surabaja and elsewhere."[10] After some initial hesitation the Soviets had begun by mid-1957 to give support to Indonesia's claim to West New Guinea. And when General Nasution left in January 1961 for Moscow to complete an additional $400 million Soviet arms credit deal, he stressed that this new arms purchase was part of Indonesia's "confrontation in all fields" in the acquisition of Irian Barat.[11]

And yet in retrospect, one is bound to note that neither the 1958 rush of Soviet weapons after the eruption of the PRRI rebellion, nor the 1961 Soviet arms credit, were at the time logistically indispensable to the Djakarta government or to Sukarno's authoritarian leadership. Without the 1958 Soviet arms deliveries and the steady arrival of MIG-15s and Ilyushin-28s for the Indonesian Air Force during the following two years, as well as of Polish submarines, and Soviet submarine chasers, naval oilers, and other vessels to boost the Indonesian Navy,[12] the campaign against the PRRI might have been slowed. But given the loyalty of the bulk of the Indonesian Army and government control of the central bureaucracy, that campaign would eventually have succeeded anyway. As for Irian Barat, Indonesian military action during the 1960-62 crisis period, as distinct from the enormously successful, political propaganda "war scare" campaign, was largely confined to small-scale, random, paratroop drops, limited commando infiltration by sea, and a skirmish with a few motor torpedo boats of the Indonesian Navy, none of which caused the Dutch forces in the disputed territory any great difficulty. On the other hand, the Soviet arms deliveries and Moscow's denunciation of the PRRI and their alleged CIA agents, as well as full throated support for the Irian campaign and the Sukarno regime generally, particularly in the United Nations, undoubtedly gave a powerful psychological and political boost to the Djakarta government. Although in May 1958, the United States also agreed to sell the Indonesian government about half a million dollars worth of small arms and aircraft parts, and although Indonesian leaders kept publicly insisting that in accord with Indonesia's "independent" foreign policy Indonesian arms shopping was not confined to the Communist bloc alone, there is little doubt that because of earlier American hesitation and strictures on arms deliveries to Indonesia (not to mention U.S. Secretary of State John Foster Dulles' criticism of the Sukarno regime at the time of the PRRI rebellion), Moscow had clearly stolen a march on its Western competitors at a critical juncture in Indonesia's early national history. The huge 1961 Soviet arms purchase was the crown on this achievement. Realization of this may well have been decisive early in 1962 by causing the Kennedy administration, then preparing to escalate the U.S. commitment in another Southeast Asian crisis, namely Vietnam, to begin exerting maximum pressure on the Dutch to surrender Irian.[13]

Questions About Soviet Influence

But could all this Soviet material and political support for the Sukarno regime really be said to have created a state of affairs in which Moscow, if, perhaps, only to a greater degree than before, was now calling the tune of Indonesian domestic and foreign policies? Or, in other words, was the new Khrushchevian policy of the later 1950s of Third World accommodation and assistance to revolutionary and/or post-colonial liberation movements on the way to "national democracy" and beyond, paying off in Indonesia? To the extent that Soviet aid and support had helped in the preservation of Sukarno's regime and its radical nativistic nationalism and in the campaign to acquire West New

Guinea, and to the degree that these developments had frustrated and embarrassed the United States and its allies, Soviet policy might be deemed successful. But considering the material expense involved, the effectiveness of the Soviet support policy might well be doubted. Certainly in the case of the suppression of the PRRI, Soviet arms supplies were not critically important; as indicated, the effect of Soviet arms aid in the West New Guinea crisis was primarily political and psychological. Could the same results not have been attained, there-fore, at considerable less cost to the Soviets?

Then, too, events were to show that the aid provided by Moscow had, at best, a short-term value. For one thing, the anti-Sukarno and anti-Communist opposition in Indonesia, though formally suppressed and contained in Sukarno's "Guided Democracy," was not destroyed. Indeed, it would erupt with explosive force by the end of 1965. The "nation building" Irian campaign and the "momentum" tactic did not end the polarizations in Indonesian political life but merely covered them over, as each of three principal Indonesian power factors, that is, Sukarno, the Army, and the PKI (by now the largest and most influ-ential party), established a precarious mutual equilibrium. Both the 1956 and the 1958 Soviet credit extensions furthermore had aroused political controversy and misgivings among the military, and the acqui-escence by Nasution and other high Army commanders in subsequent Russian weapons shipments was primarily actuated by the consideration that, since it would be impossible for top Army leaders to turn against the Sukarno regime anyway, the armed forces might as well make them-selves as strong as possible within the "Guided Democracy" system in anticipation of a widely expected, inevitable showdown with the PKI. Precisely this strengthening of the Army was what the Soviet arms shipments were helping to accomplish.

To be sure, the Soviet buildup of the Indonesian Air Force and the training of some of its pilots in Eastern Europe did, reportedly, contribute to the emergence of a leftist Air Force officers group, of which Air Marshals Suryadarma and Omar Dhani, both Sukarno favorites, were acknowledged leaders. But this leftist contingent, though aug-mented, as in the case of the Indonesian Army and Navy, by covert PKI proselytizing, comprised but a fraction of the armed forces' total. One can but speculate in some wonderment what the USSR eventually hoped to gain by building up the one, most anti-Communist element of the Indonesian power triad. Certainly there was no rapid emergence of a pro-Moscow political momentum in the armed forces. For these reasons too, the PKI leadership, still striving in the 1961-63 period to retain formal neutrality in the Sino-Soviet conflict, and engaged in an usually covert, but intensely bitter, political struggle with the Army, could not but have very mixed feelings about the massive Soviet arms aid. This, in turn, was hardly likely to make the PKI an effective Soviet policy instrument on the Indonesian scene.

Soviet Failure? The Malaysian Affair

How little leverage the Soviets had in Djakarta, despite their generosity, became apparent during 1962-63, when, virtually without shifting political gears, the Indonesian government's successfully con- cluded Irian confrontation campaign moved into a new confrontation effort, directed this time against the planned creation of the Malaysian Federation. There remains controversy over the motives behind Djakarta's sudden anti-Malaysia policy. But surely the need to preserve the highly delicate Indonesian domestic balance of power through a new foreign adventure was of critical, and probably of decisive, importance. How- ever, the campaign against Malaysia, accompanied by the same small- scale, Indonesian guerrilla and paratroop infiltrations, and the intense political and psychological war-scare tactics that Djakarta had used in the West New Guinea crisis, suited Moscow much less, and, indeed, demonstrated its diplomatic failure in Indonesia for at least three rea- sons.

First, the anti-Malaysia confrontation created a potentially serious and, in any case, an unpredictable problem at the very time that the USSR was attempting to foster a policy of coexistence with the United States in a general climate of more relaxed international relations.[14] Sukarno's new anti-Malaysia campaign was also a serious policy reversal for the Kennedy administration, which, by pressuring the Dutch to relinquish their hold on West New Guinea and by promising Sukarno a long-term development assistance program, had sought to improve the U.S.' own relations with Djakarta. The United States discovered by the middle of 1963, however, that it would have to reconsider its options in Southeast Asia at a time of an already ever growing involvement in the Vietnam quagmire. Second, the abruptness and intensity with which the organizational machinery of mass mobiliza- tion and propagandization could be and was mobilized by the Sukarno regime against a new external target, in avowed disregard of any effort at solving the deepening crisis of Indonesia's chaotic economy, sug- gested a recklessness and instability in the Indonesian leadership, which, increasingly aggravated by the bizarre bombast of Sukarno's personal political style, seemed to render the delivery of modern arms to that leadership somewhat akin to handing a loaded pistol to a mentally disturbed infant. * And, third, the enthusiasm with which the

_____

*The grave economic consequences of the Sukarnoist confronta- tion policies can hardly be exaggerated. Two authoritative economists wrote, shortly after the abortive 30 September 1965 coup, that "a pic- ture of economic breakdown has been revealed to the Indonesian people and to the world which can have few parallels in a great nation in modern times except in the immediate aftermath of war or revolution."
(J. Panglaykim and H.W. Arndt, The Indonesian Economy: Facing a New Era [Rotterdam: Rotterdam University Press, 1966], p. 7)

PKI supported the anti-Malaysia campaign (indeed, it had initiated this campaign at the close of 1961 even before it became official Indonesian policy), and the increasingly Maoist hues of PKI ideology, indicated that Indonesian Communists could in no way be counted on to lend strength to Soviet policy interests.* Moreover, because of the PKI's dynamic role in the steady radicalization of official Indonesian policies and on the political scene generally, Peking, which also had swiftly condemned the formation of the Malaysian Federation, seemed to be —and, in fact, shortly became —the natural ally of the Sukarno regime in this new "confrontation" venture.

Djakarta's Drift Toward Peking

Under all these circumstances it is remarkable that Moscow remained hopeful (or desperate) enough to continue its arms deliveries to Indonesia and even agreed to new ones, as well as to a moratorium on repayments. During his Djakarta visit in June 1964, Soviet Deputy Premier Anastas Mikoyan even managed qualified support for the anti-Malaysia campaign (provided it was carried out, he said, "with a sense of responsibility"), and proffered assurances of new Soviet supplies of aircraft, including transport planes and helicopters. The latter promise was implemented further by an Indonesian Air Force mission to Moscow the next month, when it was reportedly agreed that "the Soviet Union will also sell to Indonesia the latest weapons within the framework of perfecting the country's air defense."[15]

At this juncture, however, PKI attacks on "revisionism," a term increasingly used by the party leadership to designate the USSR, had

---

*During 1961, PKI chairman Aidit had still equivocated on the implications of the Sino-Soviet dispute, refusing to condemn Albania and acknowledging the enduring contributions of Josef Stalin, but also simultaneously acknowledging the "vanguard" role of the Communist Party of the Soviet Union and stressing the independence of the PKI "which is not led by any other party." See D. N. Aidit's essay in Serba-Serbi Dokumen Partai 1961 (Djakarta: Jajasan Pembaruan, 1962), pp. 112-115; and Strengthen National Unity and Communist Unity, Documents of the Third Plenum of the Central Committee of the Communist Party of Indonesia, Djakarta, end December 1961 (Djakarta: Jajasan Pembaruan, 1962), p. 24. During Aidit's visit to Peking in late August and early September 1963, he began to reveal a distinctive Maoist line, for example, in his emphasis on the paramount importance of armed struggle, in his subsequent identification with Peking's view of its relations with India, and with Chinese attacks on the Indian "revisionist" Communist leader S. A. Dange. See also D. N. Aidit, Langit Takkan Runtuh (Djakarta: Jajasan Pembarun, 1963), pp. 24-40.

become steadily shriller, and, like the Chinese, Aidit began stressing that "the main measure rod" of doctrinal purity of a Communist party was adhesion to the Moscow Declaration of 1957 and the Moscow Statement of 1960.[16] The PKI refused to send a delegation to the anti-Peking International Communist and Workers' Parties Conference in Moscow in March 1965, presumably because not all such parties and Socialist countries had been invited to attend. Still, it must be said that the PKI as far as possible formally maintained the proprieties in its relationship with the USSR, never attacking Moscow or Soviet leaders openly and by name.

Sukarno, meanwhile, yoked Indonesian foreign policy ever more firmly to that of Peking, closely supporting the Chinese diplomatic offensive in the African-Asian world through various solidarity conferences that sought to exclude Soviet participation.[17] Full Chinese backing for the anti-Malaysia confrontation, in turn, went hand in hand with Indonesian Communist infiltration in the Philippines, with the conduit role of PKI personnel of Indonesian consular offices in India in funnelling funds to Indian Maoists, and with the increasing warmth generally between Djakarta and various Asian Communist states. "Thus what we saw taking place rapidly," President Lyndon Johnson among other commentators was to write later, "was a Djakarta-Hanoi-Peking-Pyongyang axis, with Cambodia probably to be brought in as a junior partner,"[18] and operating strategically in a nutcracker fashion subsequently described by Sukarno as the strategy whereby Communist China struck a blow against the American troops in Vietnam from the North, while Indonesia struck from the South. In the meantime, PKI leaders and a handful of left "progressive" officers, with the almost certain foreknowledge of Sukarno, and aided by covert supplies of Chinese arms, began laying plans for a new coup attempt.

The 1965 Coup and Its Effects

The events surrounding the failure of this abortive coup, which occurred on the night of September 30, 1965, are not relevant here. It must be noted, however, that the debacle of Gestapu (from Gerakan Tiga Puluh September or "Thirty September Movement," as Indonesians customarily refer to the coup) led rapidly in subsequent months to the fall from power of Sukarno and to his replacement by General Suharto, to the banning of the PKI, to the killing and jailing of tens of thousands of PKI cadres, suspects and, it is to be feared, innocents, and, last but not least, to a drastic alteration of Indonesian foreign policies involving principally a rupture with Peking and a new hospitality to Western and Japanese development capital. In Gestapu's aftermath Indonesia's relations with the USSR were also at first subjected to new strains, but since 1972 a gradual improvement has been noticeable. The banning of the PKI and of Marxism-Leninism has made domestic anti-Communism an official (and partisan) policy dynamic in Indonesia, which has periodically resulted in charges that the USSR (and more especially the Soviet Embassy in Djakarta) has been covertly assisting the Communist underground in Indonesia and anti-Suharto elements. In turn, uncomplimentary references to the "reactionary" Suharto government and its "fascist jails and torture chambers" harboring "devoted patriots who had fought against imperialism, " as well as descriptions of the adverse living conditions generally of the Indonesian people under the Suharto regime (one Pravda account charged that 22 million Indonesian children cannot attend school because of their parents' poverty), along with warnings that the Djakarta government is abandoning its nonalignment foreign policy and is veering too closely to the "U.S. imperialists" —these became the stock in trade of the Soviet media.[19]

Repeated Soviet attempts to intercede on behalf of condemned PKI leaders charged with masterminding the Gestapu affair and alleged Kremlin efforts to exploit the tens of thousands of political prisoners in Indonesia through the organization of an international relief campaign, brought furious Indonesian press reactions. Meanwhile, Muslim groups in Indonesia protested allegedly slighting references in Soviet books to the Koran, Islam, or the Prophet Muhammad.[20]

Sources of Indonesian-Soviet Friction

Other seemingly chronic sources of contention remain, for example, the presence in Moscow and other East European capitals of Soviet-oriented PKI exiles who continue to denounce and call for resistance to the Suharto regime as well as acknowledge the party's past tactical errors because of Maoist influence. Then there is the controversy over whether the Malacca Straits should be considered a free international sea passage (as the USSR has maintained) or, on the basis of a 12-mile territorial water limit (insisted on by Indonesia and Malaysia), should be viewed as falling essentially within Indonesian and Malaysian jurisdiction. * Meanwhile, the Soviet planes, naval ships, and other military hardware given Indonesia over the years now are rapidly

---

* On December 18, 1972, the Soviet ambassador to Indonesia, P.S. Kuznetsov, was first reported to have endorsed Indonesia's 12-mile territorial waters claim. Shortly thereafter, however, the Soviet embassy in Djakarta issued a press statement saying that the Soviet position on the Malacca Straits question remained unchanged, that it considered it as a free sea passage. Antara Daily News Bulletin, vol. 25, no. 1650 (December 18, 1972) and vol. 25, no. 1658 (December 29, 1972). See also M. Leifer and D. Nelson, "Conflict of Interest in the Straits of Malacca, " International Affairs, vol. 30, no. 2 (April 1973), 190-203.

becoming, for want of spare parts, as much of a monument to obsolescence and the Sukarno past as the Polish sugar refinery in Acheh, North Sumatra, which closed two days after opening, and the Soviet phosphate plant at Tjilajap in Java, or the Soviet marine biology laboratory at Ambon, East Indonesia, both of which no longer operate.[21] Because of repeated Indonesian requests since 1966 for a moratorium on the repayment of the $804 million Indonesian debt to Moscow (as determined by the previously mentioned financial protocol of November 22, 1966), the Soviets were at first reluctant to extend new credits. However, Moscow eventually became more accommodating in working out a repayment schedule, and there have also been periodic discussions on completion or reactivation of unfinished or inoperative projects dating from the Sukarno era and new Soviet offers of help.

Still, in the context of the Nixon diplomatic initiatives toward Peking and Moscow, and the resulting general reassessment among the Southeast Asian nations of their region's security policies and needs, Indonesia, particularly since 1972, has made some effort to improve her relations with the USSR, finding the latter more than willing to reciprocate. Speaking in Djakarta on December 20, 1972, Indonesian Foreign Minister Adam Malik emphasized that Indonesia "was greatly desirous" to normalize her relations with all East European "socialist countries"; and on February 12, 1973, Indonesian President Suharto reportedly charged Indonesia's new ambassador to Moscow, Surjono Darusman, with explaining to the Soviet leaders that Soviet-Indonesian relations should not be related to Indonesia's "domestic policy" — a reference, one may surmise, to the Suharto regime's avowed domestic anti-Communism. From May 24 to June 3, 1973, a seven-man delegation from the Indonesian parliament paid a goodwill visit to the USSR, meeting with Soviet officials in what was described by the Antara Indonesian news agency as "a cordial atmosphere." Soviet spokesmen and media meanwhile — along with their usual criticism already noted — have in recent months repeatedly expressed the hope for closer relations with Indonesia, particularly in trade and, countering periodic Indonesian press charges, have stressed that the USSR is no threat to Indonesia, nor has any intention of involving itself in Indonesia's domestic affairs. According to a press statement by Malik, in December 1972, Soviet officials had assured him that the USSR would "not indulge in subversive activities against Indonesia" and was now "eager" to see Indonesia grow and develop.[22]

Despite such assurances, and notwithstanding Moscow's eventual relative flexibility in working out a long-term repayment schedule of Indonesia's formidable debts to the USSR, and even a Russian readiness to extend new credits as well as complete existing development projects like the iron and steel plant at Tjilegon,[23] powerful elements in the Indonesian political community, for example, in the Army and among Muslim groups, continue to block an acceleration of improvements in Soviet-Indonesian relations (just as they do in regards to

relations with China). The real dynamic in such an eventual improvement, it would appear, stems from the Nixon initiatives in attempting
to create a more flexible "multi-polar" international order, and from the
resulting necessity to reshape Indonesia's —and indeed Southeast
Asia's —foreign relations in more fluid terms that can accommodate and
balance the interests of the USSR as well as those of the other major
power blocs. With East-West Cold War rigidities ending, or at least
diminishing, Djakarta realizes that it must become more hospitable to
Moscow's growing presence and impact in the South Asian and Southeast Asian regions. On March 23, 1974, a new Soviet-Indonesian trade
agreement was signed in Djakarta, marking, as Indonesian Foreign
Minister Malik put it, the beginning of a "new phase" in relations
between the two countries. Indonesia has remained skeptical about
such recent Soviet policy initiatives in Asia as the collective security
proposal for the region first advanced by Soviet party Secretary Leonid
Brezhnev. But, of late, Indonesian reactions to the Soviet idea are not
as sharply negative as they used to be. The problems which the Suharto
government is experiencing in disseminating the advantages of massive
inputs of Western development capital for the benefit of all Indonesians
has also made it more sensitive to Soviet criticisms about the "one-
sidedness" of Indonesia's "economic orientation."[24]

Before underscoring the implications of all these developments,
particularly in the context of current or future Soviet influence in Indonesia, it is necessary first, however, to review briefly the pattern of
Sino-Indonesian relations.

The Scope of Sino-Indonesian Relations

There are three more or less distinctive phases in Indonesia's
relations with People's China. The first spans the period from mid-
1950, when Peking opened its embassy in Djakarta, to the beginning
of 1963, when relations, after more than a decade of alternating
tepidness and coolness, rather suddenly and remarkably began to
warm up, to the point of an alliance. The second phase, the one of
greatest amicability thus far, runs from 1963 to the Gestapu affair of
1965 and, however, brief, was of considerable significance in Indonesian policies. The third phase, finally, from the failure of the 1965
coup to the present, is a period of severe mutual antagonism, but one
which, because of the Nixon diplomatic gambit referred to above, has
shown a few signs of possible improvement.

Early Diplomatic Recognition

We are still in the dark as to just why the new Indonesian Republic, so reluctant to formalize diplomatic relations with the USSR, already in August 1950 agreed to accept an embassy of the government
of the People's Republic of China, sending its own charge-d'affaires

to Peking in January 1951. Perhaps three reasons, at least, may be hypothesized. First, Indonesia's decision to open diplomatic relations occurred in the middle of 1950, at the end of the tenure of the cabinet of Muhammad Hatta, which had to contend, increasingly, with "the rising power of radical nationalism" in the newly independent Republic, especially in the influential PNI, even then sympathetic to cooperation with the Communists.[25] Already a Communist inspired and PNI backed motion in the Indonesian parliament to recognize the Democratic Republic of Vietnam had been headed off with difficulty by the anti-Communist Masjumi party. In the complicated partisan wrangling between PNI and Masjumi, recognition of the new Chinese government was one element of a series of tactical parliamentary compromises, accepted with reluctance by the Masjumi and its allies. Second, there was the impression given by the new Chinese regime. Unlike the USSR, that regime was appreciated as distinctively "Asian," and, rightly or wrongly, as being a dimension of the modern Chinese nationalist and anticolonial struggle, which could therefore command a ready, almost obligatory sympathy among Indonesian nationalists. (The Korean War would soon change some of this latent appeal.) The present author's conversations with Indonesian students and youth of widely varied political persuasion during this period revealed a common conviction that under Mao Tse-tung Chinese Communism had somehow evolved in a unique way and was "Asian," and, therefore, notably different from Russian or "Western" Bolshevism. And, third, there was the question of the 2.5 million "Overseas Chinese" community in Indonesia whose allegedly ambivalent loyalties to the new Indonesian Republic were considered a potential danger that might be countered if Sino-Indonesian diplomatic channels were open. A common belief that during the Indonesian revolutionary struggle the Indonesian Chinese, also because of their alleged Kuomintang sympathies, had sided with the Dutch, seemed to introduce an element of retribution in the Indonesian diplomatic recognition of the new People's Chinese government.

If Indonesians had hoped that, by extending diplomatic recognition to the Peking government, the question of Indonesian Chinese loyalties was nearer an answer, they soon were disappointed. During the fifties and again since the 1965 coup attempt, suspicion of the loyalties of Indonesian Chinese closely interacted with fear of Peking's own policies in Asia, and especially of the role of its embassy in Djakarta in relation to those policies. Already in the course of 1951, the growing Chinese diplomatic staff in Djakarta, and its presumably increasing hold on the Indonesian Chinese, had produced friction with the anti-Communist Sukiman government and had led to restrictions on the further influx of Chinese consular officials. Subsequently, the reports that the Chinese embassy was assisting the PKI with money and printed matter, though denied by PKI leaders, further strained relations. With the advent of the first Ali Sastroamidjojo cabinet (1953-55), a new and atypical cordiality seemed at first to be

developing. In accord with the Ali cabinet's friendlier attitudes toward
the Communist bloc, relations with China also markedly improved, as
Indonesian officials now publicly supported Peking's position during the
crisis over the offshore islands in the Straits of Formosa. The April
1955 Asian-African Conference in Bandung, West Java, particularly
seemed to underscore People's China's rightful place in the new Third
World community and also appeared to mark a new high in a seemingly
growing Sino-Indonesian amicability.[26]

The Dual Nationality Problem

New frictions shortly appeared, however. A Dual Nationality
Treaty, regulating the troublesome question of the legal and citizenship
status of Indonesian Chinese, had been signed by Chou En-lai and
Indonesia's Foreign Minister Sunarjo during the happy flush of the
Bandung Conference. But the treaty soon became a political football in
Indonesia, delaying formal ratification; and from 1958 on a cascade of
Indonesian government measures restricting the residence, as well as
the business and educational operations of Indonesian Chinese, further
strained relations. Reportedly incited by Chinese embassy officials,
Indonesian Chinese traders resisted government orders that they move
from their rural businesses; and violent clashes resulted, especially
in Java during 1959-60. Peking's threat to withdraw altogether from
the Dual Nationality Treaty ultimately led to final implementation in
January 1960, at a time when relations between the two countries had
deteriorated considerably compared to the Bandung Conference days.
Meanwhile there had been other gyrations. Already in October 1956,
Sukarno, during a Peking visit, apparently had been promised Chinese
arms aid; but an Indonesian military mission, sent to China in May
1957, returned empty-handed. By the end of 1957, however, Peking
appeared to be relenting again, having given full support, in the
meantime, to Indonesia in the recovery of its West New Guinea
irredenta, and promising both economic aid and military equipment.
Deliveries were slow in being made, however; still, in the fall of
1968, Peking appeared to be competing with Moscow in selling rice
to Indonesia at lower prices, and in offering to build yet another steel
mill in Indonesia, after the Russians had already offered to construct
two.[27]

But in this 1950-63 period it was neither the offers of Chinese
aid, nor Chinese impatience over Indonesian reluctance to implement
the Dual National Treaty, nor again Peking's anger over the measures
being taken against the Chinese traders in Indonesia, nor even the
developing Sino-Soviet conflict that was of paramount importance in
shaping Djakarta's policies toward China. These factors were not
nugatory, to be sure. But far more significant was the more nativistic
and xenophobic nationalism which came to full prominence with the
first Ali Sastroamidjojo cabinet and later achieved dominance with

the imposition of Sukarno's "Guided Democracy" system. Indonesia's relations with both the USSR and People's China improved with the advent of this new nativistic perspective. Ironically, it was precisely because of the same perspective that the position of the Indonesian Chinese community, especially its merchants, began to deteriorate, as measures were being enacted to favor the indigenous Indonesian business man over the "foreign" entrepreneur. Anti-Chinese prejudice, long endemic in Indonesian (indeed in Southeast Asian) society, was reinvigorated as nativistic cultural policies accentuated the alleged undesirability of Chinese schools and of a distinct Chinese minority culture. Moreover, however concerned Peking might be to regulate, from time to time, the status of the "Overseas Chinese" through such means as the Dual Nationality Treaty, it could not be and was not indifferent to the plight of the Indonesian Chinese in the face of new discriminatory regulations. Peking media, in the middle of 1960, angrily noted how Chinese in West Java had been maltreated,[28] and Chinese protests inevitably produced an Indonesian reaction.

Indonesian Communism and China

The PKI was placed in a particularly difficult position in all this, not least because it had made the new nativistic policy largely its own. And so, at one and the same time, party statements (1) defended the Indonesian government's right to regulate the affairs of "foreigners" and (2) stressed that "the government of a friendly state, in this case the Chinese People's Republic, "was fully entitled to request" that the "reasonable rights of its citizens in Indonesia" be protected.[29] It would be wrong to believe that the PKI's dilemma (considering its growing power on the Indonesian political scene) had as little effect as Peking's protests and unhappiness. But in the context of domestic Indonesian politics, dominated at the time by the earlier mentioned nation-building "momentum" tactic, of which the struggle against the regional rebellions and the acquisition of the West New Guinea irredenta were major elements, relations with China were of secondary importance. Relatively, the USSR, by virtue of its huge arms grants and their international political and psychological effects, was a good deal more important at this time to Djakarta than China; moreover, viewed from the nation-building "momentum" tactic and the new nativism, particularly in Sukarno's ideology and policies, the measures against the Indonesian Chinese were both natural and essential — whether Peking liked them or not.

It was the anti-Malaysia confrontation, which is the next extension of the "momentum" policy and, closely connected with it, the quantum jump in the efforts at ideological and political radicalization of the country by the Sukarno government, that set the stage for the following phase of Sino-Indonesian relations, specifically for the emergence of the Djakarta-Peking axis. As her dispute with Moscow reached new levels of vehement acerbity, and as, in the aftermath of her 1962 armed conflict with India, Peking increasingly became a source of alarm among her Asian neighbors, so Indonesia's aggressiveness, coupled with various pronouncements by her leaders, notably Foreign Minister Subandrio, suggesting that the Djakarta government too had an as yet unfulfilled revolutionary mission in the world (an amplifica- tion of Sukarno's frequent dictum that the Indonesian Revolution was "not yet finished") strained her relations with the USSR, the United States, and others. Two "outlaw" nations, so to speak, seemed to be finding each other as Chinese spokesmen and media in the course of 1963-65 praised Indonesia's anti-Malaysia "confrontation" and began characterizing her policies as "an important force opposing imperialism and colonialism" in Southeast Asia.[30]

The Developing Peking-Djakarta Axis

At various conferences of Asian and African nations (for example, at Moshi, Tanganyika, in February 1963, and at Nicosia, Cyprus, in September 1963), a Sino-Indonesian entente became quite conspicuous, particularly in attacks on Soviet nuclear and Third World policies. By November 1963, Peking was financing the holding of Indonesia's Games of the New Emerging Forces (GANEFO), intended as an answer to the Olympics, and perhaps the first unequivocal evidence that the Djakarta-Peking partnership was attempting to create its own Third World power bloc independent of other international organizations, including the United Nations. Especially in 1964-65 Peking supported Sukarno's notion of a Conference of New Emerging Forces designed to be a radical Third World counterweight to the then Peking-despised United Nations, while Djakarta, in turn, propagated or played host to conferences of various Peking orchestrated Afro-Asian interest groups (journalists, women, youth, and so on).[31] The PKI, meanwhile, called for a new revolutionary offensive in what Indonesian Communists increasingly were beginning to describe as the Triple A (that is, Asia, Africa and Latin America), and in particular in Southeast Asia. This call openly linked PKI doctrine to the official position of the Chinese party, and appeared to be a repudiation of no less a Soviet theoretician than M. A. Suslov who, in March 1964, warned against focusing primary revolutionary attention on the Triple A region.[32]

Again, Chinese leaders in the course of 1965 supported the PKI's pet scheme of checking its opponents in the Indonesian armed forces by urging the creation of an embryo people's army of volunteers, a so- called Fifth Force, which would operate alongside the four other uniformed Indonesian services (Army, Navy, Air Force, and national Police). Even before Sukarno ultimately approved the Fifth Force idea in February 1965, over the bitter opposition of Army commanders, the PKI already had begun to form some overt "people's army" units of its own. The sinister role of these units would become clearer in subsequent months as at the time of the Gestapu affair, and thereafter they revealed themselves as the main Communist striking forces. At the end of May 1965, Sukarno in a lecture to Indonesia's National Defense Institute, said that it had been Chou En-lai who had originally given him the idea of the Fifth Force, and in early August 1965, Li Hsueh-feng, vice-chairman of People's China's National People's Congress, told the Indonesian parliament in Djakarta that a people's militia was essential and that when one was confronted by the imperialists it was "necessary to arm the people."[33]

In the meantime, Sino-Indonesian solidarity reached the point that Indonesia formally left the UN on January 20, 1965 (ostensibly because Malaysia had acquired a one-year term seat in the Security Council); and shortly thereafter in the same month, a wide-ranging Sino-Indonesian joint statement was issued in Peking, during the visit of Dr. Subandrio, Indonesia's Foreign Minister. According to this statement, Indonesia and China "stressed" that "no peaceful coexistence" was possible between "the imperialist forces and anti-imperialist forces," a policy position which, according to one authoritative writer, specifically meant Chinese assistance to Djakarta sponsored insurgencies, like that of the Malayan National Liberation League in West Malaysia.[34] It has also been mooted that Chinese leaders, pleased with their Indonesian partner, indicated on the same occasion that they were now ready to assist Indonesia in becoming a nuclear power; and certainly Subandrio's remark in June 1965, that "It was sufficient that the USSR was on our side for ten years and protected us from imperialism but that is not enough [now],"[35] suggested the new dimensions of Indonesian foreign policy. In any event, it appears that the January 1965 Sino-Indonesian Joint Statement was the visible part of a set of far-reaching agreements for political and military cooperation, including the shipment of some 100,000 small arms to Indonesia.[36]

Yet, Indonesian officials themselves seemed to become concerned over their government's drift toward Peking. In March 1964, for example, the newly appointed Indonesian ambassador to People's China, Djawoto, felt it necessary to emphasize that Indonesia had not become "the tail" of Peking, but that in fighting for the "emancipation of all nations," she was moving "equally with all countries of the world."[37] Furthermore, the Djakarta-Peking axis did not particularly affect endemic anti-Chinese hostility in Indonesia, only the official explanation of it. Thus, in March and May 1963, new anti-Chinese riots in Java left 13 Chinese dead, many wounded, and property losses estimated at 4 billion Rupiah. The causes of the riots remain obscure, and may have involved no more than the rivalry between two youths, one Indonesian, the other Chinese, over the affections of an Indonesian girl. But Sukarno officially attributed the riots to "counter-revolutionaries" and "foreign subversives." And instead of loosening its customary barrage of invective on such occasions, Peking media followed the theme of the Sukarno explanation: the riots had been instigated, according to the Chinese by "imperialists" and "counter-revolutionary groups," and had been designed to sabotage "Sino-Indonesian friendly relations."[38] The obvious effort being made by Peking and Djakarta to preserve their entente also had an impact on the Indonesian Chinese. Under the terms of the much delayed Sino-Indonesian Dual Nationality Treaty, some two-thirds (and perhaps even more) of the more than 1 million Indonesian Chinese who held or were regarded to have held dual citizenship had opted for Indonesian nationality. But not just bureaucratic delay and confusion caused many citizenship applications to lapse. Also the obvious cordiality between Djakarta and Peking seemed to Indonesian Chinese to make it unnecessary, or even unwise, to follow through on getting the necessary documents. And neither the Indonesian nor the Chinese government now pressed the matter. The result was that after the 1965 coup, the resulting rapid deterioration of Sino-Indonesian relations, and the Indonesian government's termination in 1966 of the Dual Nationality Treaty provisions, tens of thousands of Indonesian Chinese found themselves in a new citizenship limbo, at a time when their position in Indonesian society was never more precarious. But soon Sino-Indonesian relations were to change dramatically.

China and the 1965 Coup

In the course of 1964-65, PKI leaders and a handful of "progressive" Army and Air Force officers began making plans for a coup, which, according to post-coup PKI analyses, was designed to be a preliminary to the establishment of a "People's Democracy" in Indonesia.[39] Sukarno, who almost certainly knew of and tacitly approved of the coup, was, according to the coup plan, to remain as head of state. What led Chinese leaders to support the PKI coup plan, considering that Indonesian policies on the whole could hardly be displeasing to them, is still not clear.[40] Most probably it was the reports of Sukarno's rapidly deteriorating health, also confirmed by a visiting team of Chinese physicians (brought to Djakarta by PKI chairman Aidit) who examined Sukarno in August 1965, that persuaded them that a preemptive strike had become necessary in order to forestall the Indonesian Army from trying to take over after Sukarno's death. It has been contended that the decline in Sukarno's health in August would have left too little time to the Chinese to begin helping the Indonesian Communists in connection with their planned coup, particularly in providing them clandestinely with arms.[41] This contention is vitiated by reports, partly based on Hong Kong sources and appearing in the Thai and Malaysian press well before the coup, that covert shipments of Chinese weapons had already begun and were in fact being discovered by the Indonesian police:

Communist China is reported to be sending secret supplies of arms, explosives and military equipment to the Indonesian Communists who are getting ready for a showdown with armed forces. The Bangkok newspaper, Democracy, reported yesterday that clandestine shipments of arms were being unloaded at various places along the Java coast. It quoted Hong Kong sources for these disclosures, which coincided with reports from Djakarta about unusual activity around Baten and Pulabutan Batu in West Java and some smaller ports in East Java.

The Indonesian police are reported to have stepped up their investigations into these reports.

Political observers say that the Indonesian Communist Party (PKI) are fully aware that the Indonesian armed forces will resist any communist bid for power and it is getting ready for the inevitable clash.

In view of President Sukarno's declining health, the PKI have intensified its efforts to build a secret military force with Communist Chinese help. [42]

In an environment such as that of Djakarta in the weeks before Gestapu, where rumors of a coup were common, and even top Army commanders were wont to show incredible insouciance (some would pay with their lives for not having taken the coup rumors seriously), one can only speculate what effect these Thai and Malaysian reports had. The censor-ridden Indonesian press, in any case, did not carry them. But the reports were never repudiated by the Chinese. While this is not the place to assess the controversy over the evidence of Chinese foreknowledge and involvement in Gestapu, it must be noted also that subsequent to the coup, during the trials of Indonesian Foreign Minister Subandrio and other officials, extensive testimony was offered on the clandestine shipment of Chinese arms to Indonesia, unbeknownst to the Indonesian Army, and on the basis of an agreement made between Subandrio and Chou En-lai during their meeting in Peking in January 1965.[43] Furthermore, Chinese involvement in the 1965 coup has been the official position of the Indonesian government since the fall of Sukarno in 1966, and has structured Djakarta's relations with Peking ever since.

Before considering the third and present phase in Sino-Indonesian relations, it seems well to stress again the importance for Indonesia of the 1963-65 period of rapprochement with China. That rapprochement had the effect of lending significant legitimacy and providing further impetus to the latest extension of the Indonesian "momentum" policy, that is, the anti-Malaysia confrontation. The Sino-Indonesian rapprochement did not start the campaign against Malaysia, any more than that earlier, in the later fifties, a new cordiality in relations with the Soviets was responsible for the "nation-building" confrontation campaign to acquire the West New Guinea irredenta. Still, because of China's support for the anti-Malaysia confrontation campaign, that campaign, also in the context of Sukarno's own ceaseless radical ideologizing, and of the need to preserve the precarious domestic Indonesian power balance, came to be amplified in terms that ran parallel to Maoist China's own self-proclaimed revolutionary mission in the world. National self-aggrandizement found expression in ever new formulas. Thus, as Sukarno's information minister and official ideological interpreter, Ruslan Abdulgani, put it in 1964, Indonesia's future role was to be that of "the 'motor' of Southeast Asia and the Southwest Pacific."[44] A parallel role to China's was also played by the PKI whose followers operated in India and the Philippines to encourage local Maoists and their insurgents.

Domestically, the 1963-65 period witnessed in Indonesia the steady repression, through bans, censorship, and persecution, of the anti-Communist opposition. Anti-PKI organizations, such as the small "Trotskyite" Murba (Proletarian) Party, and publications, such as Western (especially U.S.) films and books, were proscribed.[45] Various Indonesian sources over the years confirmed to this author that some of these proscriptions, proclaimed by Sukarno during 1964-65, were the price exacted by Peking for the previously mentioned January 1965 Sino-Indonesian Joint Statement and related agreements; but there is no published evidence. However, Peking's ability to affect the course of domestic Indonesian politics was well illustrated by the open advocacy of Chinese leaders (and Sukarno's reference to them) of the Fifth Force idea, a move which strengthened the PKI and undercut the Army. As the Gestapu coup prevented full implementation of the Fifth Force idea, one can only speculate on the effect which such implementation would have had, along with the results of the other radicalizing PKI policies at the time — "revolutionary gymnastics" an approving Sukarno called them — on the internal Indonesian power balance. It would seem, however, that just as in the area of Indonesia's external relations, so in the field of her domestic politics, the rapprochement with Peking was accentuating the official, Indonesian-style Jacobinism that from its beginning had been the substance of Sukarno's nativist "Guided Democracy" and which, with the enthusiastic support of the PKI, was now propelling the Indonesian government toward full status as a "People's Democracy."* Yet, it cannot be overstressed that domestic

---

*One specialist observed in early 1965 that, though the Indonesian military might succeed Sukarno, "The probability that Indonesia will become a Communist state has been increased by the political events of 1964." Guy J. Pauker, "Indonesia in 1964: Toward a People's Democracy?," Asian Survey, vol. 5, no. 2 (February 1965), 95.

opposition to these developments, though repressed, remained powerful, and that along with this political opposition the Djakarta-Peking axis could not be said to have altered the old, traditional, anti-Chinese feelings that had flourished for centuries in Indonesian society. Surely the days of Sino-Indonesian warmth were too few and their political effects too ambiguous to overcome these ancient Indonesian ethnic prejudices.

Deterioration of Sino-Indonesian Relations

The Army-led or -condoned anti-Communist holocaust, following the failure of the Gestapu affair, swept Sukarno out of office, shattered the PKI and its agencies, and drastically altered relations with Peking. China and Indonesia reciprocally withdrew their diplomatic staffs from each other by October 1967. Since the coup, Sino-Indonesian relations have been in a deep freeze, and only recently have there been signs of a possible thaw.[46] "It is an established fact," declared Sukarno's successor, President Suharto, in August 1967, "that the People's Republic of China has directly or indirectly supported the September 30 Movement/Indonesian Communist Party, and during its epilogue has always launched vicious criticism toward us, and there are even evidences of subversive activities against the present New Order and Administration."[47] This pronouncement has been the leitmotiv of official Indonesian attitudes, bolstered over the years by such allega-tions by Indonesian military as continued smuggling of weapons from China to Indonesian Communist insurgents, Chinese aid to Communist guerrillas operating along the Malaysian-Indonesian border in West Kalimantan (Borneo), and involvement of local Indonesian Chinese in this Borneo insurgency.[48] Bloody pogroms of Indonesian Chinese sus-pected of Gestapu involvement ended by 1967; but anti-Chinese feeling, fed by popular suspicion of Chinese business malversations, and discriminatory treatment generally have continued.[49] The Dual National-ity Treaty was abrogated by the Suharto government and new citizenship regulations were only slow in being implemented, heightening the inse-curity of tens of thousands of Indonesian Chinese. In fact, suspicion of the loyalty of Indonesian Chinese (undoubtedly fanned by Army and Muslim circles, as well as by Indonesian business elements fearful of Chinese competition) is today the official reason why diplomatic relations will remain suspended, as the following wire service dispatch in 1973 suggests:

> Indonesian Foreign Minister Adam Malik says enough is
> enough for the moment. He turned down a Communist
> Chinese request to normalize relations between the two
> countries.
>   "I told the Chinese foreign minister it was enough
> for the moment that we have reached good understanding

with each other," Malik explained, "but as for normalization of relations, I told him that Indonesia would need
time to educate its Chinese population to be loyal to
Indonesia and not have their orientation towards Peking.
And he agreed with this."

Malik estimated it might take five to ten years to
so educate the four million Chinese living in Indonesia.50

A recent analysis of the foreign policy perceptions of the Indonesian elite confirms the depth of the current state of Sinophobia in
the country, repressed by the exigencies of the Sino-Indonesian partnership during 1963-65, but never gone and now given freer and legitimate
rein:

> Moreover, in the view of the Indonesians, there is an
> essential difference between the Chinese threat and the
> sort of expansionist danger that would come from any Big
> Power — and that difference is the overseas Chinese,
> whose presence in Indonesia was regarded as providing
> China with a ready fifth column and a potential for sub-
> version exceeding that of the other Great Powers. It is
> hard to overemphasize the importance of the overseas
> Chinese in the perception of the Chinese threat by the
> foreign policy elite. A clear majority brought the Indo-
> nesian Chinese into their discussion of China's aggres-
> siveness. A good indication of the way in which China
> and the overseas Chinese merge in the thinking of the
> Indonesians is the frequency with which they would
> respond to a question about China by talking about the
> Indonesian Chinese. A leading Islamic party figure aptly
> expressed the prevailing view: "We are not afraid of
> Mao's atom bomb; it is the overseas Chinese that worry
> us. The overseas Chinese are a Trojan horse. Back in
> the 1950s we were more concerned about the USSR than
> China, but now it is those overseas Chinese that have
> us worried."51

And yet, just as the years of warm rapprochement before Gestapu
tended to ignore the persistence of old, endemic, anti-Chinese popular
sentiments, so the present, post-Gestapu period has tended to becloud
not only the new adjustment and the ongoing "Indonesianization" (that
is, assimilation) of many in the Indonesian Chinese community after
the bloody postcoup days, but also to obscure new, powerful, international dynamics that suggest that more positive Indonesian relations
with Peking may well be around the corner. The reason is that again
the Nixon-Kissinger conception of international relations has increasingly compelled all Southeast Asian states to reassess their diplomacy

and mechanisms of individual and collective security.[52] Presumably in the context of more flexibility in international affairs, the Suharto regime's intransigeant anti-Chinese position and its presently correct but still cool relationship with the Soviets have become as outmoded as erstwhile U.S. Cold War perceptions and policies.

With respect to the USSR, it may be easier for Indonesia to develop warmer and more extensive relations than as regards China. For just as the rapprochement with China in the 1963-65 period provided legitimacy and encouragement to the Sukarno regime's policies, so the present and continuing strain in relations with Peking meshes with, and indeed is an important part of, the Suharto government's militant domestic anti-Communism and its self-conception as the great corrector of the policy follies of the Sukarno era. In this negative sense also, China and the Indonesian Chinese continue to loom in Indonesian decision-making; and Djakarta's future relations with the USSR are likely to reflect in the first instance its perception of Peking, and vice versa.

Soviet and Chinese Influence

I have no certainty (only guesses aplenty) about the thoughts and hidden motives of Indonesia's, or, for that matter, of Russia's or China's leaders during the time frame discussed in these pages. Nor am I aware of any publications, or (with the possible, and admittedly, controversial exception of the Sukarno statement on the desirability of a Fifth Force (see note 33, supra) of any public utterance by any of these leaders attributing any Indonesian policy or decision directly to the pressure or influence of the Soviet or Chinese governments. In the absence of such certain knowledge, a predicament which may perhaps parallel the experience of students concerned with alleged Soviet or Chinese influence in other countries, interpretations of the nature of Soviet or Chinese influence must, of necessity, be subjective and tentative.

Ideally, influence should be measured, perhaps, in proven causal terms, for example, a particular Indonesian policy posture becomes understandable only because of some prior Soviet or Chinese statement or action. The Indonesian record, at least as we now have it, shows no instance of this kind. Even trade data mirror changes only to a degree in the relative political warmth or coolness prevailing between the parties concerned. Thus, with the September 1956 Soviet-Indonesian trade agreement, the value of Soviet imports into Indonesia climbed steadily (from 3.08 millions of Rupiah in 1956 to 28.64 in 1959), as did the value of Indonesian exports to the USSR (from 0.11 in 1956 to 176.71 in 1959). But the 1956 trade agreement itself reflected a new, more nativistic anti-Western nationalism which had developed in Indonesia with the advent of the first cabinet of Premier Ali Sastroamidjojo. And, conversely, the anti-Communist fervor in

Indonesia following the abortive September 30, 1965, coup inevitably affected Soviet-Indonesian trade also, although Peking rather than Moscow was seen by the post-coup Indonesian regime as a hidden force behind the coup. The value in imports into Indonesia from the USSR fell from 128.9 millions of Rupiah in 1965 to 49.3 in 1969, while Indonesian exports dropped from 263.4 to 123.1 in the same period. However, in the period 1963-65, the years of Indonesia's warmest friendship with Peking, Soviet-Indonesian trade continued to expand, and not until after the 1965 coup did this trend begin to reverse itself significantly. A fluctuating pattern attributable to the political consequences of the 1965 coup has been discernible also in Sino-Indonesian trade. The values involved in this trade were much greater from the start, however, and Indonesian commerce with China was already much more significant in the early 1950s than with the USSR. Imports from China and Indonesia jumped from 40.32 millions of Rupiah in 1954 to 697.3 in 1959, while values of Indonesian exports to China rose from 31.59 to 605.03 in the corresponding period. The value of imports into Indonesia from China plummeted from 987.8 millions of Rupiah in 1965 to 430.3 in 1969, while Indonesian exports all but disappeared in the same time span, falling from 399.9 to 0.11.[53] Trade thus has followed, rather than been a harbinger of, changes in Djakarta's relations with Moscow and Peking, with the further explicit proviso that Indonesia's drift toward China in the early 1960s cannot be read at all from the commercial statistics.

Nor is it really possible to define Soviet or Chinese influence in an indirect sense, at least in the Indonesian case, and with the meager data presently at our disposal. I do not know a means of measuring degrees of indirectness in this respect. I do feel, however, that assuming that Sino-Soviet influence existed, the matrix in which that influence operated was the accelerating and radicalizing "momentum" policy of the later fifties and early sixties, and, subsequently, its repudiation in the post-Sukarno era. It is the domestic, not the foreign, policy of Indonesia that controls the patterns of Sino-Indonesian and Soviet-Indonesian relations, and, in a general sense, this is true for both the pre- and post-coup periods. One may legitimately hypothesize that Indonesian policy decisions in the later 1950s and early 1960s, particularly those enhancing Sukarno's executive powers under "Guided Democracy," the campaign against regional dissidents, the West Irian and (with qualifications insofar as Moscow was concerned) anti-Malaysia confrontations, and the articulation of a more nativistic nationalist public ideology were congenial to Peking and Moscow. But there is no evidence that the latter actually caused these various Indonesian policy decisions or that, before the coup, any significant changes in these policy decisions cannot be understood unless the roles of the Soviets and the Chinese are considered. In the absence of an adequate measure of influence, one must remain content with noting the possibility that Soviet and Chinese attitudes and statements, both toward Indonesia directly and toward international questions generally, confirmed for Indonesian leaders the desirability of their own policy positions. To the extent that such confirmation existed, or was believed to exist by the Indonesians, the latter may well have been pleased, but not necessarily influenced by the USSR and People's China.

All this is not to say that, operationally, the concept of influence is impossible to operationalize, even in the Indonesian case. It is rather, that insofar as Indonesia is concerned, available data do not permit much of a conclusion. It remains possible, however, to describe something of a theoretical model of inquiry, and consider what an application of it to the Indonesian case suggests. What follows is, paradoxically, both a counsel of perfection, in the sense that the methodological demands suggested may far exceed the empirical answers that can be provided, and a feeble preliminary design, in that much of what the term "influence" encompasses may yet escape from it. But perhaps the approach suggested in subsequent paragraphs may stimulate some discussion.

A Theoretical Model

First, determine as exactly as possible the time span in which the influence upon a particular government is to be measured, defining concisely the reasons for establishing that time span in this particular way. Second, determine in the period under consideration, if there is a basic and distinctive policy thrust, or one or more basic themes, either in domestic or foreign relations, or both, by which the major political turning points, and separate specific policy decisions of the government examined supportive of the basic theme, can be measured. It is unnecessary to elaborate here on the dangers of selectivity and of a fallacious post hoc argument in making such a determination. The most possibly complete enumeration of the principal political changes and the separate policy decisions is necessary. Also, it is assumed that a basic policy theme or themes can be found, and that the distinction between such a theme or themes and separate or subsidiary policy decisions supportive of that theme is a meaningful one. For example, in the Indonesian case, the nation-building "momentum" policy is the basic theme, while the progressive establishment by the Sukarno regime of the various instruments of "Guided Democracy, " or the confrontations against West New Guinea and Malaysia, are separate, subsidiary, but supportive decisions. The interdependence of the basic theme and the separate policy decisions is obvious: if research makes apparent that numerous policy decisions exist which contradict the basic policy theme that has been established, the need for a reexamination of the latter need not be elaborated upon. One might hypothesize that in a given time span no basic policy theme or themes at all can be found for a particular government. But this would suggest such an exceptional condition of careening anarchy as not to merit attention here.

Third, the nature of Soviet and/or Chinese relations with the government in question during the previously determined time span should be analyzed. This analysis, it would seem, should be as empirical as possible, concentrating heavily on the "nuts and bolts" of interstate relations, from data on trade and aid to specific policy statements and voting patterns in international bodies. Also, this particular analysis should be approached anew, that is, while making it one should avoid looking over one's shoulder at the data and insights gathered during the first two phases of the inquiry sketched above. For obviously the temptation to begin correlating even at this stage the major turns in the area of external relations, with what already has been developed in the previous examination of basic policy themes, is likely to grow, making for unwarranted emphases and selectivity. To the extent possible, this phase of the inquiry should, of course, note also any changes in ideological rationales or the general line of either the Soviet or Chinese Communist party with respect to international affairs. It seems well to guard especially against any possibly pre-conceived correlations between such party-line changes and official policy statements, and the remainder of what has been called the "nuts and bolts" aspects of interstate relations, for example, provisions of military and other aid or forms of cooperation in the international arena.

Fourth, and finally, there is the correlation and synthesizing of the data gathered. Two touchstones suggest themselves here. First it should be asked if the basic policy theme or themes, as defined in the second phase of the inquiry, and as circumscribed by the time span determined in the first phase, would have come into existence if any one or more of the data or patterns of data elicited in the third phase of the inquiry had been absent. In other words, can the formulation of the major policy preoccupations of a government during a definite period only be understood in the light of specific aspects of that government's relations with the USSR and/or People's China? Second, the question should be raised (and while doing so it is important to accentuate again the conceptual distinction between the defined basic policy theme or themes and the separate and specific policy decisions expressive or supportive of that theme) whether any one or more of the principal political turning points or separate policy decisions defined in the second phase of the inquiry would have come into existence had it not been for any one or more of the data or patterns of data developed in the third phase of the analysis. A corollary of both questions, of course, is the question of nuance, which may be even more difficult to answer.

The concept of influence, it is suggested, should be understood in terms of the answers given to the queries raised in the fourth phase of the analysis. A basic policy theme or themes, understandable only in light of specific data drawn from the area of interstate relations with the USSR and China, as defined in the third phase of the inquiry, obviously suggests strong influence. A theme not thus understandable, but some separate supportive policy decisions that are, suggests various gradations of strength or weakness of that influence.

Application to the Indonesian Case

To attempt to provide the complete data for Indonesia under the second and third stages of the kind of inquiry suggested above would obviously far exceed the limits imposed on the present essay; considerations of space have necessitated compression of data in the first two sections of the present paper which should ideally be developed separately, according to the indicated methodology. Even so, however, some tentative conclusions may perhaps be drawn from these earlier sections of the paper along the lines of the methodological criteria suggested in the present section. So considered, the time span of recent Indonesian history analyzed in this essay has a definite basic policy theme, namely that of the origin, implementation, and, after the Gestapu affair, repudiation of the nation-building "momentum" concept of the Sukarno era. A more convenient refinement of this time span would be the decade from 1956 to 1965, when not only the "momentum" theme itself is most conspicuous, and when various subsidiary policy decisions and major policy turning points such as the campaigns against West New Guinea and Malaysia are most clearly seen as supportive of that "momentum" theme, but when the successive rapprochements between Djakarta and Moscow and Peking, as measured by arms aid or foreign policy agreements, are also most in evidence. On the other hand, one aspect of the Sino-Indonesian interaction, namely the problem of the "Overseas Chinese" community in Indonesia, has roots that go far deeper than the time span under analysis in these pages. That interaction is, in fact, a curious variable, but one that nevertheless assumes a distinctive role, depending —as has been indicated —on whether one considers the Indonesian Chinese question in the period of implementation (1958-65) or of repudiation (1965 and after) of the Sukarnoist "momentum" policy.

The conceptual sine qua non of the "momentum" policy is the notion that Indonesia is in crisis. The Army inspired regional rebellions of the later fifties, the need to confront the Dutch and their allies in the campaign to acquire the West New Guinea irredenta, the continuing confrontation, this time of Malaysia, the "unfinished" Indonesian revolution, not just domestically but in the Southeast Asian region and indeed the world —these are all so many catalysts of real or imaginary crises. To articulate this crisis condition, and simultaneously and seemingly endlessly to provide solutions for it, was Sukarno's primary political role and the source of his grandiose oratory and of his elaborate ideological constructs and symbols. Sukarno's political role, especially his ideologizing, reflected and further augmented the new, more nativistic, Indonesian nationalism which became ascendant as the "momentum" policy and its crisis dynamic acquired normative force in the official conduct of Indonesian affairs. The major turning points of Indonesian policy, particularly in the 1956-65 period, such as the acceleration of the campaign to acquire West New Guinea, the anti-Malaysia confrontation, or the partnership with Peking, no less than numerous separate policy decisions in these years (the nativistic Indonesianizing of entrepreneurial economics, the imposition of the authoritarian 1945 Constitution, the development of mass mobilization organizations, the elimination of anti-Sukarno and anti-Communist groups and press) serve the continuation of "momentum" and are justified by the condition of national emergency. Whether the ceaseless projection of the crisis condition in the 1956-65 period was a deliberate attempt to recapture the elan of the revolutionary period of Indonesian nationalism (1945-49) and freedom struggle against the Dutch, at a time when during the fifties partisan political polarization and the spectre of civil war increasingly loomed more menacingly for the young independent Republic, or whether it was merely an instrument for the construction of an authoritarian system of government acceptable to, because designed to maintain power for, Sukarno, the Army, and eventually the PKI as dominant political party, or indeed, whether it involved both, will long be argued.

But one major effect of the "momentum" policy was to put a premium on the outer trappings of national strength, especially on the visible manifestations of power in the military and international spheres, even at the cost of meeting urgent domestic development needs, or even of short-term economic growth. An observation by the Indonesian Air Force Chief of Staff, Vice Marshal Saleh Basarah, provides a telling retrospect. Indonesia today has far too many Air Force pilots, Basarah complained, the result of the Sukarno era policies which sought to accentuate "everything huge, everything strong and spectacular," including pilot training.[54]

It was with this kind of Indonesia that the Soviets and the Chinese sought to establish close contact. Typically that contact —whether in the form of arms deliveries or support for aggressive Indonesian "confrontation" policies —was meant to bolster the state of continuing crisis and the radical nativistic panaceas presumably designed to meet the crises that were the stock in trade of the Sukarno political style. The data of Soviet-Indonesian and Sino-Indonesian inter-state relations tend to confirm the primacy of the "momentum" theme in Indonesian politics. Moscow and Peking, in the context of their own international policies, obviously saw an advantage in perpetuating a militantly truculent Indonesia, a growing source of concern for the United States and its allies. That support for the "momentum" policy also assisted in preserving the precarious domestic power balance in Indonesia was probably for both the Soviets and Chinese of lesser importance. Yet, as the "momentum" policy seemed to grow by what it fed on, and as the anti-Malaysia confrontation began to suggest a recklessness that could only play in the hands of Peking, the enthusiasm of the Soviets waned, only to be supplemented in Indonesian policy considerations by that of the Chinese. Within the time span indicated, the Indonesian case suggests or confirms that it was the brand of post-independence Third World nationalism represented by the Sukarnos and the Nkrumahs which was perceived in Moscow and Peking as a promising conduit of possible influence, but also that such promise, at least for the Soviets, was soon blighted.

It is apparent that the "momentum" policy, as a basic theme, came into existence without the kind of Soviet or Chinese contacts with the Djakarta government described in the third phase of the research model suggested above. As to major political turning points in Indonesian affairs, such developments as the campaign against the regional rebels and its corollary, the establishment of the authoritarian "Guided Democracy" construct and the reimposition of the Constitution of 1945, the confrontation against West New Guinea and later against Malaysia with all their national and international policy ramifications — these, too, must be regarded as having been initiated without demonstrable dependence on any factor in the patterns of Soviet-Indonesian or Sino-Indonesian relations. And only in the case of Sukarno's approval of the PKI's Fifth Force concept and his reference to a Chinese suggestion in connection with it, does one encounter a policy decision supportive of the basic "momentum" theme in Indonesian affairs which may be directly attributed to China. Yet even here caution is necessary, for one cannot always be sure of the truth of Sukarno's public statements.

So considered, the question of Soviet and Chinese influence in Indonesia, especially in the 1956-65 decade, becomes a matter of the nuances of specific policy formulations and their alternatives. Thus the Soviet arms credits, condemnation of the PRRI rebels, and endorsement of Djakarta's claim to West New Guinea, undoubtedly lend strength both to the legitimacy of the Sukarno regime struggling to maintain itself in a civil war, and to the stepped-up campaign to acquire the West New Guinea irredenta. But Soviet arms or Soviet support for the Indonesian claim to West New Guinea, in and out of the United Nations, in no way were a sine qua none, either for the continuation of the Sukarno government or for the new aggressive militancy in the Irian confrontation.

Similarly, Peking's approval of the campaign against Malaysia, of Sukarno's New Emerging Forces (NEFO) concept, and of Indonesia's leaving the United Nations, all undoubtedly encouraged the Djakarta government in its new self-proclaimed revolutionary mission in Southeast Asia. But the campaign against Malaysia, particularly as a tactic to preserve the difficult domestic Indonesian power balance, was initiated by the Indonesians before Peking voiced its official support. There is no evidence that — even taking the PKI's important role in the anti-Malaysia confrontation into consideration — the Sukarno regime started that "confrontation" because Peking wished it to. It is more difficult to determine, however, if such policy decisions as the propagation of the NEFO idea, or the decision to leave the UN, or the sponsorship of various African-Asian interest groups, were not taken without some awareness that they would be pleasing to Peking. It seems likely that these decisions were in fact so taken. But, again, it is difficult to demonstrate, given the character of the last months of Sukarno's "Guided Democracy," and the radicalizing effect of the anti-Malaysia confrontation, that such decisions or something like them would not have been made eventually anyway. Admittedly, without her Peking rapprochement, Indonesia would probably have been less likely to leave the UN. On the other hand, Sukarno himself had for some time toyed with the idea of setting up Indonesia-sponsored international organizations and conferences. In other words, the decisions behind the departure from the UN, or the propagation of NEFO, or of various African-Asian interest groups, are nuances of Indonesian policy in which Peking's influence is likely to be a matter of continuous speculation. Still, one must concede that it seems likely that had the Gestapu coup attempt not occurred and the existing domestic radicalization process continued, or, alternatively, if the coup had been successful, then Peking's influence almost certainly would have become stronger and more clearly definable in Indonesian policy decisions.

The post-Gestapu period presents additional difficulties. For in this period interstate relations are largely negative. Yet, Djakarta's domestic anti-Communism, especially as it affects the Indonesian Chinese, can superficially be viewed as being influenced by the mere physical existence of Peking, by past Indonesian relations with the Chinese government, as well as, but to a lesser degree, by relations with Moscow. As efforts go forward, however, to separate that domestic anti-Communism from foreign policy, this negative influence will become even more a matter of nuance. In the development of a new regional collective security system in Southeast Asia now under way, mutually competing Sino-Soviet presences may well come to be appreciated in more positive terms as a distinct strategic variable of potential advantage, while, domestically, in the Southeast Asian states the negative aspects of that presence remain articulated, at least for a while longer, in counterinsurgency and other anti-Communist programs.

In the Indonesian case, then, the operational value of the concepts of Soviet and Chinese "influence," at least in terms of the methodological design suggested here, is at best uncertain.* This

---

*In reaching this conclusion I believe that elements of the methodological design suggested here would have to be considered in any alternative research model addressed to the problem of Sino-Soviet influence in Indonesia. Such an alternative model should react also,

is not to say that it is illicit to use the word "influence" in this connection in a general descriptive sense, to indicate selected aspects of Djakarta's relations with Moscow and Peking. But precise methodological utility of the term, again insofar as the Indonesian case is concerned, is likely to remain controversial; and the more pressing research concern for some time to come, one may perhaps suggest, lies in adding empirically to the as yet meager body of specific data on Sino-Indonesian and Soviet-Indonesian relations.

Notes

1. Ruth T. McVey, The Soviet View of the Indonesian Revolution (Ithaca, N.Y.: Modern Indonesian Project, Cornell University, 1957). See also J. H. Brimmell, Communism in Southeast Asia (London: Oxford University Press, 1959), pp. 252 ff.

2. McVey, ibid., pp. 47-50; and G. McT. Kahin, Nationalism and Revolution in Indonesia (Ithaca, N.Y.: Cornell University Press, 1952), pp. 268-69.

3. Herbert Feith, The Decline of Constitutional Democracy in Indonesia (Ithaca: Cornell University Press, 1962), pp. 231, 291-92, 385.

4. On some aspects of these changes see Herbert Feith, The Wilopo Cabinet 1952-1953: A Turning Point in Post Revolutionary Indonesia (Ithaca: Modern Indonesian Project, Cornell University, 1958); Bruce Glassburner, "Problems of Economic Policy in Indonesia 1950-1957," Ekonomi dan Deuangen Indonesia, vol. 13 (1960), 308 ff; Hans C. Schmitt, Some Monetary and Fiscal Consequences of Social Conflict in Indonesia 1950-1958 (Ph.D. dissertation, University of California, 1959); Justus M. van der Kroef, Indonesia in the Modern World (Bandung, Indonesia: N.V. Masa Baru, 1956), vol. 2, pp. 305-56.

5. See Justus M. van der Kroef, The Communist Party of Indonesia: Its History, Program and Tactics (Vancouver: University of British Columbia Press, 1965), pp. 55-57.

6. Guy J. Pauker, "The Soviet Challenge in Indonesia," Foreign Affairs, vol. 40, no. 4 (July 1962), 612.

7. On Soviet aid and credits to Indonesia see, for example, Stephen P. Gilbert and Wynfred Joshua, Guns and Rubles: Soviet Aid Diplomacy in Neutral Asia (New York: American-Asian Educational Exchange, 1970), pp. 32-39; Charles B. McLane, "Foreign Aid in Soviet Third World Policies," Mizan (November-December 1968), pp. 240-43; Guy J. Pauker, "General Nasution's Mission to Moscow," Asian Survey, vol. 1, no. 1 (March 1961), 13-14; and Pauker, "The

---

as has my design, to the stimulating criteria of influence described by Alvin Z. Rubinstein in Chapter 1 of this book.

Soviet Challenge in Indonesia," op. cit., pp. 612-613; J. Panglaykim and H. W. Arndt, The Indonesian Economy: Facing a New Era? (Rotterdam: Rotterdam University Press, 1966), p. 12; and Antara Despatch, Djakarta, May 20, 1968 (1966 protocol).

8. On the "momentum" concept see especially D. Sumitro, Searchlight on Indonesia (New Haven, 1959), p. 43. Attributed to Nasution and the military, the concept applies to the Sukarno regime's policies as a whole.

9. Justus M. van der Kroef, "The West New Guinea Settlement: Its Origins and Implications," Orbis, vol 7, no. 1 (Spring 1963), 120-149.

10. Uri Ra'anan, The USSR Arms the Third World (Cambridge, Mass.: M. I. T. Press, 1969), p. 213.

11. Justus M. van der Kroef, "Nasution, Sukarno and the West New Guinea Dispute," Asian Survey, vol. 1, no. 5 (August 1961), 21.

12. Ra'anan, op. cit., pp. 225-232.

13. On this American pressure (particularly U. S. indications that Holland would not be able to count on American assistance in the event of a large-scale Indonesian attack on West New Guinea), see the memoirs of the then Dutch Foreign Minister J. M. A. H. Luns in Luns: "Ik Herinner Mij . . ." (Leyden, Sijthoff, 1971), pp. 109-110.

14. Stephen P. Gilbert and Wynfred Joshua, op. cit., p. 35.

15. Antara Daily News Bulletin, July 7, 1964, pp. 3-4; UPI dispatch, Djakarta, June 30, 1964; Ra'anan, op. cit., p. 239. See Nadia Derkach, "The Soviet Policy Towards Indonesia in the West Irian and the Malaysian Disputes," Asian Survey, vol. 5, no. 11 (November 1965), 569. On the ambivalence and reluctance of the USSR to support Indonesia's anti-Malaysia confrontation, see Antonie C. A. Dake, In the Spirit of the Red Bantang: Indonesian Communists Between Moscow and Peking, 1959-1965 (The Hague: Mouton, 1973), pp. 181, 255.

16. D. N. Aidit, Berani Berani, Sekali Lagi Berani! (Djakarta: Jajasan Pembaruan, 1963), p. 46.

17. Sheldon W. Simon, The Broken Triangle: Peking, Djakarta and the PKI (Baltimore: Johns Hopkins Press, 1969); Justus M. van der Kroef, "The Sino-Indonesian Partnership," Orbis, vol. 8, no. 2 (Summer 1964), 332-56.

18. Lyndon Baines Johnson, The Vantage Point: Perspectives of the Presidency 1963-1969 (New York: Popular Library Edition, 1971), pp. 135-36; The New York Times, September 7, 1966.

19. Foreign Broadcast Information Service (FBIS), April 25, 1972; Information Bulletin (Prague), no. 4-5 (1972), 66; World Marxist Review, vol. 15, no. 3 (March 1972), 48; USSR and the Third World, vol. 1, no. 2 (1971), 50; Pravda, November 1 and 3, 1972, in World Affairs Report, vol. 3, no. 2 (1973), 157.

20. For example, see Antara Daily News Bulletin, vol. 25, no. 1772 (May 18, 1973), for a recent incident involving alleged

"misinterpretations" of the Koran in a Soviet book which was protested by the Islamic Solidarity Committee based in Djakarta.

21. Compare the perceptive article of C. L. Sulzberger, "Monuments of Failure, " The New York Times, March 21, 1973.

22. Antara Daily News Bulletin, vol. 25, no. 1655 (December 23, 1972).

23. Robert C. Horn, "Soviet-Indonesian Relations Since 1965, " Survey, vol. 16, no. 1 (Winter 1971), 230-31.

24. Antara Daily News Bulletin, vol. 26, no. 2018 and no. 2026 (March 16 and March 26, 1974); V. Shurygin in Pravda, February 13, 1974; and Justus M. van der Kroef, "Recent Trends in Soviet-Indonesian Relations, " Pacific Community, vol. 5, no. 4 (July 1974).

25. Feith, The Decline of Constitutional Democracy in Indonesia, op. cit. , pp. 90-91.

26. Ibid. , pp. 192-93; 385-94; Feith, The Wilopo Cabinet, op. cit. , pp. 37-38; D. N. Aidit, "Pembangunan Organisasi Penting, Tapi Lebih Penting Lagi Penbangunan Ideologi, " Bintang Merah, vol. 15 (1959), 234; George M. Kahin, The Asian-African Conference (Ithaca, New York: Cornell University Press, 1956).

27. Ra'anan, op. cit. , pp. 196-203, 222-23; Kenneth Ray Young, "The Sino-Indonesian Dual Nationality Treaty: An Evaluation, " Asian Forum, vol. 2, no. 3 (July-September 1970), 172-82.

28. Peking Review, vol. 4, no. 29 (July 12, 1960).

29. PKI Politburo statement, "Settle the Question of the Overseas Chinese in the Spirit and Act of Indonesian-Chinese Friendship, " Review of Indonesia (November-December 1959), p. 3.

30. Peking Review, vol. 7, no. 16 (April 19, 1963). See also Chinese Deputy Premier Chen Yi's statement of support for Indonesia in the "struggle" to "crush the British neocolonialist tool of Malaysia" in Antara Daily News Bulletin, December 4, 1964.

31. See the Report on the Afro-Asian Journalists' Conference on Bandung in United Asia, vol. 15, no. 4 (August 1963), 589-90.

32. Compare M. A. Suslov, "Struggle of the CPSU for the Unity of the World Communist Movement, " Soviet Documents, vol. 2, no. 16 (April 20, 1964), 9, with A Proposal Concerning the General Line of the International Communist Movement. The Letter of the Central Committee of the Communist Party of China in Reply to the Letter of the Central Committee of the Communist Party of the Soviet Union of March 30, 1963 (Peking: Foreign Languages Press, 1963), pp. 12-13, 26.

33. Djakarta Daily Mail, June 2, 1965; August 10, 1965.

34. Peking Review, vol. 9, no. 6 (February 5, 1965); and Denis Warner in New York Herald Tribune, July 25, 1965.

35. Ra'anan, op. cit. , p. 242. Dake, op. cit. , p. 350. Dake has this version of Subandrio's remark: "Ten years ago the Soviet Union was a 'protector' for Afro-Asia in dealing with colonialism, but this Soviet 'protection' is no longer adequate. "

36. See the testimony of former First Deputy Foreign Minister Suwito Kusumowidagdo during the Subandrio trial in Armed Forces Daily Mail (Djakarta), October 14, 1966; and Sinar Harapan (Djakarta), October 11 and 14, 1966. For an extensive account of Chinese arms assistance, including aid in the nuclear field, see Dake, op. cit., pp. 326-36.

37. Antara Daily News Bulletin, March 10, 1964.

38. Antara Daily News Bulletin, May 21, 1963; Peking Review, vol. 7, no. 21 (May 24, 1963); and Indonesian Observer, June 19, 1963.

39. Suchahyo, "The 'New Order' in Indonesia," World Marxist Review, vol. 10, no. 10 (October 1967), 47. There is considerable literature on the September 30, 1965, attempted coup. For example, Donald E. Weatherbee, "Interpretations of Gestapu, the 1965 Indonesian Coup," World Affairs, vol. 8, no. 1 (March 1970), 305-17; and Justus M. van der Kroef, "Origins of the 1965 Coup in Indonesia: Probabilities and Alternatives," Journal of Southeast Asian Studies, vol. 3, no. 2 (September 1972), 277-98.

40. Ruth T. McVey, "Indonesian Communism and China," in Tang Tsou (ed.), China in Crisis, vol. 2 (Chicago: University of Chicago Press, 1968), p. 380. She notes that since "Indonesia was at the time playing a role entirely satisfactory to Peking," and had become China's only major ally, "it is hard to see why China would have chosen to do anything but play out the Sukarno string for as long as it lasted." The point is that with reports of Sukarno's imminent demise his "string" was believed to be played out.

41. David C. Mozingo, "China's Policy Toward Indonesia," in Tang Tsou, op. cit., p. 343.

42. Sabah Times (Kota Kinabalu), September 14, 1965. Also Le Democrate (Bangkok), September 12, 1965.

43. For other aspects of possible Chinese involvement in Gestapu, see Justus M. van der Kroef, "The Sino-Indonesian Rupture," The China Quarterly, no. 33 (January-March 1968), 17-46. Also McVey and Mozingo, op. cit.

44. H. Roeslan Abdulgani, Heroes Day and the Indonesian Revolution (Djakarta: Prapantja Publishing House, 1964), p. 127.

45. Justus M. van der Kroef, "Indonesian Communism's 'Revolutionary Gymnastics'," Asian Survey, vol. 5, no. 5 (May 1965), 217-32.

46. In the following analysis I have drawn on my "Indonesia, Communist China and the PKI," Pacific Community, no. 5 (Winter 1970), 27-42; and "Before the Thaw: Recent Indonesian Attitudes Toward People's China," Asian Survey, vol. 13, no. 5 (May 1973), 513-30.

47. Address of the Acting President, General Suharto, before the Gotong Royong House of Representatives on August 16, 1967. Antara Daily News Bulletin, Special Issue (1967), part 3, pp. 27-28.

48. For example, South China Morning Post (Hong Kong),

August 2, 1967; Indonesian Observer, January 4, 1971; The Sarawak Tribune (Kuching), July 28, 1972; and Antara Daily News Bulletin, vol. 24, no. 1556 (August 25, 1972).

49. Pakir Singh, "A Candle Glows," Far Eastern Economic Review, vol. 79, no. 3 (January 22, 1973), 22-23; and Lie Tek-Tjang, "The Chinese Problem in Indonesia Following the September 30 Movement: A Personal View," Internationale Spectator (The Hague), vol. 24 (June 24, 1970), 1145-54.

50. AP dispatch, Djakarta, April 26, 1973.

51. Franklin B. Weinstein, "World Politics and World Powers: The View From Djakarta," Asia, no. 27 (Autumn 1972), 51-52.

52. For aspects and implications of this reassessment see Lau Teik Soon (ed.), New Directions in the International Relations of Southeast Asia: The Great Powers and Southeast Asia (Singapore: Singapore University Press, 1973).

53. Yearbook of International Trade Statistics 1969 (New York: UN Statistical Office, 1971), p. 394; Yearbook of International Trade Statistics 1961 (New York: UN Statistical Office, 1963), p. 328; and Yearbook of International Trade Statistics 1958, vol. 1 (New York: UN Statistical Office, 1959), 290.

54. Angkatan Persendjata (Djakarta), June 22, 1973.

CHAPTER

4

SOVIET INFLUENCE IN EGYPT, 1967-73
Malcolm H. Kerr

Assessing the influence of the Soviet Union in Egypt is in some ways a rather straightforward, even obvious, task and in others a complex and elusive one. The main outlines of Soviet-Egyptian relations over the years since the first arms deal in 1955 are well known. There has been a massive and continuing flow of both military and economic assistance, frequent exchanges of high-level visits, and for the most part a consistently warm exchange of public diplomatic and ideological support, marked by occasional quarrels, and with some questions always open to a certain measure of "agreement to differ."

The record of Egypt's successes and failures, and changes of policy, domestically and internationally, is equally familiar. It takes no expertise or subtlety to grasp the significance of the Six Day War as the comeuppance of Nasser's activist foreign policy, or of the Soviet replacement of Egyptian losses of equipment in 1967 as an underwriting of Egypt's policy of resisting Israel's peace terms, or of Gamal Abdul Nasser's death and Anwar Sadat's succession as the end of an era of man-on-horseback politics in Egypt, and the opening up of a period of struggle for power among lesser men within Egypt and uncertainty in her outlook abroad, a situation which obviously left the Soviets at the crossroads. The crisis of 1972, in which Sadat expelled thousands of Soviet military personnel from Egypt, is a familiar one in its main dimensions, and the most important short-term causes and consequences — the Soviets' failure to help Sadat get the Israelis out of Sinai, and the reduction of the Soviet strategic presence in the Eastern Mediterranean — are well known to all. Lastly, there is the war launched by Egypt and Syria in October 1973, in which these two Arab states benefited from a massive Soviet military resupply effort and close diplomatic support, but in the aftermath of which Egypt turned sharply away from Soviet patronage and toward the United States. The long-term impact of these events remains unclear in mid-1974, and it will be widely agreed that much will depend on the course of peace negotiations with Israel.

Beyond such rather obvious outlines, the task of charting the precise mechanisms of Soviet influence in Egypt is extremely difficult. One would like to be able to pinpoint the details of behind-the-scenes negotiations, of Soviet proddings and Egyptian responses, of the calculations of leaders on each side of the likely actions of the other in specific circumstances. A flow of published memoirs of retired Soviet and Egyptian public figures, such as those that follow the retirement of every American president, would help. So would a Soviet or Egyptian counterpart of a David Halberstam, an Arthur Schlesinger, or a Jack Anderson. In the absence in each country of a parliamentary opposition party, a free press, a public archive of the private papers of a retired president, and the like, we are forced back upon three limited paths of inquiry.

First, there are the officially controlled press and the public pronouncements of the leaders, from which hints and tidbits may be gleaned. These are less likely to tell us who influenced whom and how, than to signal phases of tension and cooperation. Soviet press analyses after the June 1967 war expressing dissatisfaction over the continuing bourgeois character of the Egyptian army officer corps, for example, may have suggested some measure of uncertainty in Moscow over the utility of fully rearming Egypt; on the other hand, the Soviets proceeded to do so, and so alternatively they might be taken to reflect a Soviet warning to Egypt that in return for rearmament, Soviet military training and advice would have to be accepted more extensively. On the Egyptian side, throughout the career of Muhammad Hassanein Haikal as Editor-in-Chief of Al-Ahram, by the same token, readers followed his weekly editorials for clues of official attitudes toward the outside world. But this process, though interesting and of some analytic value, can be downright misleading, as indeed it is probably intended to be on occasion: thus on October 5, 1973, the day before Egypt with Soviet help went to war, Haikal complained of Soviet complaisance in the Middle East deadlock and stated that "the Soviet Union could have given more help to the Arabs." In short, this method of inquiry is less a method than a guessing game.

Second, there is plenty of speculation available about both Soviet and Egyptian politics in the international press; and in the Egyptian case, it is certainly worth an investigator's time to follow what is said about the affairs of Cairo in the daily newspapers of Beirut, the Arab capital of gossip and rumors. The closest follower of such gossip is admittedly better informed than others; but essentially, as compared to the imaginative study of official pronouncements, this simply adds the speculation of others to one's own.

Third, one can do what we mainly do in this essay: to piece together the sequence of known events of the past, put oneself in the shoes of national leaders, and attempt to arrive at rationally plausible interpretations of their concurrent and conflicting interests against the broad background of historical evidence. From this vantage point one can make deductive arguments about the pressures generated by specific situations upon the leaders, and about the choices they faced; one can also attempt to project a measure of this somewhat artificially assumed and incompletely substantiated rationality into areas where information is lacking, including the present and future as well as the past; and some common-sense hypotheses about patterns of influence may be drawn. Such a process does not, of course, tell us anything specific about the day-to-day mechanisms of communication by which particular decisions by particular people have been arrived at. It does have the merit of not purporting to accomplish more than is possible, and it should certainly be distinguished both from rank speculation and from simple narration.

In what follows, then, we shall not try to unearth any discoveries but to place Soviet-Egyptian relations in a perspective that may suggest the ambiguities of the overlapping but distinct interests of the two states: first, by briefly setting Egyptian-Soviet relations within the general framework of the Soviet role in the Third World and Egypt's role in the Middle East during the years prior to 1967, and second, by reviewing the major events in which they were involved together after the 1967 war.

Egypt's Place in Soviet Concerns Prior to 1967

On a general level, we may regard the Soviet-Egyptian relationship over the years as a rather typical one between the dominant Communist state and a Third World country that is relatively poor, backward, and tradition-ridden and whose leaders have no intention of espousing communism or becoming Soviet satellites but do have considerable ambitions to modernize their society and increase their international prestige in the name of revolution and national liberation, tend to see the leading Western powers as obstacles in this path, and are quite ready to profit by whatever leverage the Soviets will give them. The record of Soviet relations not only with Egypt and with certain other Arab states, but also with Ghana, Indonesia, India, Cuba, Guinea, and others has made this overall pattern a familiar one. The pattern helps us to see Soviet-Egyptian relations beyond their specific circumstantial context, especially beyond the context of the Arab-Israeli conflict which so often tends to overshadow our thinking about all Middle Eastern politics. It helps us to gain a general perspective and to appreciate that there is a more or less common list of Soviet advantages and problems, successes and failures, in dealing with Third World countries of the radical nationalist variety and in translating the various forms of aid given them into practical benefits for the USSR.[1]

Thus we know, for example, that in many instances the ability of the Soviets to move in and establish their presence in a country, with trade and aid, is largely a function of local antagonism toward the former colonial power and/or the United States; that in the early phases at least, the Soviets have the advantage of possessing no vested interests and thus nothing to lose; that the Soviet model of economic and political development, plus its status as a superpower, lend it a ready prestige with rising groups of national intelligentsia. On the other hand, we know that local nationalists tend to focus on local and regional concerns that the Soviets do not altogether share or want to get embroiled in; that the nationalists sooner or later are apt to experience some frustrations and disappointments with Soviet personnel and equipment, and to chafe at what appears as Soviet heavy-handedness; that the Soviets in turn become irritated with the inefficiency and hypersensitivity of local personnel; that national projects and national economies get bogged down in shortfalls, cost overruns, inflation, and deficits, and the Soviets sooner or later find themselves faced with the prospect of pouring in more and more money just to bail their clients out; and that in time, the local nationalists become sensitized to the idea that the Sovets' purposes and their own are ultimately divergent and that they are in some danger of being manipulated and eventually transformed into puppets or else discarded.

It has become part of our conventional wisdom, in short, to see that the Soviets have inherited difficulties comparable to our own in dealing with the Third World and in trying to translate aid into influence. Accordingly, it is not particularly surprising that their record in Egypt has been at best a mixed one, for reasons unrelated to the particular character of the international issues in the Middle East. As in the case of Soviet relationships elsewhere, there has been over the years an important coincidence of interest and ideology between Egypt and the USSR, and a readiness on the part of each partner to make use of the other, coupled with stark cultural differences and a sense of mutual irritation and mistrust.

Beyond these general considerations, however, there has been in Egypt's case the peculiar circumstance of her conflict with Israel, whose military occupation of a large expanse of her territory from 1967 onward was bound to overshadow all else as the number one national problem, regardless of who governed Egypt and regardless of all other aspects of Egyptian relations with the Soviet Union and other outside powers. Certainly there were, between 1967 and 1973, many secondary considerations which colored these relationships; but in essence we are no longer dealing with simply another instance of the mixed advantages and disadvantages facing the Soviets in Third World countries. In Egypt their prospects of influence could not but reflect their ability and willingness to help bring about the withdrawal of Israeli forces from the Sinai. As the October War broke out and ran its course, it was evident that Soviet help, and with it immediate Soviet influence, weighed crucially in the balance; while by contrast, as the tide of the war shifted and the aftermath of the cease-fire unfolded, it was equally clear that the payoff that Egypt sought was available only through the United States, and Moscow's leverage evaporated virtually from one day to the next. To what extent it might return would depend on the intent and effectiveness of American actions over a more prolonged period. For Egypt's initial success in launching the war could not be sustained to the point of a forcible reoccupation of the Sinai, but it did suffice to set in motion a process of American diplomatic pressure on Israel, whose eventual results the Egyptians were prepared to await patiently.

Both in reviewing the past and in anticipating the future, it is healthy to recognize not only that the hopes and disappointments of potential client states are apt alternately to rise and fall without final- ity, but also that in a broad sense the rise and fall of a superpower's influence does not necessarily follow an altogether parallel course. Given a broad rather than narrow conception of influence, we shall hopefully be more alive to the variety and subtlety of ways in which Soviet foreign policy purposes may be served in their relations with the Egyptian recipients of their aid and advice.

A limited and specific use of the concept of influence unquestion- ably has certain advantages for the analyst. Precision is important, and we do need to be skeptical of simple notions to the effect that the mere giving of military or economic aid, for instance, automatically signifies a dominant voice for the donor in the recipient's national affairs. It is also important to remind ourselves that weaker countries who are dependent in certain ways on stronger ones tend to resist the notion that they should be simply adjuncts of their patron's policies. There have been ample evidences in the Middle East of this need for caution. The Soviet frustrations in Egypt since 1967, for instance, are reminis- cent of those of the United States earlier in the 1960s when after pouring a flood of economic aid into Egypt, the United States found that in the process it was helping Nasser pay the bills for the pursuit of policies it did not like; eventually Nasser summed up his view of America's title to leverage by inviting her to "drink from the sea." By the same token, we need to be skeptical of the perennial notion of the "power vacuum" always waiting to be filled in the Middle East by one or another great power, a notion that implies that local regimes will naturally pay the greatest obeisance to the wishes of whichever country's armed forces are stationed nearby in the greatest numbers.

On the other hand, the more rigorous our conception of influence, the more we may risk reaching some oversimplified conclusions. A gen- eral caveat is that we should be very cautious about drawing conclusions from our study of Soviet or Chinese experience about what American foreign policy ought to be. For example, the fact that the Soviets have had considerable difficulties in Egypt has variable policy implications — for example, (1) therefore the United States can stop worrying about alienating the Arabs and may as well support Israel, or alternatively, (2) therefore Israel has little reason to feel threatened and does not need so much American support. Furthermore, Soviet or Chinese influ- ence over local countries in a given region of the Third World is hardly the only thing the United States needs to worry about in that region, for its interests there may depend as much on its own direct relationships with those countries as on the Soviet or Chinese positions. Egypt has demonstrated on some occasions that it is quite possible to enjoy strained relations with both the United States and the USSR at the same time, without moving particularly close to China either. We can no more readily assume that if Soviet-Egyptian relations are strained and Soviet influence over Egypt is small, the United States should relax and do nothing, than we could assume that whenever the Soviets exercise great influence in Egypt, it becomes incumbent on the United States to run after Egypt as competitive suitors.

Once we agree to eschew policy conclusions, other caveats remain. A country will sometimes seek, as Professor Rubinstein points out, to exercise influence in order to obtain specific, short-term advantages, or to create instances in which B adapts to A's preferences (see Chapter 1). We should avoid becoming preoccupied with this model, for it seems clear that in the Soviet-Egyptian case, one of the most substantial effects (and, most probably, purposes) of Soviet support over the years up to 1973 was to encourage the Egyptians to do what they wanted to do anyway. Professor Rubinstein defines this category as follows: "Finally, influence may be viewed within a strategic context . . . in terms of consequences that are observable only in the broader context of A's desire to have B opt for policy outcomes which B prefers, but which are made possible only by A, which believes they will redound to its long-term advantage: in other words, A is influencing B to do what B would prefer to do, but could not do without A's resources. "

This second dimension of analysis is crucially important, and should perhaps be stretched further to take account of A's support for policies which B not only prefers but is prepared to pursue if necessary with its own resources. In so doing, A not only enhances B's capability, but makes a gesture to strengthen the credibility of its own status as a benign patron, presumably in order to make it easier in the future to have its voice listened to on various matters. Thus in granting economic aid for a development program, A may not be particularly confident of B's ability to make the program a success, or that the project is even very desirable, and it may realize (like Secretary of State Rogers as quoted by Professor Rubinstein in Chapter 1 of this volume) that it will not be able to gain leverage over B in particular instances by threatening to cut the aid off. Nonetheless, A may still decide to grant the aid, hoping to enhance B's attitude of appreciation and receptivity, or to strengthen the hands of particular individuals inside B's regime whom A considers useful to it. As in the case of personal relationships, so also between governments the influence gained (or not gained) by friendly gestures may be impossible to identify but should not thereby be dismissed.

In the Soviet-Egyptian case, during the period from 1955 to 1967 (from the first granting of military assistance to the June war) the salient general fact of life was that the Soviets staked Nasser to the pursuit of his ambition to make Egypt the dominant power in the Middle East, and one of the dominant ones in the Third World generally. Egypt under Nasser was a small power seeking to become, or at least act like, a big one. This meant domestic economic development, the building up of the armed forces, the fostering of a climate of revolution and pan-Arabism under Egyptian leadership and of continuing confrontation with Israel, and active opposition to the entrenched strategic positions of the United States and her allies. This was bound to be an investment with mixed blessings from the Soviet viewpoint. The stronger Nasser became, the more he might represent not simply a conduit for Soviet influence in the surrounding region, but a substitute for it, with purposes of his own that would ultimately be likely to diverge from theirs. Alternatively, if he failed in his ambitions, he would become a political and financial millstone for an indefinite period, and might drag the Soviet Union into dangerous confrontations with the United States.

Again, with respect to the domestic picture both in Egypt and in neighboring countries, whether Nasserism turned out to be a prosperous movement or not, the Soviets had no clear basis of judging whether the resultant regimes would be better or worse from their point of view, than what might emerge if they gave Nasser no help: they could help him to launch Egypt on a "noncapitalist path of development," but whether that would lead inevitably to socialism was an open question. The important point was that once they had lent their blessing to Nasser's policies, domestic and foreign, both his purposes and his prospects were bound to be largely beyond their control. Backing Nasser was very much of a calculated risk — using the word "calculated" in the loosest possible sense. The Soviets could hope that from one occasion to the next he would pay heed to their wishes and their advice; but equally if not more important, in other matters where Egyptian-Soviet relations were not directly involved and no advice was sought or given, they could hope that on balance Nasser's conduct of affairs would serve purposes useful to them, and also that in the process the general basis for close relations would be strengthened.

Up to 1967 the record of events suggests that these hopes on the Soviet side met with a mixture of gratifications and disappointments, and generally it could be said that their "influence," broadly rather than narrowly defined, was confirmed to a moderate degree. Just how far Soviet interests might have been served by Nasser's actions if the USSR had never helped him is a moot question. This uncertainty makes the whole assessment of Soviet influence as a net factor imprecise, but that is a liability we must accept in the process of opting for the broader view. Armed with general Soviet encouragement, Nasser helped to stimulate an atmosphere of militant resistance to Western strategic aims and of radical domestic change, in the process of which Western bases and alliances, Western-style political systems and pro-Western rulers, and established Western political conceptions ("the free world," "constitutional democracy") were swept away or eroded; and conversely, the Soviet Union, its policies and its communist teachings succeeded in becoming respectable, if not whole-heartedly accepted, in Middle Eastern minds. Less welcome to the Soviet Union was the fact that Nasser developed the widely popular notion of a middle path for the Arabs independent of both great-power blocs and ideologies. Nasser's eventual setbacks in domestic economics and regional politics culminating in the 1967 war presented the Soviets with unwelcome liabilities and dangers, moreover, while also opening the door for the resurgence of conservative and anti-Soviet elements; yet at the same time it could equally be said that the door was open to the left; and in the power struggle that followed Nasser's death, chance played a major part in the rightward swing that Egypt was to experience.

During the pre-1967 period, then, we may say that Soviet influence in Egypt was not a matter best assessed in terms of specific instances in which it could be demonstrated that the Egyptian government adopted a certain course at the behest or for the sake of the Soviet Union. No doubt there were many occasions where Nasser's tactical decisions were made in the light of the advice the Soviets gave him, or of what he knew to be their wishes; but influence of that sort seems to have been of much less consequence than the encouragement they gave him to pursue a mutually advantageous general policy.

The Aftermath of 1967

After June 1967 the picture underwent a drastic change. While it still might make sense for the Soviets to underwrite Nasser in his pursuit of his own ends, the potential benefits were now much more modest, being restricted essentially to the mere survival of the Nasser regime or, at most, to a mild recuperation of its previous position. It had been one thing to invest Soviet resources in a leader aspiring to hegemony over the entire Middle East, with the prospect that his influence in the region would in a way be theirs; it was now another simply to help him stave off total collapse.

Perhaps, in the post-1967 period, the material grip the Soviets came to hold on the Egyptian government, in terms of their ability to grant or withhold help the Egyptians could not do without, was a good deal tighter than ever before; perhaps, for instance, in 1972 they could have dissuaded Sadat from expelling the bulk of Soviet military personnel from Egypt, or gotten rid of Sadat himself, by threatening to cut off the flow of all military and industrial equipment and spare parts if they had seen fit to do so. But this added grip available to Moscow was of rather little use, given the fact that the Egyptian regime after 1967, and especially after Nasser's death in 1970, had lost its old potential to carry weight in the world. Whatever influence the Soviets may have gained over the Egyptian government itself was surely more than offset in its value to Moscow by the Egyptian loss of influence in the surrounding area.

On the other hand, considering that both the Soviet and the Egyptian governments after 1967 set their sights on the same very modest aspirations (compared to those of the pre-war years) of recovering Israeli-occupied territory and preserving the main domestic accomplishments of the revolution, it was ironic that these modest goals were less plausibly attainable than the grandiose dreams of the Nasser-Khrushchev heyday had seemed to be in their time. This meant frustration for both parties, which was bound to color the mental atmosphere of the unequal relations between them and therefore the manner in which day-to-day Soviet influence could be exercised.

From the June 1967 war until Nasser's death in September 1970, the Soviets followed a two-pronged policy toward Egypt. On the one hand, they moved rapidly to rearm her;[*] beyond this, they also sent large numbers of Soviet military personnel to Egypt to retrain the army, maintain new equipment, man air and naval bases newly available to Soviet forces, etc. They gave unstinting diplomatic support to Egypt at the UN and elsewhere, in an effort to place responsibility for the war on Israel and to require her to withdraw from all occupied territories.

On the other hand, the Soviets repeatedly stressed their own preference for a Middle East settlement that would entail the recognition of Israel as a legitimate state, and systematically avoided any identification with the Palestinian or other Arab militants who opposed mediation and peace with Israel. They had indicated their support for the substance of what was to become Security Council Resolution 242 long before the Egyptians did so, although for a time they soft-pedaled this view in apparent deference to Egyptian hesitations.[+]

Furthermore, the Soviets showed no sign of interest in dislodging Israel from the occupied territories by force, and until 1973 desisted from supplying Egypt with some of the offensive weapons she would need to do so, such as attack aircraft, long-range artillery, ground-to-ground missiles, and amphibious vehicles in which to cross the Suez Canal. While building up their military presence in the eastern

---

[*]Nasser, in his speech of July 23, 1970, stated that immediately after the June war the Soviet leaders pledged that they would restore all the equipment Egypt had lost, free of charge.

[+]At the General Assembly in the summer of 1967 the Soviets and Americans both indicated support for the Latin American resolution, substantially similar to what was to become 242 in November, but the Soviets changed their mind before it could be brought to a vote. The Egyptian delegation may have been equally interested in it but had to take account of strong opposition from other Arab states such as Syria and Algeria.

Mediterranean, the Soviets appeared as concerned as the United States to avoid any escalation of the local conflict into a super-power confrontation; and it was not until the winter of 1970, when Egyptian artillery bombardments of Israeli fortifications across the Canal were being answered by Israeli "deep-penetration" air raids into the Nile Valley and the Egyptian position was becoming desperate, that large numbers of Soviet pilots were sent to Egypt to fly air-defense patrol missions, plus other Soviet personnel to install and operate surface-to-air missile batteries. Even then, as the U.S. proposal for a cease-fire and the revival of the UN mediation mission of Gunnar Jarring was put forth in June 1970, it was evident that the Soviets were eager for this to be adopted, presumably for the sake of de-escalation.*

Israel announced her acceptance of the American proposals on July 31; an American-drafted cease-fire plan was submitted to the parties, was accepted, and took effect on the night of August 7-8. Israel complained very soon afterward that Egypt was installing anti-aircraft missiles in the Suez Canal zone in violation of the "standstill" provisions of the cease-fire agreement; Egypt rejected her complaint as unfounded, but when the U.S. government —with obvious reluctance — substantially concurred in her accusation, Israel refused to proceed with the negotiations with Jarring which the cease-fire was supposed to facilitate, and which the Israeli right-wing critics of the government had been warning would be a diplomatic snare for Israel to fall into.

The whole affair had a number of important consequences. The cease-fire took effect (and remained effective on a de facto basis until October 1973), thus saving both sides, but especially Egypt, grave losses and preventing a Soviet-American confrontation. Egyptian air defenses were substantially shored up with the SAM missiles. The Israeli occupation of the Sinai continued unabated and unchallenged. The Jarring mission and the whole prospect of a concerted UN-U.S.- USSR diplomatic intervention, on which Egypt counted and which Israel

---

*Although an American-initiated proposal, it was accompanied by regular meetings in Washington and New York with Soviet representatives, and while President Nasser was spending his 19 days in Moscow in July prior to announcing Egypt's acceptance, reports circulated that his sessions with Soviet leaders were being followed by talks between Foreign Minister Gromyko and U.S. Ambassador Beam. (See London Observer, July 5 and 12, 1970.) Nasser, in announcing his acceptance of the U.S. proposal in a speech on July 23, went out of his way to praise the Soviet Union for their support to Egypt, in a manner that seemed intended to fend off Arab criticism of the Soviets for pressing the cease-fire upon them. On July 24, in a meeting with the National Congress of the Arab Socialist Union, Nasser stated flatly that the proposals "were not only the result of U.S. efforts, but also those of the Soviet Union."

feared, was aborted. The crisis in Jordan between the government and the Palestinian militants followed, distracting everyone's attention from the "standstill violation" issue. Nasser died on September 28, and the end of a major chapter of Soviet-Egyptian relations may conveniently be marked on that date.

There are numerous questions one could raise about particular Soviet and Egyptian steps taken during the 1967-70 period, and about the influences that each exerted and received, but on such a level there are very few definite answers available. What prompting, if any, did Moscow provide to urge Egyptian adoption, at Khartoum in September and at the UN in November of 1967, of the principle of the "political solution" to the problem of "liquidating the traces of aggression" (a euphemism for the negotiation of a peace settlement that would entail recognition of Israel in exchange for her withdrawal)? Did the Soviets, through their military advisors or at the governmental level, have occasion actively to restrain the Egyptians from attempting any major military actions, such as a reinvasion of Sinai or air raids against Israel? What was the Soviet view of the Egyptian decision to begin the "war of attrition" in the spring of 1969? What bargaining took place, if any, during Nasser's visit to Moscow in January 1970 over the Soviet agreement to commit air defense units to Egypt? Over the acceptance of the U.S. cease-fire proposal? How was the decision reached between Moscow and Cairo to proceed with the construction of missile sites after August 7, in a violation of the standstill clause that gave Israel the excuse to withdraw from the Jarring negotiations?

We simply do not know the answers to these questions, and it would be a matter of sheer speculation to try to trace any pattern of influence on an event-by-event basis. The most that can be said with some assurance is that the Soviets had good reason to wish to avoid escalation in the Middle East, but that they did not wish to let Egypt be further humiliated, and indeed that they regarded the latter prospect as a serious threat to their own reputation; that they did not mind any particular diplomatic concession being made by their Egyptian clients that the latter might agree to, and would welcome some Arab-Israeli settlement, provided it would not ruin Nasser's inter-Arab reputation or make him dependent on the United States; but that they had no particular reason to press hard for the conclusion of peace and were quite prepared to see the basic Arab-Israeli conflict, from which they had derived much benefit, persist once the risks of escalation were removed. On the Egyptian side, there is no particular element of these presumptive Soviet preferences that was really objectionable, but the priorities were probably rather different: what mattered most was to get Israel out of Sinai, regardless of which superpower got the credit and regardless of what dangers the Russians thought they were running. Stabilization of the status quo might suit Moscow but not Cairo. Yet there is no reason to assume that the Egyptians were much more reluctant than the Soviets to contemplate a settlement with Israel as the price of withdrawal; nor, conversely, that in the absence of the Soviet arms airlift following June 1967, Egypt would have caved in and sued for peace on Israel's terms.

Given these assumptions, we may imagine that Nasser may have pressed hard for offensive weapons he never got, and that in this and other ways, the Soviets exercised an important restraint over the Egyptian urge for revenge; and that once the Soviet air-defense units had moved into Egypt in force in 1970 (whether reluctantly or enthusiastically, we cannot tell),* the Soviets may have had to undertake some persuasion of a skeptical Nasser to agree to a cease-fire. Once the cease-fire was concluded, it would seem that the Soviets had less reason than the Egyptians to hesitate to violate it by moving the missiles: after all, what the Soviets probably wanted most was the cease-fire, while what the Egyptians wanted most was for the Jarring negotiations to proceed, since it was the latter that promised to be the eventual vehicle of international diplomatic pressure on Israel to withdraw. We might therefore suppose that the Soviets insisted on moving the missiles, overcoming Egyptian qualms, arguing perhaps that the completion of the work of construction and installation was too vital on military grounds to forego, or that everybody tacitly expected both sides to cheat on the standstill clause anyway. + But then, it is quite possible that the Egyptians drew these conclusions for themselves and required no persuasion.

---

*Professor Uri Ra'anan has argued at length that this was a calculated Soviet move, and indeed that the Soviets have always intervened abroad with their armed forces at their own initiative and for their own purpose rather than at the behest of clients. That the Soviets have minds of their own, however, is hardly the issue: their clients, like anyone else's, can get into trouble and engage Soviet prestige in unforeseen and undesired ways. Unfortunately Ra'anan's analysis, which goes so far as to offer a detailed account of deliberations within the Kremlin, is completely undocumented, and he gives no indication of the nature of his sources. While this adds up to one of the best short stories of the year, it cannot help us decide what really happened. ("The USSR and the Middle East: Some Reflections on the Soviet Decision-Making Process," Orbis, vol. 17, no. 3 (Fall 1973), 946-77, especially pp. 956-65.)

+Egyptian spokesmen during the dispute did charge Israel with violations of its own, including the strengthening of fortifications along the Canal and the sending of air reconnaissance flights over Egyptian territory; and the State Department leaked word that it possessed evidence that the Egyptian charges were correct. (New York Times, September 15, 1970.)

Soviet Relations with Sadat

On the face of it it is curious that Sadat, a relatively weak
figure, should have been more at odds with the Soviets than the
redoubtable Nasser—and, for good measure, stood his ground fairly
successfully. There are a number of variable factors that may help
explain this: for example, armed with greater experience and finesse,
Nasser may have been more adept than Sadat in avoiding confrontations
with Moscow, and the Soviets may have seen more need to pay respect
to him. Moreover, since Sadat was presiding uneasily over a coterie
of shifting rival factions whereas Nasser had dominated affairs pretty
decisively, there was now a much more plausible opportunity for the
Soviets — or other outside parties — to seek to influence Egyptian
policymaking via their selected instruments within the regime, with the
natural result that the irritations already existing between Sadat and
the Soviets from earlier times were exacerbated. (Sadat had engaged in
a widely publicized argument with Khrushchev in Moscow in 1961 over
socialism, communism, and religion.)

Then again, there is the matter of timing: perhaps, in the nature
of circumstances as they developed, if Nasser had lived he would have
ended up by 1972 in much the same sort of clash with the Russians as
Sadat did.

What seems doubtful is that Nasser would have been drawn into
the confrontation that Sadat faced in the spring of 1971, for the latter
grew out of two circumstances attributable to Sadat's particular outlook
and situation. The first was his negotiation with the United States over
the proposed "interim solution" involving the opening of the Suez Canal
and a partial Israeli withdrawal, a negotiation initiated by Sadat in
February and which brought Secretary Rogers to Cairo to visit Sadat in
May. The Soviets, by all indications, thoroughly disapproved of this
negotiation, in which they were not consulted and which seemed to
threaten to make the United States the sole arbiter in the Arab-Israeli
conflict.* This sharply distinguished the atmosphere and significance

---

* According to the Beirut magazine Al-Jumhour (issue of May 25,
1971), Sadat had been displeased when his Minister of the Interior,
Shaarawi Gomaa, visited Moscow in February without telling him, then
returned to Cairo conveying a rebuke from the Soviets to Sadat "for
making diplomatic decisions without telling anyone" (Arab Report &
Record, London, 1971, p. 273). On May 5, while Rogers was in
Cairo, the Soviet Ambassador to the UN, Jacob Malik, accused Rogers
of "unilateral meddling"; Pravda criticized Rogers' initiative on four
successive days beginning May 11. The London Daily Telegraph on
May 14 reported that the United States had embarked on a policy of
"deliberately excluding Russia from American attempts to negotiate an
Arab-Israeli settlement." As further evidence of this, it noted that the

of the "interim solution" negotiations from those over the cease-fire the previous summer, which had also been sponsored by the United States but with active Soviet cooperation.

The second special circumstance was the challenge that Sadat faced inside his own regime, which led him to dismiss, first, Vice President Ali Sabry on the very eve of Rogers' arrival in Cairo, and then, a week after Rogers' departure, half a dozen other top officials — including the Minister of Interior, the Minister of War, his principal advisor on internal security affairs at the Presidency, and the chief of the General Intelligence Agency — and a host of lesser figures.

It would be too simple to describe the ousted Sabry-led faction as "pro-Soviet." Admittedly Sabry himself, though no Marxist, had become associated over the years with the idea of "playing the Soviet card," much as Zakaria Mohieddin was identified with "playing the American card." The other two most prominent victims of the purge, Shaarawi Gomaa and Sami Sharaf, represented the internal security apparatus and the challenge to a new President's authority that naturally flowed from their independent control over an army of under-cover agents and a mass of secret dossiers and tape recordings. They were, however, closely identified with Sabry for a number of reasons, and through him to the Soviet Union; and with Sabry, they had taken up opposition both to the "interim solution" negotiation and to Sadat's project for confederation with Libya and Syria that was then in the air.

Thus Sadat had flung a double challenge in the Soviets' face. In a very short time he was obliged to pay a price, which was, however, more symbolic than real. A Soviet delegation headed by President Podgorny arrived in Cairo on May 25 to settle accounts. "No one doubts," wrote a British journalist in Cairo, "that he is here to assess the extent of what is perhaps the biggest setback the Soviet Union has suffered in her long and patient drive for supremacy in the Middle East." Ideology had had little to do with causing the crisis, yet inevitably it would be affected: "The Soviet conception of the natural evolution of the Egyptian revolutionary regime has taken a body blow."[2]

What Podgorny obtained was not a retraction of any of Sadat's actions but a compensatory gesture, in the form of a treaty of friend-ship, hastily drawn up and signed by the two leaders after only two days of meetings. The treaty in its published provisions fell short of binding the partners to a full military alliance: they agreed merely to consult each other about matters of common concern and not to join alliances hostile to each other, to cooperate to preserve the social and economic benefits of their respective revolutionary systems, and so forth; and the Soviets pledged to continue arming and training the

---

Soviet Embassy had not been invited, as some other foreign missions were, to briefings given by Secretary Rogers on the results of the trip (ARR, 1971, p. 252).

Egyptian forces "with a view to strengthening its capacity to eliminate the consequences of aggression. "[3] Still, even in this limited form, the treaty marked an unprecedented departure from the principles of "positive neutralism" and nonalignment of which Nasser had for so long made such a fetish; and the provisions, limited as they were, still implied the imposition of some significant restraints on Egypt's freedom of action, and of a Soviet right to take an interest in Egypt's internal as well as foreign affairs. Article 2, calling for cooperation to preserve the social and economic gains, etc. , could be read as an implicit extension to the Middle East of the Brezhnev Doctrine that had been invoked against Czechoslovakia in 1968, claiming for the USSR the right to intervene in a socialist state to protect the domestic system.

As if to appease the Soviets, in fact, Sadat on May 17 had already made a point of appointing a communist, Fuad Mursi, to the provisional Secretariat of the Arab Socialist Union; and in the new Cabinet another communist, Ismail Sabry Abdullah, was to become Minister of Planning. But these were token gestures. The Prime Ministry remained in the hands of Dr. Mahmoud Fawzi, an elderly retired diplomat inherited from the pre-1952 royal regime, clearly oriented toward the West in his fundamental outlook. To preside over the Arab Socialist Union, and reorganize it following its decimation in the purge, Sadat chose Dr. Aziz Sidky, a tough and loyal administrator with long experience in dealing with the Soviets. Pointedly, Sadat chose the opening day of his talks with Podgorny, May 26, to declare publicly that Ali Sabry had masterminded the plot against him that he had foiled by the purge.[4]

On the whole, the events of May 1971 seemed to indicate that Sadat was relatively immune to Soviet pressures — at least, of the magnitude that the Soviets found it politic to bring to bear on him. He reaffirmed his independence, much to the Russians' obvious displeasure, in July of the same year when he and Colonel Qaddafi of Libya assisted President Nimeiry of the Sudan in overcoming a Marxist-oriented coup d'etat and executing a number of participants.

Sadat's Expulsion of Soviet Military Personnel, July 1972

If Soviet military assistance and diplomatic support were Egypt's only instruments for defense against Israel, they were of no real use for offensive purposes. With the Soviets unwilling to help Egypt try to regain its lost territory by force, the only source of help in "liquidating the consequences of aggression" could be the United States. This gave fundamental plausibility to Sadat's participation in the "interim solution" negotiations, his invitation to Rogers, and his willingness to antagonize the Soviet leadership by carrying out his purge of May 1971. The "interim solution" failed, leaving Sadat bitter and disillusioned with the Nixon administration for its failure to press Israel to make vital concessions; but still the fact remained that if

Washington had little to offer him, Moscow had nothing much either. Beyond this, however, there was the consideration that Egypt's ties to the Soviet Union and the presence of significant Soviet bases and forces in Egypt were themselves among the reasons for American reluctance to lean on Israel. To the extent that the Soviets declined to become part of the solution, they were part of the problem.

On July 23, 1972 — the 20th anniversary of the Egyptian revolution — Sadat made his electrifying announcement that he had ordered all Soviet military installations to be handed over to Egyptian control, and for all Soviet equipment to be sold to Egypt or taken away. During the weeks that followed, explanations of the background to this decision poured forth. Among the most salient points were the USSR's alleged unwillingness to supply Egypt with offensive weapons and lack of candor as she put Sadat and his ministers off time and again with evasions and empty promises. Sadat himself had gone to Moscow in quest of arms in March and October 1971, and February and April 1972; Prime Minister Sidky followed in July. According to Sadat's subsequent recounting, clear answers to the Egyptian requests were never forthcoming, and in the meantime the idea was gathering force in Cairo that Soviet policy in the Middle East had come to rest on the cornerstone of "no war, no peace."[*] Sadat, soon after the Soviet expulsion, stated in a written statement addressed to American readers:

> There is no alternative to the creation of a credible
> deterrent to the Israeli forces on which the U. S. adminis-
> tration lavishes most "generously" its most sophisticated
> weapons. Egypt here faces an embargo imposed by the
> West. In fact she also faces a partial embargo imposed
> by the East. The Soviet Union, whose great assistance to
> us in building our defenses and in the most important
> domains of development is unforgettable (and will remain
> unforgettable), declines to provide us with the weapons
> which would constitute this credible deterrent. [5]

In a blunter statement to a Lebanese journalist, Sadat complained that without such weapons as the MIG 23, a "peaceful settlement" as advocated by the Soviets "meant surrender to American and Israeli terms."[6]

It is impossible on the basis of public information to be certain how real or significant a factor the Soviets' withholding of weapons was. Given the fact that by October 1973 the Egyptians were

---

[*] See, for example, the summary of Sadat's version of events in Newsweek, August 7, 1972, pp. 28-29. Mohammed Hassanein Haikal, in a series of articles shortly before Sadat's expulsion order, had advanced the same notion of Soviet benefit from the "no war, no peace" situation, and other expressions of this view had been aired as well.

generously enough armed to launch a successful crossing of the Canal, and indeed resupplied thereafter, it is clear that the Soviets were far from permanently inflexible on this question. Perhaps they worried less about Egypt going to war once their own combat units were removed from the country. Indeed, in some quarters it has been argued that the whole removal was the result of a calculated Soviet decision to withdraw their units from an untenable situation, in the face of accelerated American arming of Israel earlier in 1972.[*] This may be, although the Soviets could hardly welcome the humiliation of being so peremptorily and publicly expelled by their supposed client, and it is difficult to see how they could have counted on the United States to fail to take advantage of Sadat's clearly implied invitation to replace their patronage with an American one.

It seems likely that the internal mood in Egypt had much to do with the expulsion. The Russians had never been popular as visitors in the country, as the easygoing, extroverted Egyptians found them clannish and stolid; and nowhere was this unpopularity so pronounced as within the ranks of the Egyptian army, especially among officers who found their own authority preempted and their self-respect undermined by arrogant foreign instructors and advisors. Despite the private misgivings of a good many leftist intellectuals and other Egyptians who feared that Sadat had thrown away his only card without extracting anything in return from the United States, widespread press reports and observers' impressions at the time indicated a great sense of relief and satisfaction in Egypt that the Soviets had been taught a lesson. The possibility of warnings to Sadat from his military leaders cannot be excluded.

----

[*] Ra'anan, op. cit., pp. 968-69. Elsewhere in the same article Ra'anan writes: "As for Cairo's complaints that the USSR allegedly reneged on commitments to deliver certain 'offensive' weapons to Egypt, it is difficult to find an item to which this could apply seriously. Prior to the events of midsummer 1972, the Kremlin had sent to Egypt one of the Warsaw Pact's main battle tanks, the T-62, the latest all-weather versions of the MIG-21, practically the entire SAM series (2, 3, 4, 6), the Tu-16B, with a sophisticated air-to-surface missile, and other modern weapons" (p. 956, note 3). Subsequently, however, in discussing the buildup during the "twelve or thirteen months" preceding the October war (that is, after midsummer 1972), Ra'anan catalogs a long list of items shipped in unprecedented quantity by the Soviets to Egypt which, he implies, were to make a critical difference, again including the T-62, the MIG-21, the Tu-16, and various series of the SAM (p. 973). It goes without saying that if their arrival before October 1973 was so important, and heralded a new phase of Soviet policy, then their nonarrival before July 1972 was important too, and signified something else.

Egyptian apprehensions of Soviet satisfaction with the status quo
were naturally stimulated by the Nixon-Brezhnev meetings in Moscow
in the spring of 1972, and the implication arising from them that while
the two superpowers held differing views on the middle Eastern conflict, they neither desired nor foresaw a confrontation arising between
themselves. But if Sadat and his advisers hoped that their unilateral
removal of Soviet forces from Egypt would fulfill and American precondition for pressure on Israel to accept a full withdrawal in exchange for
peace, to be delayed perhaps only by the U.S. elections, they were
completely disappointed: election day and Nixon's second inaugural
came and went, but without the slightest sign of American intent to
take further initiatives in the Middle East. The opening of the Water-
gate hearings, with their promise of distraction and paralysis in
Washington for an indefinite time, rang down the curtain on whatever
vestigial expectations may have remained — until the 1973 war dramatically changed the picture once again.

Meanwhile Sadat again paid the Soviets the price of token gestures, as he had done after ousting Ali Sabry and his friends in 1971.
In October he sent Prime Minister Sidky back to Moscow in search of
a partial reconciliation, and dismissed his War Minister, General
Sadek, who had a particular reputation for hostility to the Soviets.
Sidky was received politely in Moscow, and was reassured on the
flow of Soviet spare parts; a modest number of Russian experts drifted
back to Egypt; the Soviets reiterated old statements of support for
Egypt's diplomatic position against Israel; but by December, a
journalist in Cairo could report that "Soviet-Egyptian relations remain
almost as distant as they were . . . last July."[7]

The October War and After

As the inability of the USSR to undo Egypt's defeat became
increasingly manifest, it became possible for even a modest political
figure like Sadat to defy the Soviets on occasion and to retract from
them an important part of the privileges they had gained as the patrons
of his celebrated predecessor. On the military level, the trump cards
were held by Israel and the United States, who, it appeared, could
not be challenged by Egypt and the Soviet Union respectively. Moreover, Egyptians could reason also that only the United States could (if
she chose) arrange an improvement in their situation by putting pressure
on Israel, and furthermore, that they depended as much on the United
States as on the USSR not to allow still further disasters to be visited
upon them on top of that of 1967. Egyptians and other Arabs could well
conclude that the Soviets had only second-rate gifts to bear.

Were such apprehensions as these sufficient to persuade the
Soviets to support a decision by the Egyptian and Syrian leaders to go
to war? If so, it was a striking illustration of the tyranny of the weak
over the strong, and a strangely passive acquiescence on the part of

the Soviets in the initiative taken by their clients. And yet this is as plausible an explanation as any. We might imagine, of course, that the Soviets expected that the Arab armies would again suffer defeat, that they would turn to Moscow to intervene and bail them out, and that then the USSR would have a golden opportunity to impose herself in whatever way she chose, thus delivering a master stroke of Machiavellian manipulation. But this motivation seems most unlikely, combining as it does the prospect of the humiliation of Soviet-trained and -equipped forces with that of a dangerous international escalation. It is true that on October 25, as Egypt's Third Army was cut off and threatened with destruction, the Soviets did propose to send in their own forces, thus provoking President Nixon to declare his famous counteralert. But there is no reason to suppose that this was the situation which the Soviets had sought to bring about.

Alternatively, we may imagine that the Soviet leaders willingly played their part in planning the Syrian-Egyptian attack from the beginning, many months before it was launched, in order to achieve a measure of military success for their clients, embarrass the United States, and carve out for themselves a major role in subsequent diplomatic negotiations. After all, they knowingly provided Egypt with enough military equipment to think of going to war; and they were well aware that if given enough such encouragement, the Egyptians could be counted on to make the plunge. Thus it would seem that the decision on war was at least implicitly shared between Moscow and Cairo well before October; perhaps it was also explicit.

We can imagine certain precautionary stipulations that the Soviets may have made: that Syria and Egypt would avoid any threat to the territory of Israel proper; that they accept the principle of peace negotiations with Israel; that the resupply of equipment be paid for in cash (that is, by the Arab oil states); that Saudi participation in an oil embargo against the United States be assured; that no cease-fire and no peace-keeping forces from the UN be accepted without full consultation with Moscow, etc. None of these stipulations, if made, was likely to have met with any serious objections, even the one calling for peace negotiations, considering that from an Arab point of view the purpose of the war was presumably to bring diplomacy into play under favorable circumstances.

In response, the Soviets would have had to provide Egypt and Syria with certain assurances of diplomatic support, arms shipments, and the like. It stands to reason that the Arab states would have pressed their Soviet patron for the maximum possible commitment to neutralize the United States Sixth Fleet and prevent American armed intervention; it seems highly unlikely that the Soviets would have made any explicit commitments on this sensitive and dangerous point. It is more plausible that they should have given some unspecific undertaking of intervention against Israel if necessary to prevent a repetition of the Arab disaster of 1967, subject to the proviso that such an action would not risk confrontation with the Americans. If so, and if an undertaking of this sort lay behind the crisis of October 25-26, it seems most likely that it was pressed on Moscow from Cairo and not the other way around, since the chief risks would be borne by the USSR to the benefit of Egypt. Perhaps the Soviets made the gesture of proposing to send forces to Egypt on October 25, simply in order to discharge their commitment, but without any intention of following through in the face of what they knew would be strong American objections.

In the light of what happened in the Middle East in the months following the October War, it is clear that the Soviets badly miscalculated in supposing that they stood to gain anything from it. Paradoxical as it may seem, their clients' relative success redounded not to their benefit but to that of the United States, the power that had supplied the hated Israelis during the fighting and became the target of the Arab oil embargo. This paradoxical outcome began to unfold from the moment when the United States joined the Soviet Union in imposing a cease-fire on Egypt and Israel, thereby withholding from the latter what was promising to become a crushing military victory.

As Secretary Kissinger went on in the following weeks to visit Cairo, Damascus, and other Arab capitals, the truth of the new situation became clear: the key to Israeli withdrawal was held, as always, in American hands; and now, for a change, there was a prospect that a newly concerned American government might actually do something. As Arab eyes turned expectantly toward Washington, the Soviets were all but forgotten. Egypt restored diplomatic relations with the United States; Saudi Arabia took the lead in ending the oil embargo; Kissinger was received cordially in Damascus, not once but over a dozen times; the President of the United States was invited to visit several Arab countries. All this, while Syrian and Egyptian corpses killed by American weapons rotted away. It was an extraordinary transformation of diplomatic fortunes and alignments. In helping the Arabs to launch an assault against the American-blessed status quo, the Soviets had unwittingly set the stage for a Pax Americana which could undo all that they had worked for in the Middle East for 20 years.

Of course, as at various times in the past, the pendulum can swing again. Events of the previous two decades suggest that from the Egyptian perspective, only the Soviets could be looked to to bolster Egypt's ability to wage war against Israel, offensively or defensively, while only the Americans could help them to make peace. Neither warmaking nor peace-making has been a successful enterprise in these past years, and with each disappointment it is not surprising that the Egyptians have shown some renewed interest in, and receptivity to the suggestions of, the superpower associated with the alternative policy. Thus a deterioration of the peace prospects that followed the 1973 war could well lead to a renewal of Soviet patronage in Egyptian affairs.

Notes

1. For a very useful general survey of Soviet difficulties, see Morton Schwartz's monograph, The Failed Symbiosis: The USSR and Leftist Regimes in Less Developed Countries (California Arms Control and Foreign Policy Seminar, Santa Monica, May 1973).

2. David Hirst in The Guardian (London), May 26, 1971.

3. Text of the treaty in Arab Report and Record, 1971, p. 272; also in New Times (Moscow), No. 23, 1971, pp. 8-9. See also N. Safran, "The Soviet-Egyptian Treaty," New Middle East (London), July 1971, pp. 10-13; and Robert O. Freedman, "Changes in Soviet Policy toward the Middle East since Nasser: A Case Study in Soviet Foreign Policy, 1970-72" (unpublished manuscript, Marquette University), pp. 28-31.

4. See ARR, 1971, p. 273.

5. Anwar el-Sadat, "Where Egypt Stands," Foreign Affairs, vol. 51, no. 1 (October 1972), p. 122.

6. Juan de Onis in The New York Times, October 6, 1972.

7. Henry Tanner in The New York Times, December 4, 1972.

5

SOVIET AND CHINESE
INFLUENCE ON THE
PALESTINIAN GUERRILLA MOVEMENT
Moshe Ma'oz

According to a widely-held impression, based on reports by the news media, close links exist between the Soviet Union and China on the one hand, and the Palestinian guerrilla movements on the other. As a result, it is generally assumed that both the Soviet Union and China exert considerable influence on these movements. This assumption derives from several facts: frequent visits by guerrilla leaders to Moscow and Peking, and their meetings with Soviet and Chinese leaders; the participation of guerrilla leaders in official functions in both these capitals; Soviet and Chinese declarations of support for the "struggle" of the Palestinians; and, finally, the extension of considerable military aid and some military advice by these powers to the guerrillas.

Although the organs of the Palestinians frequently express their gratitude to both Communist powers for their support, their statements suggest that the Palestinians feel more indebted to the Chinese than to the Soviets. This feeling seems to be reflected in statements such as the following: (1) Expressions of solidarity with the Chinese revolution and the struggle of the Chinese against American imperialism as well as against the "Chiang Kai-shek clique"; (2) Appeals to Arab governments, which do not have diplomatic relations with China, to recognize People's China as a reward for its policy toward the Palestinians.

Surface manifestations of what appears to be strong Chinese influence on the Arab guerrillas are often reported in Chinese publications, which say that many Palestinian guerrilla fighters ardently study Chairman Mao's works in order to help liberate Palestine. Such glowing reports are not limited to Chinese publications. On March 23, 1970, The Guardian (London), in a dispatch from its Beirut correspondent, vividly described how "Fatah guerrillas can be seen on the hillsides of Jordan with the little Red Book and [how] Chairman Mao's benign portrait smiles down from the wall of most Fatah campaign headquarters."

On the basis of reports such as these, many conclude that China's ties with the Palestinians serve to extend Chinese influence throughout the Middle East and to undermine the Soviet, as well as Western, presence in the region.

However, these impressions and assessments relating to the dimensions of Soviet and Chinese influence on the Palestine guerrilla movement lack a firm base and are probably largely incorrect. There are several reasons for this. First, they are partly derived from biased sources of information. Second, they are based on analogies with what appear to be similar situations in other parts of the world, but these analogies are partly misleading. Third, they stem from a misunderstanding of the positions of the Communist powers in the region, as well as from a misreading of the aims of the guerrilla organizations in the Arab world.

Thus Western commentators, viewing China's activities in the Middle East in the context of what they deem to be China's global aims, assume that the Chinese are striving to infiltrate the guerrilla movement in order to use it as a revolutionary instrument. This assumption is augmented in several ways: (1) by the Chinese mass media, which strives to depict China as an active, revolutionary factor in the Middle East and as a counterweight to Soviet influence; (2) by the propaganda of the guerrilla organizations, which attempt to appear as allies of the principal revolutionary power; (3) by the Soviets, who tend to exaggerate Chinese influence in order to warn the Arab states against the danger from Peking; and (4) by certain pro-Western quarters both in conservative Arab countries and in Israel which fear a Chinese-Palestinian revolutionary alliance, and try to gain Western support by playing up its threat.

The bias and the tendency toward exaggeration which characterizes many of the sources dealing with the relations of the Palestinians with China and to some extent with the Soviet Union, constitute one of the main obstacles facing a researcher in this field. Not only does the information from China and the Soviet Union come from government sources, but the news media in most Arab countries are likewise subject to censorship, and hence do not provide accurate information on this subject. The exception is the relatively free Lebanese press, as well as some organs of the Palestinian movement which appear in Lebanon. These sources provide important data. Foremost among them are ideological journals and books which are published by the guerrilla organizations and which give a balanced picture of the Palestinian attitude toward the Communist powers.

Another obstacle facing the researcher is lack of access to information relating to sensitive but important topics such as arms shipments, military advisers, and secret agreements. Moreover, since the Palestinians operate not as a state but as a guerrilla movement, the researcher is deprived of the possibility of measuring the influence of outsiders on them in areas such as economic and social policies and foreign affairs. In addition to this, since the Palestinian organizations operate within Arab states and are subject to their control, it is frequently difficult to distinguish between their relations and those of their host countries with the Communist powers. It is especially difficult to make this distinction in view of the fact that these complex relationships are often in a state of flux.

A further difficulty which has to be taken into account stems from the fact that the Palestinian movement is not uniform, but is split along ideological and political lines. Some organizations are Marxist, others are nationalistic. Compounding this difficulty is the great variety in the size and popularity of the various organizations.

This essay will focus on the two major Palestinian organizations which dominate the Palestinian movement, namely, the Palestinian Liberation Organization (PLO) and Fatah. These were the first Palestinian organizations, and they are the largest and most popular. It is with them that China and the Soviet Union have developed close ties.

The USSR and China Enter the Arab World

Since the initial appearance of the Palestinian movement, Soviet and Chinese policies toward it were derived basically from their general policies toward the Third World and their specific policies toward the Arab world. The objectives of each Communist power in the Middle East (as in other parts of the world) were to establish a presence and to exercise influence, while simultaneously neutralizing, if not eliminating, the presence and influence of the other and of the Western Powers.

Moscow and Peking have different priorities in the Middle East. For the Soviet Union, the area is essential, because relative geographical proximity affects vital security interests. Accordingly, the USSR has invested considerable political, military, and economic effort to penetrate the area. For China, however, the Middle East is distant geographically and is of secondary importance politically, strategically, and economically.[1] For these reasons and because of its limited resources China could not afford, nor did it desire, to invest heavily in the area; it was satisfied to supply selective material aid, while simultaneously launching an active diplomatic and propaganda campaign.

A new stage in relations between the Soviet Union, China, and the Arab world was ushered in in 1955. For the Soviets, after decades of frustration, it was a year of breakthrough. Beginning with the Czech arms deal with Egypt in September, the Soviet Union steadily widened its contacts in the area and within a few years established a major political and military presence in the Arab world and the Mediterranean basin. For China, too, 1955 was important. During the Afro-Asian Conference in Bandung, contacts were made between Chou En-lai, Nasser, and Ahmed Shukeiry, then serving as the Assistant Chairman of the Syrian delegation to the Conference. But China was a minor actor, since it lacked economic resources, diplomatic contacts, and, above all, the compelling interest in the Middle East of the Soviet Union.

Chinese activity in the Arab world was limited to tentative dealing with marginal issues, while the Soviet Union pressed its relations with Egypt and Syria. Furthermore, after the Suez Crisis (1956), China's relations with Egypt and other Arab countries deteriorated because of the former's unbending adherence to revolutionary ideology. China took a dim view of the "bourgeois-military" Arab regimes that oppressed their Communist parties. Relations between China and Egypt especially worsened. For its part, Egypt criticized Peking for its intervention in Tibet and India and expressed apprehension over Chinese infiltration into Iraq (which recognized China in late 1958). As a result of these frictions, China kept its contacts with the Arab countries in the years that followed to a minimum, while expanding its activities in Africa and Southeast Asia. At the height of the Sino-Soviet antagonism in the mid-1960s, China renewed its effort to penetrate the Arab world.[2] The Chinese might have mounted this challenge to the Soviet Union in the Middle East in order to ease Soviet pressure on the Chinese border in Central Asia.

During these years, China moved to foster better relations with Egypt and other Arab states, disregarding the oppression of communists in those countries (1964) and the appearance of pro-Chinese factions that had broken off from the pro-Soviet Arab Communist parties. Chou En-lai visited Egypt in 1963, 1964, and 1965; and during these years China hosted Egyptian, Syrian, and Yemeni delegations (a friendship pact was signed with Yemen in 1964). China proposed generous aid to Arab countries amounting to 32 percent of China's foreign aid budget, while the negative trade balance between China and the Arab countries became quite conspicuous.

Once again Chinese efforts to improve relations with the Arab countries faltered. A main stumbling block was Nasser's Egypt, which continued its close relationship with the Soviet Union and helped to strengthen the USSR's position in the Arab and Afro-Asian worlds, at the expense of its relations with China. A purge of pro-Chinese factions in Egypt's Socialist Union and the expulsion of Chinese diplomats from Egypt occurred in 1965.

Even the new Ba'thist regime in Syria, which was sympathetic toward China almost from its very inception, could not relinquish its ties with the Soviet Union to suit China's policy.

The coolness of the Arab countries moved China to freeze its political relations and to cut down its economic contacts with these countries, especially Egypt, in the second half of the 1960s. The Cultural Revolution also required China to adopt a hard and revolutionary line in relations with the governments of bourgeois states. Even the military defeat of Egypt and Syria in June 1967, which cast a temporary shadow on Soviet-Arab relations, did not improve China's position in the Arab world. Only after the death of Nasser in September

1970, and the expulsion of Soviet military experts from Egypt by Sadat in July 1972, did relations improve between China and some of the Arab countries, including Egypt. The termination of the Cultural Revolution in China and the worsening of the Sino-Soviet dispute gave China an additional incentive for improving relations with the Arabs. However, the limited scope of Chinese aid could not replace the massive Soviet aid to the Arab states, nor could the diplomatic support of the PRC, which became a member of the UN in 1972, replace the political clout of the Soviet Union. In sum, it is clear that the Soviet Union has an obvious advantage over China in everything concerning a presence in the area and the exercise of influence over the Arab countries.

The question arises whether this holds true for one of the important realms of Sino-Soviet rivalry, namely, in the Palestinian guerrilla movement. We shall examine Chinese and Soviet policies toward the Palestinian guerrilla movement, which both Communist powers consider as part of the revolutionary movement in the Third World and as such a target for attention.

China and the Palestinians Since 1964

Until the First Arab Summit Conference in January 1964 called for the establishment of the Palestinian Liberation Organization (PLO), the People's Republic of China, sympathetically aware of the Palestinian problem since the 1955 Bandung Conference at which Chou En-lai and Ahmed Shukeiry held talks, did not officially recognize the Palestinian Nation.[3]

In 1963 and 1964, China tried to increase its influence in the Arab world. It failed in its efforts to operate through the radical Arab governments and the Arab Communist parties, which tended to look more to the Soviet Union. Interested in weakening Soviet leadership of the antiimperialistic liberation movements in the Third World, China saw the establishment of the PLO as a new opportunity to improve relations with the Arab world and to link itself to a local national liberation movement. This was important to China especially in view of the preparations it was making for the second Afro-Asian Conference — to which the Soviet Union was not invited. At the end of 1964, Chou En-lai said to the Arabs: "We are ready to help the Arab nations to regain Palestine . . . we are ready to give you anything and everything."[4] At the time, China did not look upon the PLO as an independent, national liberation movement, nor was it defined as such in the two Afro-Asian meetings that took place under China's influence in 1965: the Bandung Islamic Conference in March and the Ghana Solidarity Conference in May.[5]

In 1965, though, China slowly began to change its position toward the Palestinian movement, seeing in it a revolutionary potential in the Arab world.

This change was also the result of the continuously disappointing attempts at improving relations on a state-to-state basis with the Arab states and of the Cultural Revolution in China, which emphasized anew in Chinese foreign policy the ideology of supporting world revolution and national liberation movements.[6] China considered the Palestinian organizations and especially the PLO and al-Fatah — and not the Arab governments — to be the principal targets of its aid in the Middle East. This Chinese position was derived from: (1) the desire to find an alternative to the bourgeois and pro-Soviet Arab states; (2) the necessity of finding a suitable ideological outlet for its foreign policy; and (3) the certainty that the Palestinian guerilla organizations represented an independent revolutionary force of great potential.

Viewing the Palestinian organizations as alternatives to the Arab governments in its competition with the USSR for influence in the area, China ostensibly had a clear advantage. Unlike the Soviet Union, it had a "clean record" concerning Israel: China did not agree to the UN resolution creating the State of Israel in 1947; it did not recognize Israel, and in theory even supported Israel's destruction, declaring from 1965 on that it would assist the Palestinian nation in regaining its full rights in Palestine.

Furthermore, China — unlike the Soviet Union — was the first power and non-Arab state to recognize the Palestinian entity, grant it official representation in Peking, and support the Palestinian guerrilla organizations. Thus, during Shukeiry's first visit to Peking in 1965, a communique was published on March 22, declaring: "The Chinese Nation will assist the Arab-Palestinian Nation in its just struggle against Israel, and will help it return to its homeland and regain its full rights in Palestine. The Chinese Nation will continue to give the Arab nation of Palestine . . . political and other aid. . . ."[7]

While the Soviet Union ignored the Palestinian guerrilla organizations almost until 1969, China gave them diplomatic and political support, as well as technical and military aid from 1965 on.[8] It exploited this situation to the detriment of the Soviet Union.[9] China maintained that its support was based on ideological principles, that the Palestinian organizations were part of the Afro-Asian, Latin American antiimperialist and anticolonialist liberation movement, which, according to Lin Piao, comprised the world's "rural" areas and which were fighting the world's "urban" areas — the United States, Europe, and Israel.[10] Paradoxically, for years China supported almost exclusively the non-Marxist, nationalist PLO and al-Fatah; it gave little aid to the Marxist-Leninist oriented Palestinian guerrilla organizations like the Popular Front for the Liberation of Palestine (PFLP), headed by George Habash, and the Popular Democratic Front (PDF), under the leadership of Na'if Hawatma. The Chinese had reservations about the PFLP and the PDF, claiming that their approach was Trotskyite deviationism. They severely criticized the airplane hijackings by the PFLP in the summer of 1970, terming them "impulsive acts" detrimental to a war of national liberation.[11]

China has reservations regarding these movements because of

their limited popular base, their marginal positions, and their tendency to fragment the Palestinian liberation movement. In contrast, the principal Chinese motive for supporting al-Fatah is the fact that this organization is the biggest, strongest, and most popular among the Palestinians, especially after the Karameh Operation (1968) and its taking over control of the PLO and the Palestinian movement in 1969. From the beginning of its activity in 1965, al-Fatah strove to work independently of, and to preempt the handling of the Palestinian struggle from, the Arab countries.[12] Its independent position and numerical strength coincided with the policy objectives of China in the Middle East. China claims that the al-Fatah represents the first stage of revolution — the national-democratic stage — after which will naturally follow the Marxist-Socialist stage. Accordingly, it has extended substantial aid to al-Fatah.

Chinese Aid

Chinese support was of two kinds: (1) military arms and guerrilla training; (2) political and propaganda support. Of the two, the latter was the more prevalent. The Chinese granted diplomatic recognition to the PLO before the USSR. The establishment of PLO representation in Peking was agreed to during a visit, headed by Shukeiry, of Palestinian students and PLO officials.[13]

Since 1964 China has granted diplomatic status to representatives of the PLO and al-Fatah and has regularly invited delegations of these organizations to celebrate official Chinese events, or simply to come on "friendly" visits.[14] Senior Chinese officials issued messages of support for the Palestinian struggle, and the Chinese press published numerous articles praising the Palestinian resistance and attacking Israel and imperialism.[15]

Chinese aid was given in the form of military equipment and medicine. Palestinians underwent training in China, primarily in the Nanking Military Academy, in six-month courses devoted to military tactics and guerrilla warfare.[16] The arms were primarily light weapons;[17] and perhaps even a small number of instructors were provided.[18] However, the Chinese did not supply heavy weapons such as tanks, [19] in part because of the difficulties raised by Syria and Iraq, through whose territory the weapons would have had to be transported. The Chinese explained this away on ideological grounds, saying that the guerrillas must depend on fighting men rather than on heavy weapons.[20]

The Palestinian guerrilla organizations depended therefore primarily on Soviet weapons, which were supplied by Arab governments or with their cooperation. This dependence on the USSR weakened China's capacity to influence the Palestinian organizations and its possibility of countering Soviet expansion in the area.

Soviet-Palestinian Ties

Long before he approached China, Shukeiry sought Soviet support.
In his autobiography, Shukeiry writes that from 1948 on he tried, as
Syria's UN representative, to improve relations with the Soviet delegation: he supported the USSR against the United States on every occasion
in order to obtain Soviet assistance for the Palestinian cause. He preferred the USSR's support to the recognition and aid that China offered
him in 1955 because the USSR was stronger and wealthier, and because
it was a member of the United Nations and was in a position to stymie
Western policies. Fifteen years later, however, when Shukeiry tried to
collect the debt he felt the Soviets owed him, he was disappointed.
From 1963 to 1965, he courted the Soviet embassies in the Arab countries, met with Kosygin, Khrushchev, Gromyko and Malik, requesting
military assistance, aid for the refugees, recognition of the PLO, and
permission to open an office in Moscow:

> For two long years (1963-1965) I knocked on the gates of
> Moscow as though I were Henry IV, standing seven hundred
> years ago before the gates of Canossa, doing penance
> before the Pope. I did not seek penance for I did not sin,
> but rather a large deposit that I made in the Soviet Union
> over a period of fifteen years; I came to request the settle-
> ment of this debt — even a fraction of it. . . . But the
> Soviet Union did not agree to the liberation of Palestine
> and did not want to recognize the Liberation Organization.[21]

Frustrated and angered, Shukeiry turned to China. However, both
Shukeiry and the Palestinian organizations continued to look to the
Soviet Union for weapons. They occasionally noted the USSR's positive
role in the UN and the Security Council in resisting American and
British attacks, and termed it "the principal support of the Arab masses."
The Soviet government continued its policy of supporting only the
legal governments of the Arab states, and for years did not respond to
the "courting" of the Palestinians. From 1965 to 1968, Soviet relations
with the PLO, al-Fatah, and the other Palestinian organizations ranged
from neglect to hostility. The organizations were disregarded by the
USSR, which was convinced that they lacked political significance and
could in no way serve Soviet interests in the Middle East.[23] The USSR
based its presence and position in the area on the legally constituted
Arab governments; it had no reason to support Palestinian movements
that were still in their infancy, notwithstanding the fact that some of
them professed Marxist-Leninist principles.
After the June 1967 war, the Soviet lack of interest in the
Palestinian guerrilla organizations was replaced for a short period by a
more pronounced negative attitude. Moscow feared that the Palestinians
would undermine the Arab countries and generate a new war with Israel.

This could have endangered Moscow's position, temporarily weakened by the Six Day War, and ended its efforts to reach a political solution aimed at preserving its status in the area. Perhaps the Soviet Union also feared that internal upheavals in Arab capitals would be conducive to the encroachment by its growing enemy — China.

The Soviet press at the time sharply condemned "adventurist" and "ultra-revolutionary" Palestinian guerrilla organizations for pressing for another round with Israel, without regard for the consequences; and it called them "backward elements of an Arab national movement that are nourished by the Chinese for their own purposes."[24]

The Soviets and the Palestinians since 1968

The increased political importance since 1968 of the Palestinian guerrilla organizations— especially al-Fatah — both in the Arab world and internationally — impelled a change in Soviet policy. Moscow acted to come to terms with a new weighty force in Middle East politics. It now considered the Palestinian movement an active, significant factor, with a broad popular base among the Arabs. Improvement in relations with the Palestinians was not a substitute for continued support of the radical Arab states, though relations with the latter had cooled somewhat. Furthermore, from the Soviet point of view, in the event of an Arab-Israeli settlement, the Palestinian guerrilla organization was apt to become an important factor. The importance of the Palestinians was enhanced because of the possibilities that they might topple the regime in Jordan, or that a Palestinian state might be established in the West Bank and Gaza. The Soviet Union was also concerned over China's growing involvement with the Palestinian guerrillas; it feared that they would become satellites of the Chinese and give them a weapon to use in the Sino–Soviet struggle for leadership of the national-liberation movements in Asia and Africa.

Soviet relations improved primarily with al-Fatah and the PLO. There was virtually no improvement in relations with the marginal extremist groups responsible for the plane hijackings and other terrorist excesses. However, the strengthening of ties with the PLO was neither executed at once nor on an official Soviet governmental level, but rather by means of public bodies serving the USSR. Moscow was chary of tying itself to the Palestinian guerrilla organizations, whose political futures seemed uncertain. Official support for them was also apt to complicate relations between the Soviet Union and the pro-Western Arab nations (for example, Jordan and Lebanon), or result in American intervention.[25]

Beginning in the summer of 1968 and increasingly during 1969, the Soviet press gave extensive coverage to the activity of the Palestinian organizations in background articles and translations from Arab newspapers. The existence of the Arab people of Palestine was noted and the Palestinian guerrillas were described as partisans.[26]

Similar descriptions have appeared in recent years, lauding "the Palestinian resistance movement" and describing operations against the conquerors and ruling circles in Israel as "desirable and legitimate revolutionary" operations.[27] The Soviet Union also improved relations with the Palestinians through Soviet public organizations and movements, such as women's, workers', and students' organizations, the World Peace Council, and the Afro-Asian Solidarity Committee. Thus, for example, a delegation of Palestinian women arrived in the Soviet Union in March 1973 at the invitation of the Soviet Women's Association,[28] and Yasser Arafat and his delegation were warmly received at the World University Games in Moscow in August 1973. The Afro-Asian Solidarity Committee invited Yasser Arafat and other Palestinian representatives to visit the Soviet Union several times and meet with the representatives of public organizations, Communist party leaders, authors, and journalists.[29]

In 1970, the USSR instructed Arab Communist parties to improve relations with the Palestinian guerrilla organizations and bring them closer to the Soviet Union. Accordingly, these parties declared their full support for the Palestinian liberation movement, though some of them expressed a more extreme line than the Soviet Union regarding the Palestinian question, and matched the Palestinian guerrilla organizations themselves in calling for the destruction of Israel. The Iraqi Communist Party, for one, declared that fedayeen activity is the realization of the Arab Palestinian nation's struggle and aspiration to liberate the homeland and reclaim its stolen rights, including self-determination in that homeland. It called on Arab peoples "to support and assist this movement (fedayeen) with neither conditions nor reservations and with all material, technical and military means, and to enable Arab youth to join the fedayeen organizations. . . ."[30] The Jordanian Communist Party publicly announced the establishment of a new, armed organization called "Quwat-al-Ansar." Among the declared objectives of the organization is an anti-Zionist and anti-imperialist campaign and the liberation of Palestine.[31]

In at least one instance, such extreme positions were criticized by the Soviet and Bulgarian Communist Parties in deliberations held in Moscow on the Syrian Communist Party's platform. Among other things, they denounced the call for Israel's destruction, holding that Israel is an existing fact, while at the same time emphasizing that "the struggle of the Arab Palestinian Nation is just and involves an integral part of the Arab and world national liberation movement."[32] In early December 1969, a Soviet bloc declaration held: ". . . there must be a just solution to the problem of insuring the legal rights and interests of the Arab people of Palestine, who are waging a courageous national liberation and antiimperialist struggle."[33] Similar declarations were made by high-ranking Soviet leaders. Alexander Shelepin, a member of the Soviet Communist Party's Politburo and Chairman of the Trade Unions, proclaimed at a World Assembly of the Communist Trade Unions in

Budapest in October 1969: "We consider the struggle of Palestinian patriots for the liquidation of the consequences of Israeli aggression as a just antiimperialist struggle and we support it. "[34] In February, Tass, the official Soviet news agency, reported an official message from the Soviet Union's UN delegation that described the activity of the Palestinian guerrilla movements as a ". . . struggle of peoples against invaders and occupiers that is just from the viewpoint of international law. "[35]

Soviet Premier Kosygin expressed similar opinions in November 1969;[36] and in October 1970, Soviet party boss Brezhnev described Palestinian guerrillas in Jordan as "troops of the Palestinian resistance movement. "[37]

Soviet support for the Palestinian guerrilla movements, semiofficial since late 1969, gained momentum after the expulsion of Soviet military personnel from Egypt in July 1972 and became fully official and explicit after the October 1973 war. A statement issued in Moscow following the Brezhnev-Tito talks in mid-November 1973, called for the realization of the legitimate rights of the Palestinian Arab nation.[38] Yet the Soviet Union held off granting permission to the PLO to open an office in Moscow. However, one was opened in East Germany.

Increased Soviet approval brought more military aid. By the end of 1968, Moscow had agreed to supply the Palestinian organizations with weapons and other equipment, though indirectly via the East European countries. The conduit was Bulgaria, Czechoslovakia, and East Germany (news of a large weapons deal between Arafat and East Germany was publicized).[39] By the end of 1971, Moscow dropped all pretense and offered military assistance directly.[40] It also offered to train al-Fatah members and to hospitalize the wounded in the USSR.[41] Al-Fatah received its first direct Soviet arms shipment, consisting primarily of light weapons, through Syria in September 1972. Among the weapons apparently supplied to the guerrillas, were also the SAM-7 antiaircraft missiles, which were found at the disposal of Black September members in Rome in the summer of 1973. Other shipments contained medical material and other equipment.[42] There were also reports of Soviet and East European intelligence aid,[43] such as the assistance extended by the Czechs to the guerrillas who overpowered a train in September 1973 carrying Russian Jews from Czechoslovakia to Austria. The Soviets interceded in Jordan for the commutation of Abu Daud and other al-Fatah members condemned to death.[44]

Sino-Soviet Competition

From an examination of the Sino-Soviet rivalry among the Palestinian guerrilla organizations it becomes apparent that the Soviet Union has not gone out of its way to compete with China by adopting extremist positions on the Palestinian question, such as calls for the destruction of Israel. The USSR has pointed out to the Palestinians that there is no contradiction between a political solution, which it

119

backs, and their national aspirations. It argues that these aspirations are likely to be realized in two stages — the first, after a return, for example, to the borders of 1967, and the second, after a return, for example, to the 1947 borders which the Soviet Union would demand after the termination of the first stage.[45]

The Soviet press tried to create the impression that the objective of the Palestinian guerrilla organizations was the implementation of the Security Council's Resolution 242, and it tended to disregard or cover up their desire to destroy Israel.[46] At the same time, however, the Soviet Union has not changed its basic policy concerning the need for a political solution, which is anathema to the Palestinian guerrilla organizations and to Communist China. While some Soviet groups expressed "understanding" of the motivation of various terrorist operations in Europe, such as Munich,[47] the Government officially condemned their methods, especially the hijacking of planes.[48] For example, Pravda's correspondent in Cairo, told an Egyptian journalist: "We, as a government and people support the struggle of the Palestinian people to free the occupied territories. There are, however, various aspects which we cannot support, e.g., we are against attacking civilian airplanes or other civilian objects . . . [because] adventurism might be a threat to Arab revolutionary progressive regimes."[49] Soviet representatives blamed China for instigating the Palestinians' adventurism. The Chinese "in every possible way encourage their extremist tendencies, push the Palestinians to lead a 'popular war' against Israel . . . lead a campaign against a political settlement of the Mideast crisis and try to introduce a split in the antiimperialist front of the Arab states . . ."[50] and also ". . . a split between the Arab states and the various Palestinian liberation organizations."[51] The Soviets did not limit their struggle against Chinese influence on the Palestinian guerrilla movements to mere words. According to one Arab source, they pressured the government of Iraq, in one instance, to prevent the unloading of Chinese arms to al-Fatah in the port of Basra.[52]

China's arms shipments to the guerrillas include sophisticated weapons and volunteers.[53] The Chinese criticized the Soviet Union for its acceptance of Security Council Resolution 242, which, according to the Chinese, guarded Soviet (and American) imperialistic interests and would eliminate the armed Palestinian struggle.[54] The Chinese accused the USSR and the United States of seeking to divide the Middle East into their own spheres of influence.[55] However, the Sino-Soviet rivalry that flared up dangerously in March 1969, abated somewhat in the early 1970s. China's military aid and political support for the movements continued, as did warm receptions for visiting Palestinian delegations in Peking. Chinese attacks against Israel and imperialism also continued unabated.[56] However, in 1971-1972, there were some signs that Peking was toying with the necessity of recognizing the existence of Israel as a fact, despite the "error" committed by its establishment. For example, it differentiated between the Israeli government, which is a tool of "aggression" and "imperialism, " and the Israeli people, who are friendly toward China. There have been reports of unofficial contacts between Chinese diplomats and Israelis and of commercial ties between the two countries.[57] According to one Palestinian source, a change in China's policy regarding the Palestinian problem took place as a result of the expulsion of the guerrillas from Jordan in 1970, Nixon's visit to China in 1972, and the seating of the CPR in the UN. The source noted a speech by the Chinese delegate in the UN in which he aligned his country with "the policy of President Sadat and his efforts toward a just peace. "[58]

The cooling off in relations between China and the Palestinian guerrilla organizations could be seen in the lesser importance of the Chinese hosting Palestinian delegations, in the composition of those invited, in the reduction in the number of Palestinian events in China, and in the decreased coverage by the Chinese press of such events. The Chinese also criticized the activities of some of the more extreme organizations (for example, Black September), the continuing and growing factionalization among the Palestinian organizations and their lack of revolutionary consciousness. Most probably as a result of this, the Chinese diminished their aid to the Marxist-Palestinian organizations, such as the Popular Front and the Democratic Front.[59]

This shift is the result of many factors — partly related to the politics of the area and partly to China's global policy. First, the termination of China's Cultural Revolution in 1969-1970 ushered in a more moderate foreign policy. This found expression both in the renewal and expansion of relations with official governments and a more restrained or selective approach to the liberation movements themselves. Thus, relations were renewed with Egypt and other countries and open support was avoided for underground organizations whose activity was opposed by countries with whom China sought closer ties, for example, Turkey, Iran, and Ethiopia. If no conflict existed between China's courtship of the radical Arab countries and the Palestinian movements, China cultivated relations with both. However, the priority was given to improving relations with all Arab governments, thereby opening the way for a weakening of ties with the movements. Ironically, this is a copy of early Soviet policy.

Despite a shift in policy, China has not become a real competitor of the Soviet Union in the Arab world. Geographically, the Middle East is strategically low on its list of foreign policy priorities. There is also China's inability to match the quantity and quality of aid that the USSR gives the radical Arab states, which regard the Soviet Union as their principal source of military, political, and economic support.[60]

As long as China was alone in aiding the guerrillas, it had a good chance to make inroads in the movement. But as soon as the USSR decided to support and strengthen them, the Chinese lost their initial advantage. It is likely that the Chinese have been disappointed by the readiness of the Palestinian organizations to deal with the USSR,

especially since it has yet to recognize them officially and support all
their professed goals.

The Dimensions of Chinese Influence

There is no doubt that the Palestinians value highly China's
military aid and its moral and political support: China was the first
power to recognize and aid them, and it is still the only one to identify
completely with Palestinian goals.[61] Palestinian leaders have often
expressed their appreciation: "The Palestinian people realize that the
Chinese are their most sincere friends."[62] Such declarations are often
couched in revolutionary jargon.[63] They laud China's ideological leadership and the thought of Mao Tse-tung: "There shines brilliantly the
great truth put forth by the great leader, Chairman Mao; 'political power
grows out of the barrel of a gun'; or 'Mao's thought is a spiritual atom
bomb of unparalleled might.'"[64] In different reports (mostly Chinese)
it was claimed that selections from Mao's works were found in Palestinian guerrilla camps and that Mao's articles on military affairs were
published in al-Fatah's newspapers and were studied by the soldiers in
discussion groups. One al-Fatah leader said: "We have been following
Chairman Mao Tse-tung's teaching on guerrilla warfare since the
beginning of our revolution in 1965. The fundamental principle we have
adopted is the sixteen-character formula put forward by Chairman Mao:
'the enemy advances, we retreat; the enemy camps, we harass; the
enemy tires, we attack; the enemy retreats, we pursue.'"[65]

Palestinian expressions of respect and appreciation for China's
friendship and aid include support for the Chinese in various realms.
Internationally, the Palestinians uphold China's struggle against the
United States and its desire to regain Taiwan.[66] Chinese nuclear power
and China's acceptance as a member of the United Nations in 1971 were
described as great victories for the peoples of the world and as a defeat
for the United States.[67] As early as 1966 the Third Palestinian National
Council had called on all Arab governments to recognize the CPR out of
respect for its stand on the Palestinian question;[68] and in 1970, al-
Fatah had pressed Jordan to recognize China and establish diplomatic
relations with it.[69]

The Chinese use Palestinian expressions of friendship to enhance
their prestige in the Third World. This support, however, was of little
practical use in the Arab world. It did not bring about an improvement
in China's relations with the conservative Arab states, which remain
suspicious of all revolutionaries and which have no desire for a Chinese
presence. Nor are the radical Arab states sanguine over the prospect
of Chinese influence among the Palestinian guerrilla organizations,
fearing that this could diminish the dependence of the Palestinians on
them.[70]

We need operational criteria by which to assess the extent of
Chinese influence. Two may be suggested: first, the extent to which

the Palestinian guerrilla organizations adapted their behavior in the realm of guerrilla warfare (as well as in the social and economic realms) to Maoist formulations and actions; second, the extent to which they accepted China's line on issues of importance to them, that is, their relations with the Soviet Union, their relations with each other, or their methods of operation.

With respect to the impact of Maoist doctrine on the military tactics of the Palestinian organizations, there is no doubt that Mao's writings have not only been translated into Arabic, but that they have also been carefully studied, in particular by al-Fatah.[71] However, Mao's works are only one — and not even the most important — source of military doctrine. Al-Fatah attempts to learn from the experience of the Yugoslav partisans, the French and the Soviets in World War II, the Algerians against France, the Egyptians against Britain in the early 1950s, and the North Vietnamese in the 1960s. But when all is said and done, that which most influences and fits al-Fatah's goals is the Cuban revolution, which contradicts Mao's theory that guerrilla warfare can only succeed in a big country like China, and not in a small one like Belgium.[72] Even the Marxist PFLP is more influenced by the Vietnamese and Cuban experiences than by the Chinese, and like al-Fatah and the PLO, it does not agree with the Chinese that one must await the ripening of revolutionary circumstances and establish a Communist party before embarking on the path of armed struggle.[73]

The guerrillas have remained open to the Soviets, even during the period when Moscow ignored them and their only aid came from China.[74]

The Palestinians Between Moscow and Peking

In 1967, a debate took place in the PLO between the Chairman, Shukeiry, who wanted to rely on the Chinese, and the head of the PLO Beirut office, Shafiq al-Hut, who favored improving relations with the Soviet Union. Hut claimed that while Peking unreservedly but theoretically supports the right of the Arabs to take back Palestine, it is Moscow that has the capability for turning support into politically significant action.[75] Arafat, Shukeiry's successor, continued his predecessor's policy toward the two Communist powers, particularly after the Soviet Union began to improve relations with the PLO. He made trips to Moscow and Peking with the aim of obtaining aid from each, but he failed (perhaps he did not try) to exploit their rivalry, judging by the minimal weaponry he received from Moscow.[76] At the end of one of these trips, Arafat announced: "Our relations with the Soviet Union are good. We have found joint areas of mutual understanding with them, [though] . . . China backs the guerrillas unconditionally and to the very end."[77]

No wonder, then, that the Palestinian organizations were more sympathetic toward the Chinese. One Fatah leader, Abu Iyad, hinted

123

at a certain reserve toward the USSR because it viewed with favor peace talks by Egypt and Jordan with Israel: "The only power which holds the commando point of view is China. . . . Our only real friend now is Communist China. "[78]

Arafat criticized the USSR because "it is for a peaceful solution and we reject such a solution. " On his return from talks in Moscow in October 1971, he announced that "Moscow snow is warmer now than it used to be. "[79] Similarly, in a conference held under the auspices of Al-Ahram which dealt with the national liberation movements and the socialist states, representatives of the Palestinian organizations publicly complained that the Palestinian issue does not receive the type of backing from the Soviet Union that other issues, in whose fate the Soviet Union is interested, like Vietnam, receive.[80]

An important Palestinian publication complained of the detached approach of Soviet leaders toward the Arab-Israeli dispute during important events like the Twenty-fourth Congress of the CPSU in March 1971; and during the visit of USSR President Nikolai Podgorny to Egypt in the summer of 1971. Although in both instances the Soviet leaders condemned Israel and affirmed the rights and legitimacy of the Palestinian people, they did not, said the Palestinian commentator, mention the Palestinian struggle.[81] In talks with Soviet editors, senior Palestinian representatives implied that the Soviet policy of permitting Jews to emigrate and of flirting with a renewal of diplomatic relations with Israel were apt to intensify Arab reactions and pressure nationalist organizations into adopting a more pro-American stance. They pointed out that the Palestinian resistance organizations are convinced that the Arab radical states, which are of the utmost importance to the Palestinians, must develop friendly relations with the Soviet Union. In this way their strength will be increased.[82]

Despite their confident posture, the Palestinian organizations generally took a defensive attitude when confronted with recurring Soviet requests to halt terrorist activities against international civilian targets, to end their factional quarrels, and to unify the Palestinian organizations for operations in the conquered territories and among the refugees in Jordan.[83] On these issues, al-Fatah and the PLO could not depend on Chinese backing. China, too, criticized the Palestinians for "recourse to spectacular but unwise and inopportune acts such as hijacking . . . the failure to keep Israel in the front as the main enemy . . . and divisions and rivalry within the Palestinian movement. "[84]

Neither the Chinese nor the Soviets limited themselves to mere criticism of Palestinian factionalism. They pressured the different organizations to unify.[85] The Chinese, who initially disregarded the Popular Front for the Liberation of Palestine, the Popular Democratic Front for the Liberation of Palestine, and the Arab Liberation Front (organized by Iraq) have since 1969 established relations with them (perhaps because of al-Fatah's changing relations with the Soviet Union) and, according to different reports, supplied them with weapons and military training.[86] The Soviet Union, following in China's footsteps, has apparently established relations with at least the Popular Front, which, unlike al-Fatah, demonstrated an almost complete identity of outlook with the Communist powers.[87]

Observations

The PLO and al-Fatah have maintained their independence in dealing with the Soviet Union and China. Though responsive to requests that are compatible with their own goals, for example, those urging unity among the guerrilla organizations, they have been unwilling to accept orders from either Communist power. The fundamental approach of the PLO and al-Fatah to them has been pragmatic, not ideological. To the extent that there now exists a process of leftist radicalization within the Palestinian guerrilla movement, it stems largely from internal developments and not from Soviet or Chinese influence. The movement does occasionally adopt Marxist-Leninist slogans, and even follows some radical-left political lines, partly out of appreciation for Communist assistance and partly out of conviction. For example, at the Tenth National Convention in April 1972, the Palestinians declared their intention of participating in the struggle against imperialism, that is, the United States. But it would be an exaggeration to attribute such a stand primarily to the influence of the Soviet Union or China.

In April 1972, the Palestinian guerrilla organizations united under a general organization called the "United National Front, " in whose structure each group could retain its organizational independence and ideology. This was actually a "federative union" of organizations. Al-Fatah's dominance was by and large maintained, and Arafat's position as leader was hardly affected. The leaders of the PLO and al-Fatah took this step on the assumption that it would enhance their image and influence both inside and outside the Arab world, and not because of Soviet and Chinese urging.

The Palestinian guerrilla movement has not fully acceded to Soviet and Chinese requests to cease terrorist activities against international civilian targets. Nominally, it has divorced itself from some operations, such as the slaying of Israeli athletes at the Olympics in Munich and the killing of American diplomats in Khartoum. But in private conversations with Soviet newspapermen, Palestinian leaders pointed out the enormous value of such operations: they struck a blow against Arab circles who pushed for severing ties with the socialist camp; spurred Egypt into improving relations with the USSR (after Sadat had expelled Soviet military personnel in July 1972); forced the United States and Israel to recognize the political existence of the Palestinian entity; and raised the morale of the Palestinians in the Arab countries.

The Palestinian movement has demonstrated its independence from the Soviet Union and China by insisting on maintaining relations with each over the opposition of the other. It is by no means a Marxist revolutionary movement, controlled or led either by Moscow or Peking. It does not follow Soviet or Chinese policies in its struggle against Israel, nor has it fulfilled their expectations for carrying on a popular war in the conquered territories. Neither can it be said that the movement has contributed to a more pro-Soviet orientation by the radical Arab states. Certainly, it has done nothing to create a pro-Chinese orientation in any of the countries in which it has been active.

There are important factors that prevent the Palestinian movement from advancing Soviet and/or Chinese interests in the Middle East. Its world outlook is primarily Arab nationalist and Islamic, and almost completely devoid of any Marxist-Leninist component; its purpose is the liberation of Palestine and not the promotion of Communist strategic interests in the region. In the radical Arab states, where the organizations function in relative freedom, they are to a great extent dependent upon the good will of the existing regimes, which, for their own interests seek to limit the spread of Soviet and Chinese influence.

One can differentiate between China and the Soviet Union regarding the extent of its influence on the Palestinian guerrilla movement. China has gone further than the Soviet Union in its open diplomatic and political support, but its material aid has been limited and it has not been able to establish a major presence in the Arab world. It enjoys a considerable verbal esteem, but little actual influence. By contrast, the Soviet Union has been more restrained in the diplomatic sphere and has consequently been received with reserve by the Palestinian groups. However, as the principal military and economic supporter of key Arab countries and as the main source of weaponry for the Palestinians, the Soviet Union has greater potential influence over the movement — and that may increase, since the Soviet Union is a regional power and thus better able to intrude itself at critical moments.

The October 1973 war strengthened relations between the USSR and the Palestinian movement. The war enabled the Soviet Union to demonstrate not only its credibility as an ally against Israel, but also its strong support for the Palestinians. For the first time, the Soviet Union came out openly for the establishment of a Palestinian state on the West Bank and the Gaza strip. Conceivably, this could become a base of future Soviet influence in the Middle East. At a minimum, it can be used to undermine any Egyptian-Israeli and Jordanian-Israeli settlements reached under the auspices of the United States.

The Palestinians' attitude toward the establishment of a state of their own will, however, be determined by their own aims and internal political compromises, and not by Soviet or Chinese pressures. Yet they are likely, in the future, to rely heavily on either or both of the Communist powers for military, political, and economic support.

Notes

1. For a thorough analysis of China's Arab policy, see Y. Shichor, "The Middle East in the Foreign Policy of China" (in Hebrew), unpublished M. A. Thesis, The Hebrew University, Jerusalem, 1972. I have relied extensively on this thesis in the preparation of my paper.

2. Ibid., pp. 35 ff.

3. Ahmad Shuqayri, min al-qimma ila al-hazima (From Summit to Defeat) (Beirut, 1971), p. 218.

4. Information Bulletin, Embassy of the People's Republic of China in Cairo (December 24, 1964), as quoted in J. K. Cooley, "China and the Palestinians," Journal of Palestinian Studies, vol. 1, no. 2 (Winter 1972), p. 24.

5. D. Kimche, "The Afro-Asian Movement: Ideology and Foreign Policy in Afro-Asia," unpublished Ph. D. Thesis, The Hebrew University, Jerusalem, 1969, pp. 257-60.

6. C. Nauhauser, Third World Politics: China and the Afro-Asian People's Solidarity Organization (Cambridge, Mass.: Harvard East Asian Monographs, 1968), p. 61.

7. Shuqayri, op. cit., pp. 251-54.

8. For example, The New York Times, May 13, 1969; al-Hawadith (Beirut), November 5, 1971; Cooley, op. cit., p. 26.

9. Hsinhua News Agency (China) [henceforth referred to as HNA], January 26, 1969, and December 21, 1971.

10. Al-Nahar (Beirut), November 21, 1971.

11. Ibid.

12. There are reports that China started to support al-Fatah in 1964. See Cooley, op. cit., pp. 24, 26.

13. Shuqayri, op. cit., p. 254.

14. HNA, April 29, 1969; Al-Hurriyya (Beirut), June 14, 1971; Egyptian Gazette (Cairo), January 31, 1973; New China News Agency [henceforth referred to as NCNA], March 1, 1973.

15. HNA, July 9 and 24, 1971; Egyptian Gazette, July 6, 1971; Al-Ahad (Beirut), April 25, 1971; Radio Peking, May 12, 1971.

16. Al-Hawadith, November 5, 1971; Shuqayri, op. cit., p. 279.

17. HNA, September 26, 1970. Some sources claim that the arms were delivered free of charge: Daily Telegraph, August 26, 1970; Radio Free Europe (RFE) report, September 1, 1970. Other sources say the organizations paid for the deliveries: Cooley, op. cit., pp. 26-28; Talal Salman, m'a fath wa'l-fid'yin (With Fatah and the Guerrillas) (Beirut, 1969), p. 19.

18. Egyptian Gazette, November 25, 1971; Ha'aretz (Tel-Aviv), February 22, 1973, claims that Chinese volunteers were found in the Palestinian army camps in North Lebanon during the Israeli raid there.

19. Some sources claim that 200 Chinese tanks were sent via Algeria and were held by the Syrian authorities: The Times, July 7, 1971; Daily Telegraph, July 5, 1971.

127

20. RFE report, September 1, 1970.

21. Shuqayri, op. cit., pp. 214-18.

22. Ibid., p. 270.

23. Shichor, op. cit., pp. 57, 79.

24. Compare Oded Eran, "The Soviet Union and the Palestine Guerrilla Organizations, " The Shiloah Center, Tel-Aviv University, 1971, p. 3.

25. Ibid., p. 5; also see references quoted by Cooley, op. cit., p. 28.

26. Radio Moscow, March 11, 1973, as cited in USSR and the Third World, vol. 3, no. 3 (1973), p. 182. Also The New York Times, June 7, 1969.

27. Eran, op. cit., p. 8.

28. Pravda, August 29, 1972; Al-Hadaf (Beirut), December 16, 1972, reported on a meeting in Moscow between Soviet journalists and a delegation of the Palestinian resistance movement.

29. TASS, March 14, 1973, as cited in USSR and the Third World, op. cit., p. 182.

30. See Soviet News, February 24, 1970; International Herald Tribune, October 2, 1971; Al-Anwar (Beirut), November 4, 1971.

31. Al-Akhbar (Beirut), March 1, 1970.

32. Al-Nida (Beirut), March 7, 1972.

33. Al-Ra'ya (Beirut), June 26, 1972.

34. Soviet News, December 2, 1969.

35. TASS Press release, February 28, 1969.

36. Daily Telegraph, December 11, 1969, reported that Kosygin had affirmed Soviet support for the just struggle of the Palestinians against Israel.

37. Pravda, October 3, 1970, quoted in L. Romaniecki, The Arab Terrorists in the Middle East and the Soviet Union (Jerusalem: The Soviet and East European Research Center, The Hebrew University, 1973), p. 3. According to Dr. Romaniecki, in late 1969, the USSR, in line with its new attitude toward the Palestinians, espoused in UN discussions the right to armed struggle by "peoples who are under colonial domination. "

38. See text of a discussion between editors of Soviet newspapers and a delegation of Palestinians, in al-Hadaf, December 23, 1973.

39. Ha'aretz, August 21, 1973.

40. Egyptian Gazette, November 11, 1971; International Herald Tribune, November 4, 1971, quoting Fath journal.

41. The New York Times, December 30, 1971; Ha'aretz, August 21, 1973. Compare, Kul Shay (Beirut), March 4, 1972.

42. The New York Times, September 18, 1972; Daily Telegraph, September 28, 1972; Ha'aretz, April 4, 1973.

43. International Herald Tribune, August 30, 1972; Egyptian Gazette, April 21, 1973; Ha'aretz, March 15, 1973; Kul Shay, March 4, 1972.

44. TASS, March 11, 1973; Ha'aretz, March 15, 1973.

45. Eran, op. cit., pp. 9-10.

46. Ibid., pp. 8-9.

47. al-Hadaf, December 10, 1972.

48. Pravda, September 29, 1970, quoted in Eran, op. cit., p. 9.

49. Al-Jumhuriyya (Cairo), July 10, 1969, quoted in A. Y. Yodfat, "Moscow Reconsiders Fatah," The New Middle East, no. 15 (December 1969), p. 17.

50. V. Rumyantsev, Za Rubezhom, no. 26 (June 1969), quoted in ibid., p. 16. Compare The Observer, May 18, 1969; The New York Times, May 13, 1969.

51. Novosti News Agency, September 2, 1969.

52. Yodfat, op. cit., p. 16.

53. Daily Telegraph, May 26, 1969; August 19, 1969. The Observer, May 18, 1969, reported that China might have sent missiles to Syria for use by the Syrians and the Palestinian guerrillas. Compare Egyptian Gazette, November 25, 1971; The Times, July 7, 1971.

54. HNA, January 26, 1969; December 21, 1971; al-Hawadith, November 5, 1971.

55. The New York Times, July 31, 1970; Shuqayri, op. cit., p. 231.

56. Statement of the Government of the People's Republic of China, September 21, 1970; al-Dustur (Jordan), April 9, 1970; al-Hurriyya, June 14, 1971; HNA, March 19; April 1; and August 27, 1972.

57. Shichor, op. cit., p. 93. See article by Francesco Gozzano (who accompanied Pietro Nenni on his tour of China), "China's Stand on the Middle East," New Outlook, vol. 15, no. 1 (1972), p. 41. Compare al-Ahram, February 23, 1973.

58. Shu'un filastiniyya (Palestinian Affairs) (Beirut), no. 4 (September 1971), p. 194; Cooley, op. cit., p. 21.

59. Shu'un filastiniyya, no. 6 (January 1972), pp. 218-19.

60. Shichor, op. cit., pp. 22, 91. The Guardian, May 14, 1971.

61. For example, in 1972, Egypt's trade with the USSR reached 575 million dollars, whereas the trade protocol signed between Egypt and China for 1972 provided for a trade level of only 80.5 million dollars.

62. RFE report, September 1, 1970; Abu-Ayad quoted in The Daily Express, January 5, 1971.

63. HNA, April 4, 1972; see also HNA, May 29 and June 11, 1970.

64. Radio Peking (in Arabic), March 26, 1970; Cf. Munazzamat al-tahrir al-filastiniyya wa-jumhariyyat sin al-shabiyya (The Palestine Liberation Organization and the People's Republic of China), n.d., pp. 3-4.

65. HNA, January 3, 1970; October 1, 1969.

66. HNA, January 3, 1970; May 24, 1971; September 19, 1969.

67. NCNA, January 1, 1970. HNA, June 3, 1970. Compare Asad

Zaghlul Fuad, al-fidaiyyun al-filastiniyyun fi maydan al-qital (The Palestinian Guerrillas in the Battlefield) (Damascus, 1968), p. 55.

68. Munazzamat al-tahrir, op. cit., p. 5, quotes a resolution passed by the Palestinian National Council at its Third Convention in Gaza in May 1966.

69. Egyptian Gazette, October 29, 1971.

70. Munazzamat al-tahrir, op. cit.

71. Egyptian Gazette, July 1, 1970.

72. Shuqayri, op. cit., pp. 270-71.

73. Asad Zaghlul Fuad, op. cit., p. 54. Cf. Y. Harkabi, Fedayee Action and Arab Strategy (in Hebrew) (Tel-Aviv, 1969), pp. 48 ff.

74. Fuad, ibid., pp. 52-57, 161-62. See also a survey on the development of the Palestinian movement from 1948 to 1967 by Hasan at-Rashad in al-Yawm (Beirut), November 7 and 14, 1967.

75. Harkabi, op. cit., pp. 48-49.

76. Shichor, op. cit., p. 38, quotes Palestinian guerrillas saying, "We read Mao but actually he is irrelevant." Harkabi, op. cit., p. 49.

77. Shichor, op. cit., p. 57.

78. Ibid., p. 79.

79. RFE report, September 1, 1970.

80. UPI from Cairo, April 5, 1970.

81. The Daily Express, January 5, 1971.

82. Shu'un filastiniyya, no. 5 (November 1971), p. 199.

83. Shu'un filastiniyya, no. 3 (July 1971), pp. 159-60; no. 4 (September 1971), pp. 193-94; no. 5 (November 1971), p. 212. See also al-Hadaf, December 23, 1972.

84. Radio Moscow (in Arabic), April 5, 1972; Soviet News, August 8 and September 5, 1972; Le Monde, August 31, 1972.

85. Christian Science Monitor, November 13, 1970; al-Nahar, November 21, 1971.

86. The Observer, May 17, 1969; The Times, August 19, 1970; The New York Times, January 7, 1971.

87. The Guardian, October 27, 1971; Ha'aretz, August 23, 1973.

6

SOVIET AND CHINESE INFLUENCE IN THE PERSIAN GULF

Bettie M. Smolansky
Oles M. Smolansky

Any attempt to analyze the nature of the influence-building process by a great power in a Third World area must be preceded by an examination of the likely aims and interests which generate the quest for influence: only through an understanding of the motives of the influence-seeker is it possible to evaluate his activities. Admittedly, perception of the motives that stimulate a nation's policy is not an easy task; indeed, it is almost as difficult as the measurement of influence itself. Nevertheless, since this argument is based on the assumption that some understanding of motives is necessary as a ground for assessing influence, the effort must be made. In spite of the fact that there is no sure method for comprehending the aims of a nation's policy in the absence of candor on the part of its leaders, one approach does seem feasible. Specifically, an analysis of the military-strategic, political, and economic interests which a nation could reasonably be expected to have in an area (that is, its "objective interests"), coupled with its past actions there and the relevant pronouncements by its ruling elite, should project at least the broad outline of the considerations that motivate its policy.

A case can of course be made that the super powers seek influence for its own sake, and indeed this type of approach to world politics seems to have had powerful adherents in both Washington and Moscow in the first two decades of the Cold War. However, the United States as well as the Soviet Union have had their fingers burned so often and have gained so little in the way of measurable positive results from their efforts in this sphere, that both now seem inclined, if not to

The authors wish to express their gratitude to the Research Institute on Communist Affairs and the Middle East Institute of Columbia University, where the initial research for this paper was undertaken, and to Sir Geoffrey Arthur, Ambassador Abdulla Bishara, John Duke Anthony, and Patrick O'Ferrall, who commented on an earlier draft.

abandon, at least to modulate the intensity of the contest between them. (China's efforts have by necessity been considerably more modest than those of the United States and the USSR; but Peking, too, has had its share of disappointments. The fiasco it suffered in Indonesia in the wake of Sukarno's overthrow is the most obvious example.)

Reason alone would suggest the likelihood that all the major participants must by now be reevaluating (if they had not already done so) their involvement in the contest for influence in the Third World. For instance, the alacrity and relative good grace with which the Soviet policy-makers accepted their 1972 ouster from Egypt suggest that they may finally have come to appreciate that their patron status vis-a-vis Third World clients is not only a two-edged sword but is often one not worth honing.

The ultimate problem for the superpowers is that the tangible benefits which each enjoys from its "victories" in the contest (trade, occasional diplomatic support, access to port facilities, and the like) are won only at what is often considerable hidden cost. Specifically, these benefits accrue as one establishes a client relationship with a developing nation, but this same process leads to a reduced potential for policy flexibility. (After all, one now has a stake in the area; that is, commitments to honor and investments to protect.) Thus, the real question becomes whether or not the benefits which result from increasing one's influence are worth the loss of policy flexibility and thus ultimately the potential threat to national security which such a loss may ultimately entail. For, as most people would admit, no stake in the Third World is worth a superpower confrontation, let alone a nuclear holocaust. Such considerations gain even greater potency when accompanied by the realization that victories can be reversed at the whim of one's frequently unstable clients.

The Importance of the Gulf

Thus, while a detailed analysis of the potential importance of the Persian Gulf* to the Soviet Union and the People's Republic of China lies outside the scope of this paper, a brief look at the region's significance to each of the Communist rivals seems necessary. The factors, which have traditionally been thought to lend to the Middle East generally and the Persian Gulf specifically a unique importance in world politics and have made it an area of major concern to the great powers (and thus an area where the quest for influence appeared a worthwhile pursuit), have been examined in some detail before.[1] That analysis demonstrated that factors such as military-strategic considerations,

---

*The Gulf, as referred to in this paper, includes Iran, Iraq, Saudi Arabia, Kuwait, Bahrayn, Qatar, the United Arab Amirates, and Oman.

transportation and communications, and international trade have lost much of their salience due either to circumvention by technology or shifts in the world's power balance. It is not argued that these factors are now entirely lacking in importance; rather, it is contended that the means by which the superpowers' interests may be most readily secured and maintained have shifted. Both the United States and the Soviet Union must now confront the possibility that establishment and maintenance of a physical presence in an area like the Persian Gulf may not be the safest and the surest road to the exercise of influence. No question more clearly illustrates this point than that of the controversy which surrounds the one factor that gives the region most of its current intrinsic importance — oil.

Some sixty percent of the world's known petroleum reserves lie under the sands and off the shores of the riparian states of the Persian Gulf. The region is the major oil supplier to Western Europe and Japan and is rapidly growing in its importance for the American market, facts which became starkly clear in the aftermath of the October War. This situation has led some commentators to postulate the likelihood of Soviet efforts to become the dominant power in the Gulf in order to control the valve to the primary source of Western fuel. Such scenarists typically ignore the fact that the means to achieve such an objective peacefully are beyond current Soviet capabilities and that efforts in that direction would undoubtedly produce more negative complications than successes.* Certainly any attempt to take over the region by force either directly or through client states would heighten the risk of nuclear war to unacceptable levels.

A more serious controversy among Western scholars has revolved around the question of whether or not the USSR will need to become a major importer of Middle Eastern oil in the foreseeable future. For, while efforts to dominate the region in order to deny its resources to an adversary would probably enjoy a relatively low priority in Soviet thinking, a direct need for Middle Eastern petroleum for Russia's own use would clearly increase that priority substantially.

Until very recently, the evidence for each side of the argument appeared to be equally weighty. (The Russians, typically, have been reticent about their own projections.) Thus, it has been clear for some time that the USSR possesses enormous petroleum deposits in Siberia, and some experts have expressed confidence in Moscow's determination to utilize these resources to help maintain "energy independence" at almost any cost. It has been equally apparent, however, that the

---

*The reasons for this assertion will be examined below. The recently ended Arab embargo demonstrates Moscow's current impotence vis-a-vis control over the oil flow. The Arabs began the embargo without consulting the USSR and ended it at a time when Soviet Arabic language radio broadcasts were urging its continuation.

extraction and particularly the transportation of Siberian oil to the industrial areas of the USSR was likely to be an extremely expensive operation, requiring a capital investment of a magnitude that some experts contended Moscow could not afford given the other essential demands on its budget. More precisely, proponents of the view that the Soviets will need to be net importers by 1980 or soon thereafter have cited the economics of the situation as well as the following considerations in support of their contention: the Russians have begun importing Iranian natural gas, they have concluded an agreement with Iraq to help develop the North Rumaylah oil fields in return for payments in oil, and, most importantly, they have encouraged their East European satellites to begin looking elsewhere for petroleum supplies.

Until recently, the tide in this controversy appeared to be running with proponents of the latter view. Even if they had prevailed, the question of whether the USSR would adopt what John A. Berry described as the "colonial" or the "commercial" pattern in order to secure the oil it would need becomes the next controversy to be settled. (Berry makes a convincing case for the view that a simple commercial arrangement would be the Soviets' likely choice. The other alternative is fraught with incalculable and hence unacceptable risks.)[2] In any case, this question may well become moot if recently begun Soviet negotiations with the Western powers bear fruit. Showing a cunning akin to good old "capitalist ingenuity" the Kremlin is attempting to reach agreements with the Japanese to underwrite the expense of building the eastward pipeline (connecting the Tiumen' fields with the Soviet Far East) and with American oil companies to finance the western link, both in return for petroleum and natural gas. The deliveries, to be stretched out over a 20-year period, would not begin until the pipelines are completed. Thus, while there may be an interim period during which some importation of oil will be necessary (in which case it would almost surely be secured by simple cash or barter deals with Middle Eastern producers), these projected agreements show a long-term commitment by the Russians to development of their own energy resources and preview an era when they will not only not need Middle Eastern oil but may well compete with the major exporters for a share of the world's petroleum markets. This does not mean, however, that all oil or natural gas imports from the Middle East would be discontinued. Barter agreements involving Iranian natural gas in exchange for Soviet heavy machinery and other Soviet economic aid make good sense economically, while the Iraqi oil is situated in relative geographic proximity to major processing and refinery installations in the Baku region, where local petroleum reserves are slowly being depleted.

Negotiations between the Soviets and Americans are currently stalled. While a number of major oil companies have expressed an interest in the deal, none appears willing to rush into it — the results of the famous wheat deal have no doubt had a cautionary impact. Moreover, Western sensitivities on energy matters have been immeasurably heightened by the events of late 1973-early 1974. Indeed, it is ironic that Moscow has once again been negatively affected by the behavior of the Arabs, that, is, the recent actions of the latter have increased Western reluctance to enter into any but the most ironclad forms of agreement on issues where a degree of potential energy dependence on a foreign power is involved. Thus, while a number of U.S. companies still view the possibilities with some interest, Soviet negotiators now have the difficult task of concluding a mutually beneficial agreement with bargainers for the other side who approach their task in a more clear-eyed and hard-nosed fashion than might have been the case earlier.

There is little or no controversy concerning the current Chinese stake in the Persian Gulf. It is minimal and definitely smaller than that of the Soviets. For, compared to the USSR, China does not have the same regional proximity, the kind of extensive trade, transportation, and communications networks to maintain and protect, nor, as yet, the type of developed industrial system which produces a seemingly insatiable thirst for oil. Indeed, Peking's primary interest in the region thus far and for the foreseeable future, given the enormous domestic problems that it must solve before developing the kind of full-scale global interests which characterize the superpowers, appears to be in not letting its rivals, above all Moscow, have life too easy.

The Internal Situation in the Gulf

Yet another task remains before the problem of influence can be approached directly, namely an examination of the internal situation in the Persian Gulf itself. For, no matter what the aims of Soviet or Chinese policy in the area may be, they will be constrained by the limits which local conditions inevitably set. This is especially true in an area where internal and regional rivalries entangle and intertwine, sometimes running parallel, sometimes intersecting, and where they typically operate on multiple levels simultaneously.

Dating back to the nineteenth century and until the end of World War II, much of the area known as the Persian Gulf was a de facto part of the imperial preserve of the British Raj. Great Britain signed its initial treaty with the Imam of Musqat in 1798, followed by a succession of treaties with other local rulers, enforcing respect for its wishes by gold and occasional use of "gunboat diplomacy." As a result, the Gulf became a virtual British "lake." Even after Iran, Iraq, and Saudi Arabia had gained their independence in the pre-World War II period, Musqat and Oman, the Trucial Shaykhdoms, Bahrayn, Qatar, and Kuwait remained "protected states" which had in varying degrees relinquished their external sovereignty to London. This meant that, until 1961, when Kuwait acquired its independence, Great Britain conducted the foreign affairs of these "states," was responsible for their security, and had considerable influence on their domestic policy as well.[*] These special arrangements continued in force with the remaining localities (Bahrayn, Qatar, the Trucial Shaykhdoms, and Musqat and Oman) until the early 1970s, when all four reluctantly set themselves up as independent states in response to the announced British intention to withdraw from areas "east of Suez." This closed another chapter in the annals of British policy in Asia, ending a period of influence unparalleled in the modern history of the Gulf, an area which, technically, had never been a colonial possession of Great Britain. The same withdrawal has created, if not the classic power vacuum to which many analysts allude, at least the necessity for major shifts in the relational system between the states of the area. Certainly the governments of the Gulf states are inclined to regard public references to a vacuum as overdone if not outright insulting. Iran, Iraq, and Saudi Arabia in particular, as the larger and more powerful states of the region, have taken great pains to let the rest of the world know that no vacuum exists and that whatever power shifts are necessary are the problem of the littoral states.

Whether or not these problems can be solved by the Gulf states themselves depends on two basic factors: the viability of their current regimes and the nature of their relations with each other. There are both positive and negative signs concerning these factors. Specifically, some of the more stable regimes clearly have somewhat conflicting views on the shape of the Gulf's future, while the fragility of some of the other regimes calls into question the value of their cooperative spirit. Since the issues involved are complex, a brief examination of the internal situation in each state, followed by a review of the likely sources of intraregional conflict, is necessary at this juncture.

The Shah has been assiduously solidifying his internal position over the past two decades, and few doubt the short-range stability of his regime. Moreover, Iran's considerable oil revenues allow him to maintain an impressive military establishment, far and away the strongest force of any of the Gulf states.[3] While Iran has been generally regarded in the postwar era as an American ally, it has, in recent years, been subtly shifting toward a more pragmatic, neutralist stance. This diplomatic maneuvering in the context of the East-West competition has been accompanied by efforts in the Gulf itself to establish, if not the hegemony which some critics claim, then at least a position as the "first among equals."

As could have been predicted in the light of the long-standing rivalry between the two countries, Iraq has responded negatively to the Shah's initiatives and has begun asserting its own interests in the

---

[*] According to the terms of the Friendship Treaty, concluded shortly before the granting of independence, Great Britain remained responsible for Kuwait's security.

Gulf with increasing vigor. However, Baghdad's ability to press its case is impeded both by its military inferiority vis-a-vis Tehran and by domestic difficulties. While the Ba'th has for many years been entrenched as the ruling party, it has historically been plagued by and will probably continue to be subject to frequent intraparty upheavals. This friction and the changes in government which it produces make it more difficult to cope adequately with the country's internal problems,* but the basic leftist orientation of Iraq and the nominally pro-Soviet tone of its international policies do not appear to be threatened by intra-party disputes. However, the motivations of Iraqi policy in the Gulf are much more strongly influenced by the ruling elite's hostility toward Iran and the feeling of isolation from the other Arab states in the region than by ideological considerations or general foreign policy requirements. Thus, while Baghdad pays lip service to the promotion of internal order in the Gulf,[4] it seems less willing to act with restraint in protecting its own narrow interests than most of the other states of the area. For one thing, Iraq appears to have initiated the March 1973 border incidents with Kuwait. It has encouraged the formation of Ba'thi cells in Bahrayn, Qatar, and Abu Dhabi and has also lent some support to the revolutionary "Popular Front for the Liberation of Oman and the Arab Gulf" (PFLOAG).

The behavior of Saudi Arabia in the early days of the post-British era in the Gulf has been in marked contrast with that of Iraq. Admittedly, King Faysal can afford substantial generosity and forebearance toward his neighbors, given the overwhelming wealth of his realm. As the most conservative of the larger states of the area, a high degree of regional stability is unquestionably worth some sacrifice to the Saudis, and thus they have been busily cementing good relations with most of their neighbors save Iraq and, further south, the People's Democratic Republic of Yemen (PDRY), whose "radical Arabism" is a source of considerable distaste to Faysal. This trend is likely to continue to dominate Saudi policy so long as the current ruling elite remains in power. At this stage, the King appears to be in control of the domestic situation despite the occasional rumors of an impending coup. However, he is no longer young, and his death could result in a succession crisis — considering the relatively tight-fisted economic and social policies of

_____

*These problems are considerable and include the need for improved living standards and for development of the oil industry to finance such improvements. (The June 1972 nationalization of the Iraqi Petroleum Company, while politically popular, produced a period of substantial economic dislocation and resulted in considerable income loss.) Another domestic problem which admits no easy solution is the Kurdish question. The issue appeared settled after a decade of intermittent bloodshed, but strains reappeared in late 1972, leading to the outbreak of hostilities in early 1974.

the ruling family and the vigor with which it has suppressed dissent,
it is not unreasonable to assume that there must be internal dissatisfaction with the current regime.

Kuwait, as the oldest and most stable entity of the group, has, in
recent years, acted as a kind of combination of cheerleader, mediator,
and father confessor to the other new "ministates" of the Gulf. It has
enjoyed the fruits of enormous and wisely administered new wealth, and
its stability and prosperity have come to serve as a model for its neighbors. Moreover, it has the widest circle of friendly relations both in
the Arab East and in the world at large of any of the Gulf states and
has, in recent years, been successfully transforming its status from a
British protected state to that of a neutralist nation.* Internally, one
of the rulers' main problems appears to be the presence of a large non-
native population. The government has begun to show signs of concern
about the situation and is now attempting to severely restrict immigra-
tion. The largest non-Kuwaiti group is comprised of Palestinians; but,
in making sizable contributions to the PLO, the authorities have succeeded in diffusing the potential dissidence which would otherwise
probably emanate from that group.

Although originally part of the abortive effort to establish the
Federation of Arab Amirates in the late summer of 1971, Bahrayn and
Qatar each decided to go it alone. One of the factors which caused
the failure of their efforts to federate with the Trucial Shaykhdoms also
made them relatively good candidates for independent status; that is,
the fact that they are somewhat more populous, wealthy, and, in the
case of Bahrayn, "modern," than the Shaykhdoms made it difficult to
arrive at a mutually agreeable internal distribution of power. Moreover,
each has a solid economic base due to substantial oil production in the
case of Qatar and the combination of modest petroleum extraction and
a relatively well developed commercial and industrial system in Bahrayn.
In any event, on August 15, Bahrayn, and on September 1, Qatar proclaimed their independence, followed by the signing of friendship
treaties with Great Britain. Within a month, both had been granted
membership in the UN and the Arab League and had received messages
of congratulations and recognition from most of the world's governments with the notable exception of the People's Democratic Republic
of Yemen (PDRY).+ Since that time each has endeavored to cultivate
good relations with neighboring states‡ and to attend to domestic

---

*Kuwait is still basically pro-Western but has been moving gradu-
ally toward a more centrist position on the East-West continuum.

+The reaction of the PDRY, a strong backer of PFLOAG, which has
aspirations in the Gulf, was predictably negative. In contrast, both
Peking and Moscow sent congratulatory messages.

‡Bahrayn's agreement, in December 1971, to lease part of the
naval base vacated by the British to the U.S. Navy caused some

problems. In the case of Qatar, the latter took a relatively dramatic turn in February 1972, when the ruler was deposed by a cousin in a bloodless takeover.

For the most part, a similar situation has prevailed in the more recently formed United Arab Amirates (UAA). Comprised of at first six, and later seven, shaykhdoms of the Trucial coast which stretches along the Gulf's southern shore,* the UAA came into existence on December 2, 1971, as the deadline for Britain's military withdrawal was rapidly approaching. The predictable signing of a friendship treaty with Britain took place on the same day, and UN and Arab League membership came within a week. As in the case of Bahrayn and Qatar, diplomatic recognition was forthcoming from most of the states of the area. This time, however, the abstention of the PDRY was augmented by Iraq's refusal to recognize the new entity as a protest against the UAA's failure to react more forcefully against Iran's occupation of Abu Musa and the two Tunb islands a few days before the Union was formally announced. (Baghdad later relented after its efforts to involve the UN in the matter failed, and the first Iraqi ambassador to the UAA presented his credentials on June 12, 1972.)[5] Internally, the UAA faced its first crisis soon after its inception. An attempted coup in Sharjah in January 1972 was successfully put down, though not before the ruler had been killed. While the conflict was primarily the culmination of a family quarrel, some evidence indicates that, had the coup succeeded, Sharjah might have withdrawn from the UAA and joined in a smaller union with Ra's al-Khaymah. However, the plot failed and a successor who happened to favor continued adherence to United Arab Amirates was chosen. Shortly thereafter, Ra's al-Khaymah dropped its objections to the union. The second crisis occurred in June 1972 with an outbreak of hostilities between tribesmen in the Sharjah-Fujayrah border area. It was successfully put down by the Union Defense Force, which, at the time of independence, had been formed around the nucleus provided by the former Trucial Oman Scouts. Since then, relative peace has reigned in the area, though ancient rivalries and hostilities continue to bubble beneath the surface.

---

negative reaction; but, since it simply formalized a preexisting arrangement, nothing came of the verbal protests. However, the agreement has been cancelled in the wake of the October War.

* The original six were: Abu Dhabi, Dubai, Sharjah, Ajman, Fujayrah, and Umm al-Qaywayn. Ra's al-Khaymah joined belatedly in February 1972. Abu Dhabi and Dubai, as the most populous and richest of the seven, dominate the union with Shaykh Zayd Bin Sultan, Amir of Abu Dhabi, acting as its first president and Shaykh Rashid Bin Sa'id, Amir of Dubai, as the vice-president. It was primarily dissatisfaction over the internal allocation of power that led to the original holdout by Ra's al-Khaymah.

The most enigmatic and potentially most troublesome territory in terms of threats to regional stability is the Sultanate of Oman which, with Iran, guards the southern access to the Persian Gulf. Now ruled by Sultan Qabus, who overthrew his archconservative father in July 1970, Oman has at long last begun to emerge into the twentieth century. Qabus, a graduate of the Sandhurst Military Academy in England, appears committed to modernizing his nation and improving the standard of living of his people, but his efforts in that direction are complicated by the drain on resources necessitated by the fight against the Dhufar rebels (of late PFLOAG).* While there was a long history of regional rivalries and open conflict in the former Imamate of Musqat and Oman (especially between mountain and coastal areas), the current struggle is relatively recent in origin and has been complicated by some initial Chinese and Soviet backing of the rebels. Such aid, including sanctuary, has been channeled through the leftist government of the PDRY. On the other side, the Sultan's forces are led by British officers, some seconded from Her Majesty's armed forces and others serving under contract, and include large numbers of Baluchis as well as some troops supplied by the Shah and King Husain of Jordan.+ As of now, the fighting appears stalemated, with each side controlling portions of Dhufar. In the course of 1973-74, Qabus enlarged his area of control; but the rebels enjoy the usual advantages of guerrilla movement, especially in the mountainous regions. It is noteworthy, however, that in early 1974 there appeared to be signs of strain and internal dissent within the rebel movement. As of now, Oman faces an uncertain future.

Finally, the general picture for long-range domestic tranquility in the newer Gulf states (and, to an extent, Saudi Arabia) appears to encompass a number of factors which could threaten the status quo:

(1) Each state is beginning to play host to large numbers of aliens who could well become a source of significant discontent even though they are, for the most part, being carefully kept out of positions of power.

(2) As oil revenues grow and the standard of living improves, there will inevitably arise a newly educated class attracted to "foreign ideas." In this context, increasing militancy in the Arab-Israeli dispute is likely to become a requirement for survival on the part of

---

*While Oman is currently enjoying a substantial economic boost due to the increasing production of recently discovered oil, approximately one-half of the national budget is being used to combat PFLOAG.

+The rebels are widely believed to have aspirations in the rest of the Gulf as well as Oman; that is, they presumably would like to conquer Oman first and them move up the coast through the UAA, Qatar, and Bahrayn partly in order to control that area's oil resources. The Shah feels threatened by these developments and his aid to Sultan Qabus is intended to prevent them.

the established regimes. (The response of area states to the October War bears witness to the recognition by their rulers of this fact.)

(3) When the armed forces of these states will come to be led, as they probably will, by members of the indigenous population without strong ties to the ruling families, these officer corps will constitute a separate and important element of power whose interests may vary from those of the rulers. (This process appears to have already begun in Abu Dhabi.)

It should also be kept in mind, however, that these factors are counterbalanced, at least for the short run, by two other considerations: (1) most of these states have highly efficient secret police establishments capable of detecting and suppressing internal dissent. Moreover, (2) to the vast majority of the inhabitants of this region, intrafamily, intratribal, and intertribal quarrels hold far greater interest than the ideological and/or nationalistic struggles of the outside world. Nevertheless, the latter factor could prove to be a not unmixed blessing. While such disputes could serve to siphon off whatever fighting inclinations are present, they might also be manipulated by those bent on different types of struggle. For example, some observers report that ancient feuds have been used by the Marxist leaders of the Dhufar rebels to recruit adherents to their cause.

Intraregional Relations

Superimposed over this intricate and, in many cases, potentially explosive domestic situation is an equally complex network of possible intraregional conflict. Although some of the troublesome issues, such as Iran's claim to Bahrayn, have, for the most part, been settled, a sufficient number of other disputes, controversies, and feuds remain to challenge previous efforts at conciliation.* Not surprisingly, Iran, as the area's only non-Arab state, and Iraq, as its only leftist regime, figure prominently in most of the major controversies. Indeed, some of the most bitter disputes of the past have erupted between the two of them. Their long-standing feuds over navigation rights in the Shatt al-'Arab and Iraqi discontent over Iranian sovereignty in Khuzistan remain unresolved. Moreover, each has accused the other of fomenting internal minority strifes. When exacerbated by other problems, these long-term differences periodically lead to public exchanges of invective,

---

*The shallowness of the Gulf has precluded the application of the standard international law provisions for determining where a nation's continental shelf ends. Therefore, substitute arrangements have had to be used and have been arranged by bilateral treaties between Iran on the one hand and Saudi Arabia, Bahrayn, and Qatar on the other. The remaining Arab states have as yet reached no such arrangement with Tehran.

severing of relations, and troop buildups along the frontier. One such episode, involving navigation privileges in Shatt al'Arab, flared up in 1969 and yet another series of border incidents occurred in early 1974. While tempers have since cooled, the underlying disputes have not been settled and tension could erupt again at any time. Even when the issue does not directly involve the two, Tehran and Baghdad often wind up heaping verbal abuse upon one another. Thus, after November 30, 1971, when Iran occupied Abu Musa and the Tunb islands, over which Sharjah and Ra's al-Khaymah had previously claimed sovereignty, Iraq's reaction was more negative and protracted than the subsequent response of the UAA. It might be noted in passing that, while no particular efforts are under way to reverse Tehran's occupation of the islands, Ra's al-Khaymah has not formally relinquished its claim to the Tunbs. Sharjah, in contrast (though admittedly having little choice in the matter), had signed a treaty sharing control over Abu Musa with Tehran on the day before the Iranian occupation. Since that time, oil has been discovered in the island's offshore area, and, by prior agreement, Iran and Sharjah are to share the revenue from its extraction.

While Baghdad-Tehran relations are the poorest of those between any two Gulf states, Iran does not have exclusive call upon the disputative energies of Iraq. Given the length of their mutual border and the differences in their ideological perferences, there exists a predictably deep mistrust in the relations between Baghdad and Saudi Arabia. Further, while it appears to have abandoned its earlier claim to the whole of Kuwait, Iraq, in March 1973, staged military maneuvers in the border area and, in the process, encroached on Kuwaiti territory. This latest episode appears to have reflected an effort to obtain control of Warbah and Bubiyan, two islands which control access to the Iraqi port of Umm Qasr. Sovereignty over them would also strengthen Baghdad's claim to offshore oil.[6] While Iraqi troops have been withdrawn from Kuwaiti territory, no final resolution of the conflict has been reached.

In the lower Gulf, at least for the time being, a spirit of cooperation seems to be the order of the day. Thus, in an interview of December 12, 1972, the Saudi Foreign Minister said that the dispute between Saudi Arabia, Abu Dhabi, and Oman over the Buraymi oasis could best be settled by a referendum.[7] Equally significant is the apparent determination of the various members of the UAA to submerge territorial disputes between them and between the individual shaykhdoms and Oman for the sake of regional order and stability.

Nevertheless, given the number and depth of these rivalries, as well as the enormous new wealth of the area, the substantial, emerging arms race between the countries of the region comes as no surprise.[8] There can be no doubt that the quest for modern weapons has been engendered, in part, by aspirations of "neighborhood prestige." However, since none of the Gulf's military establishments could hope to withstand an assault by a great power, these arms are ultimately designed to protect their respective national interests in intraregional disputes.

Moscow and Peking in the Gulf

In the face of the difficulties which such intraregional complexity inevitably poses for an outsider, it is not surprising that, with one notable exception (Iraq, to be discussed below), both Moscow's and Peking's efforts in the Persian Gulf have been rather tentative. (Some observers might be tempted to predict that the Soviets would use local quarrels to their own advantage, but the cross pressures are so intricate as to encourage only those who seek anarchy for its own sake. For instance, while Moscow's status as the champion of the Arabs in their conflict with Israel is the source of much of whatever good will exists in the Arab East toward the USSR, it also makes it more difficult for the Soviets to maintain their traditionally hostile line vis-a-vis the conservative monarchies of the Gulf since they have emerged as the major financial backers of those Arab governments and organizations directly affected by the Israeli policies.) Indeed, in the southern Gulf, the most striking feature of Soviet and Chinese policy is the relative dearth of the sorts of economic, military, diplomatic, cultural, and political activities which are the symptoms of direct efforts to gain influence.

Thus, neither has an embassy in Oman, the UAA, Bahrayn, Qatar, or Saudi Arabia. Moreover, there is little trade* and no aid agreements with any of these states. The relative paucity of official visits and cultural exchanges between the USSR and these countries is especially striking when measured against the frequency of such events in most other Arab states. This dearth of activity is primarily a result of the suspicion and hostility toward the Soviet Union and Communist China which is widespread in the ruling circles of the area. Such negative feeling is partly the result of ideological differences[+] and partly of the hostile treatment which the local rulers have traditionally received at the hands of Moscow's and Peking's propaganda organs.[+] More recently, mistrust of Communist intentions was augmented by what was seen as support for the Dhufar rebellion. Sultan Qabus has vowed that there will be no cooperation by Oman with either the USSR or the PRC due to their backing of the insurgents. Since PFLOAG has announced designs on the other smaller states of the region as well, there is a natural

---

* Since the mid-1960s, Saudi Arabia has been engaged in very modest trading with the Soviet bloc. From 1966 through 1971, Soviet exports to Riyadh increased in value from 2.6 to 5.4 million rubles; but in each case the figure represented only about .8 of one percent of total Soviet exports to the Arab world. Saudi exports to the USSR during the same period were also negligible.[9]

[+] The Saudis especially are wont to remind their fellow Arabs that Communism, as an atheistic system, is incompatible with Islam.

[+] The line has been somewhat muted since the 1967 war, but the rulers of the area are not likely to forget the excesses of the past.

inclination among the current rulers not to cooperate with those whom they believe have supported forces seeking their overthrow. However, while the Chinese formerly made no secret of their backing of the Popular Front, extending aid in the form of arms, advice, and moral support, they have recently reversed their course, primarily as a concession to the Shah of Iran with whom they are assiduously seeking improved relations. Moreover, although there have been reports concerning the capture of some Soviet weapons by the loyal Omanis, Moscow's actual support for the rebels has been primarily verbal and somewhat halfhearted at that.[10] It might be of interest to note that, even though soon after its inception the UAA had expressed a willingness to establish diplomatic relations with the USSR, it backed out of this arrangement in response to Saudi pressure.

The Soviet dilemma in the Gulf is thus illustrated by the fact that, while the Kremlin feels compelled to give moral (and, perhaps, some physical) support to the Marxist revolutionaries spurred both by Chinese sniping about its ideological apostasy and its own emotional preferences, experience has no doubt dulled the Russians' appetite for yet another client who would be difficult to control and whose prospects for success are so uncertain.

Kuwait has much in common with the other southern Gulf states, especially in terms of emotional attitudes toward the two Communist giants. Nevertheless, its approach has been more pragmatic. Indeed, Kuwait's relations with both might best be characterized as correct and businesslike. It opened diplomatic relations with the USSR in 1963 and allowed Peking to replace Taiwan in 1971. While Kuwait needs and receives no aid of any kind from either, its trade relations with each are growing steadily though Soviet efforts in this respect are naturally more advanced than those of the Chinese. Thus, by 1971, Soviet exports to Kuwait comprised about 2.6 percent of their Arab world total,[11] after having increased seven-fold between 1964 and 1969.[12] Moreover, in October 1970, Kuwait and the USSR signed a mutually beneficial agreement to supply oil to each other's customers.[13] The number and significance of cultural contacts in which Moscow has been able to interest the Kuwaitis have thus far been minimal and have consisted of only a few visits by journalists, scholars, and dignitaries, including the Soviet Mufti, as well as the granting of a small number of scholarships for Kuwaitis to study in the USSR. Lest it grow complacent about its "successes," the Kremlin finds interspersed with the announcements of these agreements and visits what appears to be an orchestrated chorus of warnings and reminders from editors and members of the Kuwaiti parliament about the negative nature of Soviet intentions in the Arab East. Probably in recognition of the relative superficiality of relations between them, Soviet press comments on Kuwait have, in recent years, been remarkably restrained.[14]

The Chinese, as latecomers to the scene, have an even less impressive record than the Russians. Thus, a visit by the Kuwaiti

Minister of Trade and Industry to Peking in December 1972, resulting in a contract for Chinese purchase of 600,000 tons of fertilizer, has been one of the largest deals to date.[15]

The realism which marks Moscow's attitude toward Kuwait has, in recent years, also begun to characterize Soviet relations with Iran. While the two states have long maintained correct diplomatic relations, this tradition has typically been overmatched by the suspicion and hostility with which the Iranians have historically regarded the giant looming on their northern border. One of the most dramatic developments in Moscow-Tehran relations in the postrevolutionary period has been the depth and range of economic ties established during the past decade. While in dollar amounts U.S. aid continues to outweigh heavily that of the USSR, the Soviets have, in the last 10 years, outstripped the Americans by emerging as Iran's major trade partner.[16] Moreover, Soviet aid and trade investments in Iran are particularly impressive when measured against Moscow's efforts in other developing nations.[17] Much of the aid has taken the form of loans which Tehran should have no difficulty in repaying, given its ever growing income from oil. Still, the aid agreements have given the USSR an important role in such development projects as a natural gas pipeline, the Isfahan steel mill, machine tool plants, a hydroelectric dam, port expansion, and the fishing industry. Moreover, involvement in the Iranian economy has directly benefited the Soviet Union in that repayment in natural gas has been arranged on terms beneficial to Moscow. One of the most noteworthy agreements between the two countries in terms of symbolic significance, however, entailed the Iranian purchase in early 1967 of $110 million in Soviet military equipment. Tehran thus became the first formal member of a Western military alliance (CENTO) to purchase Soviet arms. Even though the deal constituted a significant departure for the Shah, it must be noted that the equipment in question consisted primarily of military vehicles and in no case necessitated training by Russian personnel. Nor has the detente in Soviet-Iranian relations altered the Shah's firm political commitment to the West as well as to the resolute suppression of the indigenous Communist party. Moreover, Tehran will probably be somewhat tougher in any future economic negotiations with the Soviet Union since recent reports indicate considerable Iranian resentment both with the terms of the natural gas arrangements, which are now seen as much too generous to the Russians, and with the relatively obsolete and low quality equipment used in several Soviet-built projects, above all the Isfahan steel complex.

Similarly, close economic association with the USSR has not prevented the Shah from normalizing relations with China. The Chinese established diplomatic ties with Iran during their post-Cultural Revolution drive to gain recognition in the outside world, but thus far the new arrangement has produced little more than a few ceremonial exchange visits and, as noted, Peking's agreement to drop its backing of the

Dhufari rebels. The two parties are obviously engaged in an extended process of "feeling each other out. "

Though their economic efforts in Iran have been relatively success ful, the Soviets' strongest commitment in the Gulf region has been to the leftist Ba'thi regime in Iraq. In the diplomatic sphere, Moscow appeared to have scored an impressive success on April 9, 1972, with the signing of a 15-year Treaty of Friendship, similar to the one entered into earlier with the Egyptian Arab Republic. The signatories promised not to conclude any agreements with third parties that were incompatible with the goal of "permanent, unbreakable friendship" between them and to consult with each other if the peace of either was threatened. Not coincidentally, soon after the signing, a new reshuffled cabinet, which included two members of the Iraqi Communist party, was announced in Baghdad.

While the monetary value of Soviet aid to Iraq has been smaller than that to Iran, this is more a reflection of the differences in the two countries' economies than of the extent of Moscow's interest. Moreover, the bulk of Soviet aid to Baghdad has been military, and has involved a substantial advisory role by Russian military personnel.[18] As a result of close diplomatic and military ties, Soviet naval vessels have made a number of "courtesy calls" at the Iraqi Gulf port of Umm Qasr.

While, as mentioned before, trade relations with Iraq are not yet as extensive monetarily as those with Iran, they are substantial; Iraq is second to Egypt among the Arab states as a recipient of Soviet exports. Moreover, Moscow's involvement in the country's economic development encompasses many more diverse types of projects than in Iran. A partial list includes fisheries, communications, agriculture (especially land reclamation and irrigation), electrical power plants, merchant shipping, mineral extraction, ship building, and manpower training. The single most important agreement, signed in 1969, involves Soviet cooperation with the Iraqi National Oil Company (INOC) in developing and exploiting the North Rumaylah oil fields. In return for its aid the USSR is to be paid in crude oil.*

The nature of the developing economic ties between Baghdad and Moscow is best exemplified by the fact that in October 1972 Iraq applied for membership in the Comecon with "observer" status. While no formal agreement has yet been reached, Iraq is the first non-Communist state to ask and receive serious consideration for membership. (In 1972 Finland became an associate member.)

The above activities have been accompanied by a large volume of travel by diplomats, economists, scholars, technicians, and other

---

*Paralleling the situation in Iran (see above), rumblings of discontent over the poor quality of Soviet equipment are now being heard among officials and technicians of the INOC.

personnel between Moscow and Baghdad. Hardly a month passes without one or more such visits being announced. Moreover, large numbers of Iraqi students have been granted scholarships for study in the Soviet Union.

Needless to say, the Chinese have not been nearly so active as the Russians. However, they have established cordial relations with Baghdad and are slowly developing enlarged trade links.

Evaluation

In the light of the preceding discussion it is possible to approach the next question: what have the Soviets and the Chinese gained from their efforts in the Persian Gulf? While China's efforts have been more substantial in only one respect, that is, its initial support for PFLOAG, the limited nature of Peking's objectives means that its quest for influence has been relatively more successful than that of the USSR. Put differently, the Chinese appear to seek primarily a form of "negative influence," whose main aim is embarrassment of their adversaries and, in an area as rife with internal dissension as the Persian Gulf, such an objective is readily attainable.

On the other hand, for those like the Soviets who seek a more permanent position of influence in a stable relational system, the Gulf is a sea of troubled waters indeed. Given current local conditions, Moscow's efforts to acquire influence in the lower Gulf states would almost surely be wasted. For this reason, the Russians have been only minimally active there and have instead rested their Gulf position on their relations with Iran and Iraq. Having done so, however, has provided the Kremlin with a dilemma that will admit of no short-term solution. Since influence is a two-way street, Soviet attempts to build up dependence upon the USSR by these traditional and bitter enemies has subjected Moscow to conflicting pressures for support in their feuds with each other. The discomfort to which Moscow has been subjected by this dilemma is nowhere more amply demonstrated than in the occasionally shifting but generally cautious language of the joint Soviet-Iraqi and Soviet-Iranian statements on the Gulf.

The current problems of the Persian Gulf were first officially mentioned by the Soviets in the joint communique of August 5, 1970, published during the visit to the USSR of Iraqi Vice-President Saddam Husayn al-Takriti. It noted, in part, that both governments favored the removal of foreign troops from the region (including Musqat and Oman) "in order to enable the Arab peoples of the Gulf to gain their independence and freedom."[19] A subsequent communique, issued in the wake of Husayn's next stay in Moscow on February 17, 1972, differed from the previous formulation in that the sides condemned "imperialist intrigues and plots" in the Persian Gulf and expressed their "full support for the struggle of the Arab states and peoples of the . . . region for the right to decide their fate by themselves."[20]

On the basis of these documents it is possible to argue that the USSR was willing to lend the Arab, and particularly the Iraqi position in the Gulf a measure of its moral backing. Still, it must be noted that the initial wording indicated Soviet support for "the Arab peoples" of the Gulf and, since no one claimed that "Arab peoples" were denied "freedom and independence" by the Shah, it could be reasonably held that the first communique did not in fact refer to Iran. Subsequently, however, when the above formulation was broadened to include both "peoples" and "states" it is reasonable to assume that, since most Arab states (and above all Iraq) were openly critical of Tehran's policy in the Gulf, Moscow had agreed to back their position vis-a-vis Iran.

Nevertheless, it is equally noteworthy that the USSR has exhibited a clear determination not to become involved too deeply in the disputes of the Persian Gulf. Thus, references to independence, freedom, and self-determination dealt with principles so broad and vague as to be meaningless in the context of the communiques. This tendency to steer clear of a firm commitment to the Arab position in the Gulf made itself evident also during Husayn's February 1972 visit to Moscow. While Husayn, in a speech at the ceremonial Kremlin breakfast brought up the subject of the Gulf and of Iraqi-Iranian relations in general, Premier Kosygin in his reply made no reference to it at all.[21] Similarly, the subjects of Baghdad-Tehran relations and of the Gulf were not mentioned in Soviet accounts of Kosygin's April 1972 visit to Iraq for the signing of the Treaty of Friendship and Mutual Cooperation.[22] It should also be noted that the Kremlin has adhered to its caution in spite of Baghdad's repeated attempts to draw it out, as, for example, during President Hasan al-Bakr's mid-September 1972 visit to Moscow. In one of his speeches, in a clear reference to Iran, the Iraqi President spoke of "actions against the historical rights of the Arab nation" in the Persian Gulf, insisting that these (unspecified) "actions" required "even greater solidarity and cooperation between our two nations. . . ."[23] Another indication of Soviet reluctance to go beyond what could be interpreted as limited support of Iraq has been the consistent reference to the Persian, and not the Arab, Gulf in Russian public statements and in speeches by Soviet dignitaries as well as in Russian versions of speeches by Iraqi officials. Moreover, the September 19, 1972, communique, issued at a time when the Kremlin was preparing to receive the Shah, reverted significantly to the original formulation: support was promised once again only to "the Arab peoples of the Persian Gulf," struggling "to repulse the aggressive imperialist plans which threaten their freedom and independence."[24]

However, probably the clearest illustration of Moscow's moderation was provided by the treatment of the Gulf's political problems contained in joint Soviet-Iranian statements and public speeches of the leaders of the two countries. It should be noted at the outset that the formula, contained in the communique of October 21, 1972, published during the Shah's state visit to the USSR only four weeks after

Bakr's departure, has been adhered to without change ever since that time. Because of its relevance, it deserves to be quoted in full: "The Soviet Union and Iran expressed firm conviction that questions concerning the Persian Gulf region must be resolved in conformity with the principles of the UN Charter and without outside interference by the states of the area themselves."[25] One could well argue that the phrase "without outside interference" represented an obligation on the part of the USSR to stay out of regional feuds and that Moscow was thus prepared to let Iran and the Arab states resolve their problems by themselves. The same could be said about inter-Arab disputes in the Gulf. In any event, while outwardly a concession to Iran, the phrase no doubt reflected the Soviet desire not to become too deeply involved in the region's politics.

Moreover, the two parties agreed that their relations would be based on principles of "equality, respect for sovereignty, independence, territorial integrity, and non-interference in internal affairs [of the other country]."[26] Coming in the wake of Tehran's occupation of Abu Musa and the Tunb islands, Soviet expression of "respect for . . . the territorial integrity" of Iran can be interpreted as acquiescence in the islands' occupation — a position which Iraq clearly disapproved.

It may thus be concluded that, while outwardly lending a degree of moral support to the Iraqi position in the Gulf, the USSR was prepared neither to adopt an open and clear-cut pro-Arab position nor to intervene there directly. In pledging itself to let the states of the Persian Gulf work out their problems "without outside interference," as stated in the October 1972 communique and subsequent pronouncements,[27] the Kremlin offered reasonably conclusive evidence of its desire to remain aloof. It is significant that this attitude, which clearly displeased Iraq without securing any tangible benefits in Tehran, has not, so far, been affected by the strong displeasure at Iran's continuous allegiance to CENTO shown by Kosygin during Premier Amir Abbas Hoveyda's August 1973 visit to the Soviet Union, and at periodic displays of anxiety in Tehran about Soviet intentions in the Persian Gulf and the Indian Ocean.[28]

Thus, on balance, the considerable outlay in Iran has netted the Kremlin some favorable trade relations which are counterpoised by Moscow's frustration over the Shah's continuing adherence to the Western alliance and his newly developing relations with Communist China. Moreover, these same economic ties are undoubtedly a result of enlightened self-interest on the part of both governments rather than of Soviet leverage in Tehran.

In Iraq, though the commitment is more substantial, it is also hard to see impressive victories for Soviet influence. While the Ba'thi regime has, in recent years, initiated a number of reforms that have pleased the Russians (implementation of the land-reform law, a temporary end to the war in Kurdistan, which broke out again in early 1974, and cooperation with the Iraqi Communist Party), these moves have typically been dictated by local and regional developments rather than by Moscow's pressure. Also, while Baghdad has generally expressed diplomatic support for Soviet foreign policy initiatives, this behavior is probably more a result of its nonaligned, "antiimperialistic" status than of any direct Russian leverage. Further, Iraq can, on occasion, be disconcertingly independent, especially with regard to the affairs of the Gulf, where Baghdad views itself as a directly involved participant and the Soviet Union as a mere "outsider." Thus, the Ba'thi government withheld recognition of the UAA at the time of its formation even though the USSR sent early messages of congratulations and support. Finally, Iraq maintains cordial relations with the Chinese in the face of Soviet misgivings.

In the economic field, the Kremlin and the Iraqis have concluded a number of barter deals (which the Russians prefer for obvious reasons); but these, too, resulted from unusual local conditions; that is, Baghdad encountered difficulties in marketing its oil in the period following the nationalization of the assets of the IPC and thus was willing to barter with the Soviet bloc nations. However, now that the problems between the government and the Iraqi Petroleum Company have been settled, the Ba'thi regime, in a move obviously aimed at Russia and its satellites, has announced its intention not to enter into any more barter agreements.[29] Parenthetically, the nationalization episode illustrates the contention that, even when a client like Iraq acts as the Soviets have long advised and cajoled, the result may prove a mixed blessing for the USSR. In the short run, the nationalization and the ensuing inability to market petroleum produced some favorable barter arrangements. However, it also deprived Iraq of hard currency payments, part of which had heretofore been transferred to the Soviet Union in exchange for military and economic aid. In the long run, nationalization will remove from the Middle Eastern scene a favorite Soviet whipping boy, "Western oil monopolies," long cited as one of the demons against whom the Arabs have needed Russian support.

Some observers might see the growing Iraqi dependence on Soviet arms supplies and advisers as an indication of Moscow's increased influence in Baghdad. That may be, but thus far this influence has yielded no Soviet bases. Moreover, as the Egyptian example illustrates, such arrangements can be altered at the whim of the client state. In addition, whatever influence the Kremlin may wield proved insufficient to prevent the Iraqi instigated border skirmishes with Kuwait in the spring of 1973 — a turn of events of which the USSR disapproved because diplomatic support of its client would have brought Moscow into an open conflict with Kuwait.

While Iraqi willingness to engage in cultural exchanges is occasionally seen as a sign of Soviet influence, it is subject to fluctuations and is conditioned by the ebb and flow of good feeling between the two states. Moreover, different facets of cultural relations represent likely sacrificial lambs in both internal politics and

150

foreign relations. For instance, the precipitous closing of Soviet and satellite cultural centers in Baghdad in the wake of the abortive coup in the summer of 1972 was intended to demonstrate the regime's political independence to both domestic rivals and the great powers alike.

Perhaps the single most significant accomplishment of Soviet influence in Iraq has been in earning an unprecented degree of recognition for the local Communist party. The timing of the gesture (in the wake of the signing of the Treaty of Friendship) leaves little doubt that Moscow's pressure was an important factor in the Ba'thi decision to admit two party members to the subsquently formed cabinet. Even here, however, there are facets of the situation which detract from its ostensible significance: (1) no amount of Soviet influence would have succeeded had not the Iraqi Communist Party (ICP) been a factor in Iraqi politics in its own right, leading the Ba'th to conclude that the party might be easier to control if allowed a high degree of legitimacy and a stake in the current regime; (2) such decisions are easily reversible; and (3) of the various pro-Soviet Communist parties in the Third World, the ICP has tended to be one of the more unruly, often ignoring Moscow's wishes when local issues were at stake. Indeed, one wonders whether the Kremlin would consider the ICP an issue worth pressing were it not for the goad of Chinese accusations charging callousness vis-a-vis fellow-Marxists in the developing countries.

In conclusion, while the Soviets have enjoyed improvements in their position in a number of Gulf states, most notably Iraq and Iran, of the sort which have traditionally been assumed to yield influence, the changes have for the most part not been translatable into influence as a tangible product. Those positive results which have emerged appear mostly to be consequences of coincidences of interest rather than exercises of influence. While the heaviest investment is in Iraq, it may well be that Moscow is more interested in Baghdad as a potential counterweight to Cairo's influence in the Arab world than as a gateway to the Persian Gulf. If so, this may serve as another indication of the relative lack of success of Soviet Middle Eastern policy: for Iraq, serving as it does as the focus of much regional ill-will, has little save availability to recommend it as a political and strategic salient for Moscow's policy in the area. (Soviet overtures to Iran in the last decade are probably in some part a result of Russian realization of that fact.)

Thus, if the current Chinese position is characterized as one of negative influence, the Soviets may be said to have moved one degree higher on the influence scale to a point marked preventive influence. They have established themselves in sufficient strength (at least in the political sense) in the Persian Gulf to enjoy an "immunity" from the necessity for attempts to exercise influence directly. That is, they now enjoy sufficient status in the region to guarantee that their wishes and potential objections must become yet another factor to be weighed before policy decisions affecting the Gulf can be reached either by the local states or the rival great powers. However, an objective observer cannot help but wonder whether their investment in the area was necessary to achieve such a position or whether it might not have been theirs automatically as a result of their status as one of the world's two superpowers.

Notes

1. See O. M. Smolansky, "Moscow and the Persian Gulf: An Analysis of Soviet Ambitions and Potential, " Orbis, vol. 14, no. 1 (Spring 1970), 94-97.

2. For details, see his "Oil and Soviet Policy in the Middle East, " The Middle East Journal, vol. 26, no. 2 (Spring 1972), 149-60.

3. For some details on Iran's military build-up, see J. C. Hurewitz, "The Persian Gulf: British Withdrawal and Western Security, " The Annals of the American Academy of Political and Social Science, vol. 401 (May 1972), 115.

4. See, for example, a Baghdad Radio report of December 12, 1970, as quoted in Arab Report and Record (London, henceforth referred to as ARR), issue 23 (1970), 662-63.

5. Ibid. , issue 11 (1972), p. 290.

6. For a more detailed analysis of the dispute, see R. M. Burrell, "The Gulf Pot Begins to Boil Once More, " The New Middle East, no. 56 (May 1973), 37-38.

7. See ARR, issue 23 (1972), 583-84. Superficially, this appears to be a major conciliatory gesture by the Saudis considering the intensity with which the Buraymi setback at the hands of the British in 1955 has since rankled in Riyadh. (The resultant enmity has particularly strained relations between King Faysal and Shaykh Zayd of Abu Dhabi.) However, many observers see this Saudi "concession" as only a tactical maneuver in a long standing quarrel whose end is nowhere in sight.

8. For some details, see Anthony Mascarenhas, "Gulf Arms Race Threatens World's Main Oil Source, " The Times (London), June 6, 1973.

9. For more details, see ARR, issue 15 (1970), p. 464; issue 16 (1972), p. 419; and Stephen Page, "Moscow and the Persian Gulf Countries, 1967-1970, " Mizan, vol. 13, no. 2 (October 1971), 75-76.

10. For details, see Page, op. cit. , pp. 72-73.

11. ARR, issue 16 (1972), 419.

12. For details, see Page, op. cit. , p. 77.

13. ARR, issue 19 (1970), 554.

14. For details, see Page, op. cit. , pp. 77-79.

15. ARR, issue 24 (1972), 600.

16. According to Rouhollah K. Ramazani, The Persian Gulf: Iran's Role (Charlottesville: University Press of Virginia, 1972), p. 86, 22.06 percent of Iran's total exports went to the USSR in 1970/71, while only

8. 71 percent went to the United States. Moreover, the Soviet figures represent a steady increase in recent years, while the American trend is downward. Iran is now believed to rank second only to Egypt as a non-Communist customer for Soviet exports.

17. According to Abraham S. Becker, "Oil and the Persian Gulf in Soviet Policy in the 1970s, " (Santa Monica: The RAND Corporation, May 1972), p. 32, Soviet aid to Iran is exceeded only by that to Egypt and India.

18. Robert S. Walters, American and Soviet Aid: A Comparative Analysis (Pittsburgh: University of Pittsburgh Press, 1970), p. 84. In contrast, as noted, the vast majority of aid to Iran has been strictly economic. Moreover, while Iran has received more total aid, the difference between the two totals has not been large. Becker, op. cit., p. 33.

19. Text in Pravda, August 6, 1970. Emphasis added. A similar formulation was contained in the communique issued at the conclusion of a visit to Baghdad of a Soviet government-party delegation, headed by Vice-Premier and member of the CPSU Central Committee, V. N. Novikov. Text in ibid. , June 26, 1971.

20. Text in ibid. , February 18, 1972. Emphasis added.

21. Pravda merely noted the fact that Husayn addressed himself to this topic but, in contrast to the other sections of his speech, mentioned no details. Ibid., February 12, 1972.

22. Ibid. , April 10 and 11, 1972.

23. Ibid. , September 15, 1972.

24. Ibid. , September 20, 1972.

25. Text in ibid. , October 22, 1972. Emphasis added.

26. Idem. Emphasis added.

27. See ibid. , March 18 and August 13, 1973.

28. Text in ibid. , August 7, 1973.

29. The New York Times, April 1, 1973.

7

SOVIET AND CHINESE INFLUENCE IN BLACK AFRICA
Robert Legvold

The period of intense interest in Black Africa in the early 1960s occurred not only because decolonization thrust so many new African nations into international politics at this point, but because one set of national powers, the Soviet Union and China, thought they could exercise considerable influence in this area; and the other set, led by the United States, feared that they might be right. If it had not been for the specter of the Soviet Union or China ingratiating itself with revolutionary nationalists, exploiting political instability wherever it might develop, and perhaps benefiting from the fascination of many in Africa with the Soviet and Chinese political and economic experiences — all in order to secure greater, perhaps decisive, influence over these new governments — the United States would never have given Africa the attention that it did in the beginning.* If Africa seems less central today, it is not merely because Africa has become intrinsically less important to the ambitions of the major powers; but because the major powers have learned how limited their influence can be. In both instances Africa's place in their calculations and, hence, place in international politics has been critically a function of the levels of influence mustered by one or the other side.

Strange, then, that phenomena so much at the heart of understanding Soviet, Chinese, or American relations with Africa have never been explored. Strange that no effort has been made to look systematically at the sources, nature, and application of Soviet and Chinese influence in Africa. Strange, that is, until one realizes that the general theoretical framework for doing so does not exist. Next to no rigorous thinking has been done on the problem of influence in

---

*Nor would some of our most eminent Soviet specialists have bothered with the subject. Zbigniew Brzezinski's (ed.) Africa and the Communist World (Stanford: Stanford University Press, 1963) is a good case in point.

international politics.[1] Even less have foreign policy specialists, most particularly students of Soviet foreign policy, wrestled with the problem of devising a conceptual scheme for analyzing or criteria for evaluating one nation's influence over another. The deficiency diminishes our understanding of Soviet policy in every area and toward all countries but especially in Africa where academics and policymakers have been so easily distracted by the possibility that Soviet actions do or may shape local policy choices.

To define influence as the act of and success in affecting, altering, or controlling the action and attitudes of others immediately betrays the difficulty of giving the concept practical application. How does the analyst decide what nation B has done or thought differently from what it would have done or thought but for something that nation A did or was? His problems are twofold and both are fundamental: First is the problem of access, of knowing what in fact motivated nation B. Even when B's behavior conforms to the wishes of nation A, B may have been simply acting out its own preferences and in no way responding to A's influence. The second problem is in disentangling effect. A may well have influenced B but in a way unanticipated by A and, therefore, to the extent that B's behavior diverges from A's apparent wishes, A's influence is obscured.

There is no solution to these problems. Someone interested in analyzing the Soviet Union's or China's relative influence in a country or region must simply beg the question — in the first instance, by arguing circumstantially or from inference and with a high probability of error and, in the second instance, by ignoring this dimension and, hence, distorting actual influence.

Even to get that far, however, one has to start almost from scratch in creating a framework for argument. In the case of this essay the conceptualization will be modest. Rather than trying to break new ground, it is an attempt to squeeze further use from familiar notions, to pick over others' ideas and to fashion from them some serviceable approach to a practical problem. Its methods will be at best impressionistic. So the reader is forewarned: This is half theory applied to incomplete data, and he has no chance of gaining a more elaborate or powerful theory of influence in international politics. Hopefully, however, he may be inspired to a more subtle appreciation of the Soviet and Chinese relationship with this one region of the world.

We begin with two formulations: The first is the distinction between power and influence. Since power is often defined as the ability to affect the will and mind of others, it closely resembles the definition applied a moment ago to influence. But there remains an important difference which will serve us in this essay. If influence is, as Rubinstein points out in Chapter 1, both a process and a product, a verb and a noun, an act and an outcome, then power becomes the commodity by which that process is undertaken and the product achieved. And influence becomes both the application of power and the return from the application of power.

The distinction relates, in turn, to a second, more central aspect of the argument. To get at the nature and level of Soviet or Chinese influence most meaningfully, I have focused on what might be termed the "influence setting" — that is, the relationship between the range of payoffs sought (not necessarily achieved) and the range of available resources applied. It is oblique; but I have taken as my point of departure the kinds of payoffs inspiring Soviet and Chinese policy and, from there, have worked my way back through the three variables determining the payoffs actually realized: First the resources each possesses (power, according to our first formulation); second, the talent of each in applying these resources (a special aspect of influence as a process); and third, the peculiar environmental factors through which an influence "attempt," to borrow David Singer's term, is refracted, that is, on the one hand, the peculiar character of the nation (or regime) to be influenced and, on the other, the susceptibility of that object nation (or regime) to the influence of third parties.[2] To oversimplify, I am interested in evaluating influence as a product by discussing the limitations of influence as a process. Keeping in mind a second purpose of these essays, my approach is also comparative; as much as possible, I have tried not merely to assess the point to, manner of, and rewards in either Soviet or Chinese efforts to influence Black Africa but to compare one with the other in each respect.

Payoffs

Soviet or Chinese objectives can be looked at from several perspectives: First, as positive or negative. Although of limited application in superior-inferior power relationships — as the Soviet or Chinese relationship with an African nation usually is — the classification distinguishes the application of power to induce the other nation to do or think what the Soviet Union or China desires from the application of power to prevent the other nation from imposing its will on the Soviet Union or China. On occasion — when an Nkrumah has sought to push the Soviet Union into salvaging an ailing Ghanaian economy or when a Houphouet-Boigny has attempted to control the portrayal given his country in the Soviet press by severing diplomatic relations — Soviet leaders have developed negative or preventive objectives. But far more commonly, they and their Chinese counterparts have needed to worry only about positive objectives. In the Soviet case the predominance of positive over negative objectives reflects the assertive quality of a global power's foreign policy; China's case of an even higher proportion of positive objectives, however, stems from such different factors as the narrower number of countries with which China has interacted, the tendency to deal with countries unlikely to pursue objectives directly contrary to Chinese interests, and ironically the limited resources China brings to its relations with Africa, diminishing the claims African nations can make on them.

Objectives can also be viewed according to whether they are predominantly intended to secure a gain for oneself or to deny a gain to a
third state. Because of both the Sino-Soviet conflict and the earlier
political mercantilism of the Cold War (the zero-sum game) this is a
somewhat more useful classification than the first. By its terms early
Soviet and Chinese involvement in Africa had a double purpose: On the
one hand, to displace Western influence and, on the other, to ensure
that the erstwhile socialist ally did not profit more from the West's exit.
Western influence, however, was not easily displaced and more recently
that purpose has converged: Not only are the Soviet Union and China
concerned with containing the other's influence but now also with preventing resilient Western, particularly, former colonial powers from
reestablishing their influence where revolutionary regimes have been
ousted and from enlarging their influence where nonrevolutionary regimes have lingered.

A third more rewarding way of looking at Soviet and Chinese
objectives cuts across these and several other classifications — that is,
by time frame or in terms of short- and long-range objectives. The
classification comes close to another based on minimum and maximum
objectives. In the short run (and at a minimum), Soviet leaders likely
seek to satisfy immediate needs — specifically, the need for policy
support, that is, support for their approach to the issues of the day — a
Berlin crisis, the Arab-Israeli dispute, arms control, a more open
Common Market, Chinese territorial claims against the Soviet Union;
second, the need for service facilities — an airline route, access to a
port's repair and refrigeration facilities, a radio monitoring station, or
some other such aid to intelligence gathering as the use of Guinea's
major airport to fly military reconnaissance missions over the South
Atlantic. The Chinese, having less use for port and airport facilities,
have found a substitute need, at least in the past, for camps to train
local insurgents. Third, there is presumably the need to derive as
much economic compensation as possible for Soviet largesse; Soviet
leaders can scarcely expect to realize equal economic advantage from
their trade and aid with Black Africa — particularly when the main
compensation is conceived as political — but the opportunity to obtain
Guinea's high-grade bauxite, Nigerian columbite and perhaps petroleum,
and Moroccan cobalt speaks for itself.

The kind of objective mattering most to the Soviet Union depends
on perspective and the country involved. Looked at as a group, Black
African governments have doubtlessly been chiefly valued for the support they can lend Soviet foreign policy. Individually, however, their
importance has related to the nature of the African state involved:
Regimes considered progressive have, throughout most of the period of
the Soviet involvement with this area, been most appreciated for their
political saliency, for the boost that they give to Soviet efforts to
rally these nations behind Soviet policy. Those judged less progressive
and with no particular inclination to see international problems as the

Soviet Union does have been more appreciated for the practical advantages associated with the second and third kinds of short run objectives. Because, until recently, the Chinese dealt with a more selective group of African nations — partially of choice, partially of necessity — their short run objectives have been skewed all the more in the direction of recruiting policy support. Where China did not wish to be selective in the countries with which it dealt, the objective was still basically to secure support for policy; in this case the preoccupying concern of whittling away Taiwan's international status and breaking its own isolation.

While Soviet and Chinese leaders are attending to their short-term interests, they are also pursuing longer range objectives. For example, over time they expect to see and perhaps to help with the erosion of the American and West European presence in much of Black Africa. They recently have refined these expectations — given the durability of the special relationships that the British and French, in particular, have preserved in many of their former colonies — but both leaderships remain dedicated to encouraging African nations to free themselves of neo-colonial dependence on the major capitalist powers.

Over time, they also hope to assist in a basic transformation of African political societies, promoting modernization along the lines of their respective versions of socialism. In the long run, therefore, both anticipate a fundamental change in the nature of these societies, not only to give more support to their short-term objectives, but to confirm their essential faith in the historic direction of events. Slow and hazardous as the process may be, the Soviet leadership still counts on Third World regions like Black Africa to validate the Soviet experiment. Thus, while Soviet observers have over the last decade lost any illusions of the ease and speed with which Africa will take to "scientific socialism," part of Africa's importance to them is as visible evidence of a progress that they cannot dream of witnessing in advanced capitalist centers. Since the conditions of the Chinese revolution bear an even more legitimate resemblance to those of Africa, China's potential psychological stake in Africa's socialist revolution is all the more intense.

These longer range objectives have shorter range equivalents linked to and embellishing the highly instrumental short-term objectives mentioned a moment ago. Thus, if in the long run the Soviet leaders hope to see scientific socialism realized in Black Africa, in the short run they must first worry about the most promising regimes undermining their own future with hasty, shallow, or fraudulent revolutionary programs. Just as earlier Soviet expectations for a rapid reformation of African nations' external relationships and internal structures have waned so have these apprehensions mounted. China, never having made much of an effort to come to terms ideologically with self-professed revolutionary regimes and maintaining a more rigorous sense of the ways the socialist revolution is to be made, has shown less concern over the political and economic stability of these regimes. China may have good practical reasons for regretting the overthrow of Nkrumah or Keita, but apparently the frustration of an ideological commitment is not one of them. Or so it would seem, to judge from the little effort Chinese commentators have made to analyze the failure of these regimes in contrast with their Soviet counterparts.

Similarly, if in the longer range both countries would like to close the West out of this region, in the shorter term both find it more relevant to think in terms of enhancing their own regard in African eyes. Improving their own image in Africa is preliminary to achieving anything beyond the most limited of their short-term objectives. The Soviet Union has worked at this longer, harder, and with a wider circle of African countries than the Chinese; but, since the conclusion of the Cultural Revolution, China, too, has begun to concentrate on creating the basis for acceptance and, as much as possible, sympathy among a variety of African regimes.

According to a classic attribution in Power and Society, Kaplan and Lasswell identified the three primary qualities of influence as scope, domain, and weight.[3] The weight of influence, they said, is the "degree to which policies are affected"; domain, "the persons whose policies are affected"; and scope, "the values implicated in the policies." The same qualities apply to the objectives of influence, serving particularly well to summarize the differences in the "payoffs" sought by the Soviet Union and China in Black Africa. Thus, the character of Soviet objectives is broader than those of the Chinese both in scope (Soviet objectives have traditionally been more differentiated) and in domain (they have also been pursued among a more diverse set of states). The Soviet Union has sought a full range of short-term instrumental objectives — the Chinese, far less so; and while both have been motivated by what Arnold Wolfers called "milieu goals," that is the desire to alter or control political environment, the Soviet pursuit of milieu goals has been accompanied by a more complicated set of intermediate objectives inspired by the practical problems of economic and political modernization in sub-Saharan Africa. So, too, has the Soviet Union been more deeply involved with a larger number of African states reflecting a far broader spectrum of external and internal policies. Not only has the Soviet Union dealt with a majority of Black African nations — and, until recently, the Chinese, with a minority — but its relationship with the few nonrevolutionary governments with whom both have had contact, such as Mauritania, Dahomey, the Central African Republic, and Senegal, has been significantly more elaborate. Since the conclusion of the Cultural Revolution and, particularly, since the opening of American policy toward China, that situation is rapidly changing.* Normalizing relations with much of Africa,

---

*I am grateful to my colleague Donald Klein for the information

however, simply puts China where the Soviet Union was a decade ago when it gradually began to create "businesslike" ties, as the Soviet phrase went, with a host of moderate regimes. As the Soviet Union then and since, China will be taxed to match more complicated and diffuse objectives with an appropriately refined and varied capacity to apply influence.

Resources

Not surprisingly the resources and instruments of influence brought to the task by the Soviet Union generally exceed those of the Chinese in both depth and variety. It is not merely that between 1954 and 1970 the Soviet Union gave twice as much economic aid to a third again as many Black African states, and that the actual draw-down rate on Soviet credits (about 45 percent) surpasses the Chinese figure to an unknown but presumably substantial extent;* that, as late as 1970, Soviet trade with Black Africa was still twice that of China; that from 1955 to 1971 it gave more than $50 million in military assistance to seven Black African governments while China gave a far smaller — though undisclosed — sum to two African governments. Or that the Soviet Union has trained more than 14,000 Africans in its universities and institutes since 1956 and China, a few hundred at the most, and none of these since the opening of the Cultural Revolution.[4] Totals like these tell only a part of the story. Over the years, in aid and trade, in educational and cultural exchange, Soviet involvement with Black Africa has been noticeably larger than the Chinese. Presumably this reflects either a greater reservoir from which the Soviet Union can draw in developing these resources or a greater opportunity to apply them, or both. But it does not mean that in several of these areas China cannot compete effectively with the Soviet Union. The $402 million committed to the Tan-Zam railroad — a sum nearly four-fifths of all the aid the

—————————

that of the 29 governments (including Guinea Bissau) with which the Chinese now have relations, relations with 18 of them have been established since 1970, and the bulk of these in 1971 and 1972.

*The figures for Soviet aid from 1954 through 1969 are $553 million; for the Chinese, $224 million. In 1970 the Chinese obliterated that difference with the $402 million in credits promised Tanzania and Zambia for the Tan-Zam railroad, the largest commitment to a single development project in the history of Communist aid giving. Because this single agreement accounts for nearly two-thirds of the aid that China has given Africa over the last decade and a half and because it is so recent and so concentrated, I lopped 1970 off from my reference period for both countries. (Source: T. R. Buchanan, "Research Study," RECS-15, Bureau of Intelligence and Research, Department of State, September 22, 1971), p. 2.

Soviet Union has extended Black Africa in the last 14 years and ten times larger than any project it has considered — disproves that. So does the fact that the Soviet Union's larger trade with Africa results only because it is willing to outbuy the Chinese — because indeed, the Chinese outsell the Soviet Union in Black Africa (in 1971, by $188 million in exports to $167 million).

Nor does it mean that in still other areas, such as technical assistance and radio broadcasting, the Chinese do not fully match the Soviet effort. Since China began extending technical assistance to Black Africa in the late fifties it has kept roughly the same number of technicians, teachers, medical personnel, and laborers in the field as the Soviet Union. With the start of the Tan-Zam railroad project, Chinese numbers have in fact surged past those of the Soviet Union. According to an official American estimate, China's 6,960 economic technicians in Africa in 1970 outnumbered their Soviet equivalents by nearly 3,000.[5] Or, as in the case of radio broadcasts to Africa, the Chinese have traditionally been on the air as long, often, and in as many languages as their Soviet counterparts.

Were the Soviet Union to turn the use of these resources into an open-ended contest, the Chinese would be at a severe disadvantage. But as long as the Soviet Union places sharp limits on the scale of their use or, with the same effect, as long as Africa's capacity to absorb these resources remains limited, the issue of how much China has will matter less than how well it is employed — the topic of the next section.

If being outdistanced in the basic resources of influence in a crude absolute sense is of marginal importance to the Chinese, then their inferiorities in other areas, particularly, in the instruments of influence seem to me more consequential. Lacking resources is one thing. That is, having less to grant in economic, military, technical, or educational assistance, or less to trade, or, at least, being less willing to buy, can be offset by the talent with which limited resources are deployed, with one exception: Over the years the Soviet Union has had one peculiar resource that China has denied itself and that has given the Soviet Union a distinct advantage with the more radical African regimes — namely, a readiness to manipulate ideology. Unlike China, the Soviet Union has compromised theory in a manner designed to legitimize the ascendance of "revolutionary democrats," as they are called, in places like Guinea, Mali, the Congo Republic (Brazzaville), Tanzania, and Ghana before March 1966, and, under Khrushchev, even to accept their pretensions of being "scientific socialists."[6] By thus giving the profoundest stamp of approval a Marxist-Leninist state can give, the Soviet Union has doubtlessly gratified its revolutionary friends in Africa.

In a sense — not necessarily a conscious sense — the Chinese have compensated for demurring here by ingratiating themselves with several regimes sponsoring armed struggle against neighboring governments. These were not national liberation groups fighting against white rule in Rhodesia, Angola, Mozambique, or South Africa — groups with whom neither China nor the Soviet Union has been notably more generous — but the Watusi guerrillas operating out of Burundi against Rwanda in late 1963 and early 1964, the rebels in the eastern part of Zaire in 1964 in whose success Congo-Brazzaville had a strong interest, and the "freedom fighters" Nkrumah trained from Niger, the Ivory Coast, and Cameroon. All the better from the Chinese perspective that in this instance it was an opportunity abdicated by the Soviet Union.

Lacking the mechanisms by which influence is brought to bear is quite another matter. That China's mechanisms of influence are more rudimentary than the Soviet Union's is clear and so is the restriction that this places on its capacity to affect the actions and attitudes of African governments, a restriction less easily circumvented by the talented use of what there is. Not merely are the conventional channels of influence more highly developed for the Soviet Union, but it profits from a richer assortment of ways for exerting influence so essential in the pursuit of differentiated objectives. Thus, while the Chinese have some of the same kinds of propaganda facilities — such as foreign news agencies, wire services, book displays, movies, and radio broadcasts — these usually have less of an impact (with the exception of the Congo Republic [Brazzaville], Tanzania, and Mali). China is simply less evident in more of Africa, including those countries with whom China has diplomatic relations, a circumstance partially explained by the Soviet Union's willingness (and ability) to go to such lengths as surreptitiously purchasing media space in order to get its message across.

Second, not only has China fewer embassies in Black Africa, but rarely do Chinese ambassadors develop the entree with African leaderships that a Rodionov has had with an Nkrumah or a Romanov with the Nigerians.* Third, while both countries utilize cultural exchange programs to enhance their image among African publics, again, the Soviet Union has formal cultural agreements with nearly twice as many countries as China and generally does a great deal more under each agreement. Particularly since 1966 the contrast has been marked between the scattered appearances of Chinese photo exhibits or song and dance groups and the fairly steady stream of trade union, youth, parliamentary, Muslim, and "friendship" delegations sent by the Soviet Union. Scarcely a month passes without the appearance of the Leningrad-Kirov ballet, a variety show, or a platoon of Soviet tourists; and, if a Soviet film festival, educational display, or new cultural center is not opening, then an African soccer team or group of municipal officials will be touring the Soviet Union.

---

* China's first ambassador to Tanzania (Tanganyika at the time, 1962), Ho Ying appears to have been something of an exception. See George T. Yu, "Peking's African Diplomacy," Problems of Communism, 21 (March-April 1972), 18.

Fourth, although technically both countries have access to radical African leaderships and revolutionary groups through the Afro-Asian Peoples Solidarity Organization and its more specialized counterparts, the Afro-Asian Journalists Association and the Afro-Asian Writers Association, these gatherings have generally been far more sympathetic to Soviet positions than those of the Chinese.* So much was this the case that by 1962 the Chinese began to assail the link of Soviet-dominated front organizations like the World Peace Council, the World Federation of Trade Unions, and the World Federation of Democratic Youth with the Afro-Asian movement.

Beyond Soviet superiority where the two depend on the same kinds of mechanisms for applying influence, the Soviet Union has also enjoyed avenues of influence virtually unavailable to the Chinese. Such was true of the opportunity to affect the political education of African elites in the higher party schools that it alone has helped to establish in Mali and Ghana and by introducing a limited number of African representatives to the CPSU's own Higher Party School. Similarly, its lines of communication with the single parties dominating the political structure in several African countries has been uniquely enhanced by the formal ties of the CPSU with them and of the Komsomol with their youth apparatuses. And, for whatever its dubious value, the Soviet Union clearly commands the loyalty, if perhaps not always the sympathy, of nearly all those ragged African groups professing a commitment to Marxism-Leninism. With the exception of several groups in Mozambique, Angola, and South Africa, a faction in Congo-Brazzaville, and a handful of disaffected members of the Parti Africain de l'Independance (Senegal) who in 1965 issued several "anti-revisionist" challenges to the parent group and then expired, most of these parties have lined up with the Soviet Union.

If there is an advantage to this circumstance, however, it is largely in the context of the Sino-Soviet conflict, not in terms of the leverage yielded the Soviet Union over African developments. Hence, in those places guided by "revolutionary democrats" — generally in North Africa, but also in Guinea, Mali, and Congo-Brazzaville — Soviet advice to their Marxist-Leninist friends is to disband and, as individuals, "to join the 'national-front' party with a view to exercising influence within its ranks."[7] In less revolutionary states, such as Nigeria and Senegal, the Soviet Union has been even less impressed with the potency of groups like the Nigerian Socialist Workers and Farmers Party or the PAI and, as a result, has provided little beyond bare subsistence.

The Soviet Union had still other channels denied the Chinese. Until China's admission to the United Nations in 1972, the Soviet

---

*The last Fifth Afro-Asian Writers Conference met in Alma Ata in September 1973. Its first meeting in 1958 was in Tashkent. It has never met in China.

Union lobbied among African members with little other than the impediment of Albanian censure and, in Africa itself, Soviet representatives have commonly succeeded in establishing more elaborate workaday relationships with ministers and middle-level administrators than their Chinese counterparts, again, with the partial exception of Tanzania and Congo-Brazzaville.

Several preliminary points are suggested by this inventory of comparative advantage in the resources and mechanisms of influence. First is the obvious theme of Soviet advantage all along the line. The Soviet Union has more of almost everything and in greater variety. In effect, this is simply saying that the Soviet Union has had more of an opportunity or chose to exploit more the opportunity to extend economic aid or to trade or to give ideological guidance. As a practical consequence, the Soviet Union appears to possess greater aggregate influence or, at least, potential for influence in Africa; that is, in Black Africa taken as a whole, the Soviet Union appears to be more predominant, and, indeed, its presence is more widely established. But in any particular instance this contrast may be meaningless. China has more than matched the Soviet "presence" (or, potential for influence) in Mali, Tanzania and Congo-Brazzaville.

Second, the contention that Chinese inferiority in resources matters less than its disadvantage in the mechanisms of influence needs to be refined. At a fairly low level of involvement, such as has generally been true of Soviet relations with most of the so-called moderate African states, the Soviet Union's capacity to buy, to extend economic assistance, or to use other conventional resources gives these bilateral relationships their essential character. Cause and effect is not easy to determine, but China has been missing in exactly these respects. On the other hand, the kinds of mechanisms of influence in which the Soviets have the greatest advantage are useful primarily in the more revolutionary states and not much beyond. This is particularly the case with things like ties between the CPSU and Africa's "revolutionary democratic" single parties, Soviet work with local higher party schools, and the contact achieved through such Soviet-dominated international front organizations as the WFTU, WPC, and WFDY.

Third, and more fundamentally, the propositions not raised by a comparison of Soviet and Chinese potentials for influence may be considerably more important. That is, the answers to two key questions are not in the comparison: (1) How much influence does either of them actually wield, or, what benefit if any does the Soviet Union enjoy from its relatively greater potential for influence? and (2) How does either's actual influence stack up against the influence of other major third parties? The answer to the first question, such as we can supply it, begins with an examination of the way China and the Soviet Union have utilized their resources and instruments of influence — their success in matching both to appropriate payoffs and, in this match, how much is wrung from each — the problem to which we now turn.

The answer to the even more difficult second question is saved for the last section where I have ventured several tentative conclusions on the impact of a particular environment, including the prominence of third parties, on the influence achieved by the Soviet Union or China.

Influence as a Process: Applying Resources

The second critical variable determining the level of Soviet or Chinese influence is the skill with which each employs the resources and, to a lesser extent, the instruments of influence. Skill, in this sense, is of course a difficult quality to measure. If the attempt to educate Africans at Chinese universities collapses after only a few years amidst complaints of racism, inferior instruction, and language difficulty, or, if the Soviet ambassador's efforts to give a satisfying turn to student-teacher demonstrations in Guinea in 1961 results only in his being tossed out, one does not need to know the aim of the initiative to judge it a failure, an unskillful exercise of influence.[8] The potential for influence has been destroyed literally before it could be employed. But, when an influence attempt has run its course, discovering which results owe to which initiatives and, hence, how skillful an initiative has been presents a far more difficult challenge.

When Soviet or Chinese uses of power (or techniques of influence) are considered, one is immediately struck by the relatively small portion of the spectrum represented. Of the four traditional uses of power — persuasion, rewards, punishment, and coercion — the Soviet Union particularly and, to a lesser extent, China have largely denied themselves the latter.* Even when the Soviet Union has been sufficiently frustrated in its relations with an African nation to make retaliation a natural response, it has restrained itself. Its reactions to Nkrumah's overthrow in February 1966 and to the Ivory Coast's decision to break relations in May 1969 illustrate the point well. When the Ghanian military and police chased Nkrumah from power and Soviet experts, · advisers, and diplomats from Ghana, dismantled his "revolutionary democratic" regime, and hauled foreign policy back toward collaboration with major Western powers, the Soviet Union might have been expected to unleash a bitter propaganda campaign against the new regime, or to refuse recognition, or to help with the arming of his sympathizers, or to reject further economic cooperation and harrass the new regime over the aid obligations Nkrumah had contracted. With the exception of a critical treatment in the press, it did none of these things. Instead it yielded to a Ghanaian ultimatum to extend recognition,

---

*Techniques of influence are different from "uses of power" in this last instance. Coercion is really to remove any choice of action from the object country; and so, in terms of techniques of influence, the equivalent would have to be the threat of coercion.

doing so a day after 20 Soviets, including top embassy people, were expelled for alleged espionage activity. (China did not and was forced to close its embassy eight months later.) Despite Ghanaian suspicions, it carefully avoided giving material assistance to Nkrumah's supporters in Guinea, refusing even to repeat the former Ghanaian leader's revolutionary exhortations to the people of Ghana. And eventually it even agreed to complete a number of interrupted aid projects. Similarly, after Houphouet-Boigny severed relations — to make matters worse, on the basis of an offending Novosti press report which now appears to have been a forgery — the Soviet Union went out of its way to contain the damage done.

China has been willing to make fewer concessions to temperance when things have gone badly in Ghana, Burundi, or the Central African Republic; but its reaction scarcely adds up to an attempt to inflict punishment. When China has resorted to techniques resembling those of punishment — such as the patronage of insurgents — this seems to be less a measure directed against Rwanda, Niger, or the Ivory Coast than a means of rewarding the leadership of Burundi or Ghana. To the extent that it represents more than the use of power to reward, it is likely a genuine commitment to revolutionary change — not an attempt to influence the government of the target state.

Two things are involved: First, both countries fancy their relations with Third World countries as fundamentally cooperative. Thus, punishment and coercion appear to be inappropriate resources even with the most unreceptive among them. For either to begin throwing its weight around would complicate the celebration each makes of the natural alliance between socialism and these former, sometimes continuing victims of colonialism. Second, and more to the point, each may have felt that in any of the specific instances the use of power to punish or to coerce or to threaten one or the other would have been useless. In short, each may have recognized that it was not able to threaten a level of punishment adequate to influence an African regime's behavior. Coercion or the threat of coercion — even if any action of any African regime could matter enough to prompt its consideration — raises the further problem of drawing in third parties and provoking great power confrontations.

The notion that neither of these two countries is in a position to punish (or to coerce), however, goes to the heart of the question of influence. It is arguable that without the capacity to punish severely, the influence of one nation over the other will remain marginal and confined to the realization of marginal objectives. What de Gaulle threatened and then did to Toure's Guinea after the 1958 referendum, what the West did to Lumumba's government in 1960, or what the British could have done to Nkrumah's government had they chosen to after 1963, amounts to a magnitude of leverage neither the Soviet Union nor China has ever achieved over any Black African country. At that, applied too ambitiously, even this level of influence will fail,* but the mere possibility of so sharp an escalation heightens the effect of influence at every other level.

Perhaps China is, for the first time, moving toward this level of influence by providing Zambia the lifeline it requires; but this is a single country and the Tan-Zam railroad is a great yet single item of leverage whose duration is not likely to last longer than the time it takes to complete the project. Interestingly, the Soviet Union has declined the one opportunity it had to put itself in a position to achieve comparable influence. When, in 1965, a relatively desperate Nkrumah turned to the Soviet Union for the substantial economic relief refused by the IMF, the United States, Great Britain, and the Federal Republic of Germany, Soviet leaders were anything but eager to accommodate him. True, they may have doubted their chances of making sufficient inroads to challenge the residual Anglo-American presence, even if they were to extend large scale economic support. But more likely they simply saw the returns to such influence as vastly inferior to the burdens of sustaining it.

Without these alternative uses of power, the Soviet and Chinese ability to influence Black African regimes has remained marginal. The more far-reaching the payoffs sought, the more evident this has been. Thus, the issue of Soviet and Chinese skill in employing the resources and mechanisms of influence must be resolved at two levels: Not only in the narrower and more literal sense of excellent execution but in the broader and, I think, more essential sense of adapting ends to marginal means. For example, the Chinese have been unquestionably more adept in extending economic assistance. The terms of Chinese loans have been more attractive, the goods employed, of higher quality and more appropriate to the conditions of underdeveloped societies, and the conduct of aid personnel (the requirement that they have the same standard of living as their African counterparts), more appealing. As a result Chinese aid projects have been well received in the few countries where they have been undertaken. Those of the Soviet Union have not always been.

But this is only one side of the problem. The other more important consideration is whether the aid that either gave helped in the pursuit of particular objectives. Since there may be more than one reason for giving aid, the question is, for how many objectives was aid the appropriate means of influence? Giving aid to promote economic ties, either for their intrinsic merit or as a further source of leverage, is one matter. Giving aid (for state farms or higher party schools) to speed a

---

*And de Gaulle failed only partially. Toure was not deterred from organizing a "no" vote in the 1958 referendum, but out of this episode de Gaulle's influence over the remainder of Afrique occidentale francaise increased.

country's socialist transformation is quite another. In between aid as "rent" for Aeroflot landing rights or on port facilities is equally different from aid to buy policy support. The real issue of skill is the number of objectives that are well matched to means and the importance of the mismatches.

In this comparison, it seems to me that the Soviet Union comes off more poorly than China. Until recently, it had a somewhat greater tendency than China to overestimate the utility of this or that resource or instrument of influence in promoting its objectives. In part, this has been a natural byproduct of the most excessive of Soviet expectations. The fairly constant Soviet fascination with effecting profound changes in milieu under the leadership of Africa's bourgeois nationalists has sometimes stimulated inflated notions of how much the Soviet Union could help in the process.

Both the Soviets and the Chinese have wanted to see Western influence in Black Africa weakened (along with each other's) and the socialist revolution promoted. But the Chinese have been more wary than the Soviets of confusing the wish with reality. They, to say the least, were skeptical about the concept of national democracy, the 1960 theoretical invention by which the Soviet Union sought to rationalize its relations with the most progressive among African regimes and, at the same time, move them to a still greater defiance of the Western powers.[9] Thus, Soviet theorists insisted that a national democratic state struggles against imperialism, strengthens its independence by abstaining from military blocs and by denying military bases to imperialist powers, minimizes Western economic influence, and reinforces the state sector of the economy. The Chinese were scarcely more enthusiastic about Khrushchev's later and even more remarkable ideological manipulation — the notion of "revolutionary democracy" which credited the most advanced among African states with actually having begun the transition to socialism.[10] By one, Soviet leaders hoped to encourage the further displacement of Western power from Africa; by the other, Africa's rapid progress toward socialism.

In both cases the Chinese thought the premise was faulty and, therefore, saved themselves from misunderstanding the effectiveness of other resources and instruments of influence. For surely one of the major reasons that the Soviet Union granted its economic aid so casually in the beginning related to the exuberance of its expectations. The way the Soviet Union gave its aid had some of the flavor of the manner in which corporation executives gift their most valued customers, not so much as an essential part of the business they do, but as a symbol of their confidence and pleasure in the relationship. It was no accident, therefore, that when Khrushchev's successors confessed the foolishness of those hortatory formulas predicating a fundamental socialist transformation in Africa's most advanced states, they also rejected his offhanded approach to economic assistance. The debate over "our primary internationalist duty" that unfolded during Khrushchev's last year and then, with his removal, that went to those who had contended that the best way for the Soviet Union to fulfill its "internationalist duty" was first to build its own strength paralleled the controversy evidently stirred by the pretension that countries like Ghana, Mali, and Algeria were "building socialism," not under the guidance of Communist parties but their equivalents, the Convention People's Party, Union Soudanaise, and the National Liberation Front, respectively.[11]

Two things have happened to the Soviet Union's maximum objectives, both partially inspired by the inappropriateness of the resources and mechanisms of influence on which Soviet leaders had relied: In the first place, the explicit prospects of rapid progress toward socialism are no longer terribly enticing. Soviet policymakers, as a result, judge the Soviet stake in an African society far more on the basis of that state's intrinsic importance than on the basis of that state's potential for socialism. (Compare the Soviet Union's interest in strengthening its presence in Nigeria with its conspicuous lack of interest in the Congo-Brazzaville leader Marien Ngouabi's latest professions of commitment to Marxism-Leninism.) Second, the earlier vision of "rolling back" the West in Black Africa has gradually given way to seizing particular opportunities for what they may add to the Soviet presence in Africa's most important nations. The West's historic defeat in Africa is less the inspiration — because no longer is it perceived as within easy reach — than is the conventional desire to be where power is or will be.

In the case of the Soviet Union's shorter-term versions of its maximum objectives, the influence that it has tried to employ has been more inadequate than inappropriate. Before Soviet leaders could dream of a socialist future for Africa, they have had to ensure that the impetuous program of Africa's revolutionary democrats or their failure to match word with deed would not sabotage the whole enterprise. Their recourse demonstrates how little influence they in fact possess. In Nkrumah's Ghana, where the issue was the most acute and the Soviet presence the most extensive, they were almost completely stymied. Nkrumah simply ignored the counsel of the Soviet adviser assigned to his secretariat as well as of the team of Soviet experts sent in 1965 to survey the ailing Ghanaian economy.[12] There was nothing more the Soviet Union could do to avert the disaster. When they began their public analysis of the shortcomings of the revolutionary democrats, they were resorting to an even weaker form of influence. This kind of instruction bore little relevance to the situation in Keita's Mali and could have little effect in Guinea where the leadership had already shown itself to be a notoriously poor pupil.

Here, however, it is less a question of the Soviet Union being unskillful in its attempt to influence than being deprived of adequate resources or mechanisms for exerting influence. The Chinese have been scarcely more successful. In Ghana, Guinea, and Mali, their helplessness has exceeded that of the Soviets. In Congo-Brazzaville, where their involvement is more important, the Chinese contribution is somewhat beside the point for a regime that suffered four unsuccessful coup attempts in the first two years of its existence.

As for the preliminary aspect of the other maximum objective (enhancing one's own image as the first step toward reducing Western influence in Africa), the impression made by either China or the Soviet Union depends very little on specially devised instruments. The Ivory Coast government does not form an opinion of China by listening to Chinese radio broadcasts or watching song and dance groups; rather, as Houphouet-Boigny made plain in his September 1965 speech to the Fourth Congress of the ruling PDIC, its unfavorable judgment had much more to do with China's support for Nkrumah's "subversion camps." So, too, when Nkrumah returned much impressed from his first visit to the USSR in 1961, his enthusiasm may well have stemmed less from what he had been shown or told, than from what he wanted to believe before he ever left Ghana. It is, in short, difficult to imagine that cultural exchanges or book displays have had more than the minutest impact on the popular and official consciousness of any African state. Unless I am utterly mistaken, it matters little whose public relations effort is more tasteful or engaging.

We have now worked our way back to the first or minimum level or Soviet and Chinese concern in Black Africa, back to the question of how well either has employed its influence to secure such practical conveniences as port facilities, landing rights, and the benefits of trade and, above all, support for its foreign policy. Port facilities and the like seem to me the natural outgrowth of "business-like" relations with an African state. They neither confer nor are conferred by the resources and mechanisms of influence. They are rather the substance of normalized relations. When the Senegalese government comes to open Yoff airport to Aeroflot and to service Moscow with Air Afrique, it is not yielding to the promise of aid, a foreign minister's visit, or the fear that otherwise the Soviet Union will arm the PAI. It accepts this kind of cooperation out of the confidence built through contact over time and because it finds its own utility in the arrangement. By the same token, the Soviet Union had no resource nor mechanism of influence by which it could have compelled Guinea during the 1962 Cuban missile crisis to let Soviet aircraft use the airstrip that Soviet assistance had only a few months earlier converted for jet traffic. Perquisites like these are overwhelmingly a function of the overall character of a relationship, and with Guinea in 1962 that relationship was not auspicious. What is true for the Soviet Union is equally true for China.

In the short term, however, the critical measure of influence has always appeared to be a nation's capacity to rally support for its foreign policy. The proposition deserves challenging. Thus, while in almost every respect, the basic Soviet approach to international problems has enjoyed greater sympathy than the basic Chinese approach, there are good reasons to hesitate before concluding that Soviet influence must also be greater. In some instances Soviet influence has been clear and effective: Ambassador Georgii Rodionov used to be able to have his way with Nkrumah on specific issues: If the Soviet government was unhappy with a remark of Ghana's representative to the UN on paying debts for UN peacekeeping operations, a visit from the Ambassador to Flagstaff House would rectify matters; or he might appeal to Nkrumah to intervene with personnel at the Ministry of External Affairs who were eager to postpone an AAPSO conference wanted by the Soviet Union; or ne would persuade Nkrumah to begin assailing American plans for a multilateral nuclear force for NATO as the Soviet Union's own campaign against MLF reached a crescendo.[13] But in many respects this was a rare, indeed, bizarre circumstance and, to my knowledge, no other Soviet ambassador has achieved this level of influence in any other Black African state.

Yet even in the Ghana of Rodionov's day, the basic thrust of Nkrumah's foreign policy derived little from Soviet influence. If Ghana took a line on Berlin, American intervention in Stanleyville in 1964, or Vietnam distinctly more satisfying to the USSR than to the United States, this had much more to do with Nkrumah's general disposition than with the Soviet Union wielding some manner of influence. Without minimizing the significance of the specific initiatives Soviet representatives put him up to, I am convinced that Nkrumah would have signed essentially the same communiques in Moscow and his media would have written the same of American neocolonialism had the Soviet Union never sent a Rodionov, granted a ruble of aid, or broadcast a word to West Africa.* To the extent that any side influenced Nkrumah's basic foreign policy orientation, in a powerfully negative fashion, it was the West.

If Ghana's attitude on peaceful coexistence, the benefits of disarmament, or open polemics within Afro-Asian organizations pleased the Soviet Union more than China, again, this scarcely proved the superiority of Soviet influence. In general, Nkrumah was less inclined to view international affairs from the Chinese perspective. If any side reinforced this disinclination, it was the Chinese. As one of Scott Thompson's official Ghanaian sources reported: "Basically he feared them. He instinctively trusted Russians; he instinctively distrusted Chinese. He was, simply, scared that the Chinese did not have his own best interests at heart, and I had clear instructions to watch their movements closely."[14]

The same basic argument can be made, I think, wherever Soviet policy interests have fared well. True, in Congo-Brazzaville, Mali, and Tanzania, where the Chinese are the most active, the Soviet position is less favored, but cause and effect may not be what it seems; on the contrary, the Chinese quite conceivably have been able

---

*This, of course, begs the question of the negative consequences of a Soviet failure to do these things.

to become more active precisely because they were more warmly regarded by these leaderships. (This is not to deny that the two are interdependent for clearly well-timed Chinese help has fostered sympathy.)

There is one piece of evidence suggesting that Soviet leaders would agree with this analysis: To the extent that they once regarded their aid program a suitable means of promoting congenial African foreign policies, the tighter and increasingly conventional economic criteria now applied to aid imply that the consideration no longer holds. That seems an even fairer conclusion to draw from the Soviet readiness to spend money in countries like Nigeria sooner than where foreign policy comes closer to their preferences.

The Impact of Environment

Thus, in Black Africa, a comparison of Soviet with Chinese influence leads only to paradoxes: The Soviet Union possesses greater resources and mechanisms of influence but not necessarily greater influence — not where the two compete, at least. China has outperformed the Soviet Union in applying its influence, at least in the basic sense of matching means to ends; yet, where the short-term payoffs count the most, the Soviet Union has been more blessed. And, where the Soviet Union has most succeeded, it owes its success less to its own influence than to the (negative) influence of others.

When the comparison shifts to Soviet or Chinese influence and Western influence, however, there are no paradoxes. The essential disadvantage of China and the Soviet Union is perfectly straightforward. For most of the postindependence period the influence of both has been as vulnerable as the revolutionary regimes on which it has depended. When a Lumumba, Odinga, or Nkrumah fell, whatever potential for influence that China or the Soviet Union had fashioned also disintegrated.

The frustrations of tying their positions to the fortunes of an individual leader doubtlessly has prompted them to seek a broader and more permanent footing in countries where a few years ago they would have concentrated on immediate gains. In watching their unruffled reaction to Keita's overthrow in 1968 and, even more, their efforts to keep a safe distance from Ngouabi, both seem to be trying to free the process of "influence-building" from the vicissitudes of local politics.

This, however, is an enormous challenge. For nothing has been clearer than that the success and the inferiority of Soviet influence (in the nonspecific sense of presence) are bound up with the careers of revolutionary democrats. As far as the Soviet Union or China has gotten in Mali, Ghana, or Congo-Brazzaville that far the revolutionary democrats have carried it; where the growth of its "influence" has stopped, there the will or capacity of the revolutionary democrats to carry it further has stopped. There was something extraordinarily superficial about Soviet influence in Ghana even while Nkrumah ruled. Despite the number of Soviet technicians spread from the Tema seaport to the

Tamale airfield, the radical message of the media, the swath cut by the Soviet ambassador, the activity of the Winneba Ideological Institute, the idea that Nkrumah depended on Soviet personnel for his own personal security, and all the other signs of apparent preeminence, the profoundest sources of influence remained with the old colonial master.

It was not merely that $150 million in British investments and a third of Ghanaian trade had their own imperatives, notwithstanding the image Nkrumah was determined to give Ghana in international affairs. There was the whole weight of historical association, cultural imprint, education, and professional style that intervened. If Ghanaians are something other than Ghanaians, they are British — as Malians are French, or the Congolese, Belgians. It was not the kind of advantage that could always be easily converted to specific leverage to induce a particular action. (In this sense it would fail our original definition of influence.) But its effect was in many ways more devastating. The capacity to induce an act or a thought becomes somewhat extraneous if someone is predisposed to do essentially what you would like him to do. And the vast portion of the Ghanaian civil service, foreign office, and business community were predisposed to defend moderate internal and external policies. Nkrumah's ruling party, someone said, "remained a ship floating on the surface of society."[15] Soviet influence in Ghana traveled on that ship.

Ultimately, however, it is the revolutionary democrats themselves who sanction the continued prominence of the former metropole. Barring a basic rupture in relations, as between Guinea and France in 1958 or between Tanzania and Great Britain in 1965, even the most radical regimes move slowly to reduce their dependence on London or Paris for aid, monetary support, trade, and technical assistance.

Elsewhere that dependence becomes overwhelming. As Waldemar Nielsen writes, "private interests from the metropole came to dominate banking and every aspect of the modernized sector in commerce, manufacturing, and agriculture. Since independence their position in most of the Francophone states has been only slightly prejudiced," and he could have said much the same for English-speaking Black Africa.[16] Trade, technical assistance, the education of elites, military hardware, and even sometimes defense — for all these things the majority of Black African regimes rely heavily on the former colonial power. The difference between a French conseiller technique sitting in his office in the Senegalese Ministry of Interior and a group of Soviet experts planning a Senegalese tuna-processing complex is fundamental; so is the relationship that Senghor had with Pompidou fundamentally different from his relationship with Brezhnev; and so is the constant French interaction with Senegalese elites fundamentally different from the limited, formal contacts Soviet embassy people have with a small number of Senegalese officials. This is not to say that the Soviet Union (or China) is more disadvantaged than other outsiders, for example, the United States; but in the competition with the French it is incomparably inferior.

What all of this adds up to is problematic. Identifying the mechanisms and resources of Soviet and Chinese influence in Black Africa poses no particular problem. Nor does it require much ingenuity to get some sense of each side's relative strength in these general categories. How these mechanisms and resources are applied and with what success are another matter. I have been arguing that without the enormous residual "influence" enjoyed by France and Great Britain in many of their former colonies or without the capacity to punish severely, Soviet and Chinese influence must remain marginal. This, however, represents no more than a hypothesis. If it is correct, then attempts to use any of the resources or mechanisms of influence to affect basic foreign policy orientations, domestic political transformations, or the status of third parties only promise failure. In the past, Soviet leaders appear to have understood this fact somewhat less well than the Chinese — but, perhaps, only because the temptation to misunderstand has been greater.

This still leaves room for important accomplishments within the margin in which influence can be brought to bear. A promise of minimum aid evidently swayed the Central African Republic to switch its recognition from Taiwan to the People's Republic of China in 1964.[17] The goodwill banked in Nigeria because of Soviet willingness to supply aircraft in the early stages of the war against Biafra will presumably have its payoffs. And the specific adjustments of Ghanaian behavior that Rodionov was able to arrange certainly served Soviet interests. But accomplishments like these are better achieved through the frugal and discriminating use of the resources and mechanisms of influence. Judging from their present approach to Black Africa, the Soviet Union and China have come to recognize this.

Notes

1. Interesting efforts by J. David Singer, "Inter-Nation Influence: A Formal Model, " American Political Science Review, 57 (June 1963), 420-30, and James G. March, "An Introduction to the Theory and Measurement of Influence, " American Political Science Review, 49 (June 1955), 431-51, open the topic but presumably these authors would not pretend that their work offers an adequate design for evaluating national influence.

2. Ibid., p. 422.

3. Harold D. Lasswell and Abraham Kaplan, Power and Society (New Haven: Yale University Press, 1950), p. 73.

4. Bruce D. Larkin maintains that China's academic program was closed out soon after 1962 following only a two-year trial. (See his China and Africa, 1949-1970 [Berkeley: University of California Press, 1971], pp. 142-43.) "Research Memorandum, " RSB-80, Bureau of Intelligence and Research, Department of State, July 21, 1967, p. 8, suggests that there were 280 African students in China as late as 1966.

5. Buchanan, "Research Study, " p. 10.

6. For this episode, see Uri Ra'anan, "Moscow and the 'Third World, '" Problems of Communism, 14 (January-February 1965), pp. 22-31.

7. Colin Legum, "Africa's Contending Revolutionaries, " Problems of Communism, 21 (March-April, 1972), 8.

8. Larkin, China and Africa, p. 142, citing John Emmanuel Hevi, An African Student in China (New York: Praeger Publishers, 1963).

9. See William T. Shinn, Jr., "The 'National Democratic State, '" World Politics, 15 (April 1963), 383.

10. For evidence of Chinese criticism see V. Solodovnikov, "Afro-Aziatskaya solidarnost protiv kolonializma i neokolonializma" (Afro-Asian Solidarity Against Colonialism and Neocolonialism), Aziya i Afrika segodnya, no. 5 (1965), p. 27.

11. For details see my study, Soviet Policy in West Africa (Cambridge: Harvard University Press, 1970), pp. 230-34.

12. W. Scott Thompson, Ghana's Foreign Policy, 1957-1966 (Princeton: Princeton University Press, 1969), p. 401.

13. See ibid., p. 295; and Legvold, Soviet Policy in West Africa, p. 247.

14. Ibid., p. 297.

15. Lutfi El Kholi, "The Current Phase of the Anti-Imperialist Struggle, " World Marxist Review, vol. 10, no. 1 (January 1967), 4-5.

16. Waldemar A. Nielsen, The Great Powers and Africa (New York: Praeger Publishers, 1969), p. 103.

17. Larkin, China and Africa, pp. 129-30.

8

SOVIET INFLUENCE ON THE
INTERNAL POLITICS OF CUBA
Andres Suarez

Between 1966 and 1968 many friends of the Cuban Revolution
rekindled their admiration for Castro: like he had done before against
Yankee imperialism, fearless Fidel was now revolting against Soviet
revisionism, as he once more upheld the independence of his country
and his revolution. However, since 1968 a new switch in Soviet-Cuban
relations has almost extinguished such enthusiasm. Starting in 1970
Fidel Castro increasingly became one of the most orthodox followers of
the Soviet model and, if we are to believe his speech during Brezhnev's
visit in early 1974, one of the foremost devotees of the General Secretary of the Communist Party of the Soviet Union.[1]

The radical shift in Soviet-Cuban relations reflected in those
opposite reactions seems to offer an excellent case study for those
interested in the analysis of influence relationships. The personal
actors involved in the relationship have not changed; geographical
distance remains the same; the disparity in resources between the two
national units is as conspicuous today as it was in 1966-68; and the
American threat instead of increasing has been fading out. Why then
did Soviet influence in Cuba decrease markedly from 1966 to 1968?
And why has it been constantly growing since 1970, reaching the high
levels apparent in the spring of 1974?

The present essay seeks to explore some of the factors impinging
upon these ups and downs in the exercise of Soviet influence. First,
in search of relevant hypotheses, it looks to some of the literature
available. Next, it will test the validity of these hypotheses in the
context of the Cuban situation between 1966 and 1973. Finally, particular attention will be devoted to domestic factions, since the
linkages between Soviet influence and Cuban factions are assumed to
have both explanatory and predictive utility for understanding the
Soviet-Cuban influence relationship.

Some Hypotheses

A noticeable weakness in the study of influence relationships is the lack of general hypotheses which can outlast testing in different contexts. One recent article by Howard A. Wriggins can serve as an illustration. The author hypothesizes that "a weak regime has little difficulty exerting leverage in bargaining over aid levels [if the regime] that is heavily dependent upon foreign assistance is located near the prospective donor's principal opponent."[2] Clearly the triangular relationship, Cuba-USSR-United States, falsifies that hypothesis. Under the pressure of domestic factors, our Cuban foreign policy, boycott, has acted as an intervening variable denying Castro not only the potential advantage postulated by Wriggins, but probably having detrimental effects upon Cuban leverage to negotiate with the Soviets. Obviously the present state of research recommends, as Professor Rubinstein has suggested in the Introduction to this book, to concentrate in the elaboration of "working models," preferentially oriented to the explanation of the case under study, instead of attempting universal generalizations.

Several analysts have recommended the introduction of the concept of costs in the study of power: "Such a concept could be useful to students of international politics in describing situations in which A cannot get B to do X but can make B pay a high price for refusing to do X."[3] It seems to me that such recommendation is also pertinent for the study of the concept of influence. It helps to stress one aspect that is not always perceived in the asymmetry that is essential to the definition of the relationship, that is, the inequality of resources. From 1966 to 1968 Castro openly rejected some of the "preference patterns" most dear to the Soviets. As will be seen later there are no indications that the Soviets seriously tried to prevent this behavior. Probably they were waiting for the Cuban leader to exhaust his resources. In effect the costs began to be unbearable in 1969, and the following year Castro was again more receptive to Soviet advice.

There is a trend to look at international politics in terms of a simple dichotomy between success and failure, when it would be more realistic "to think in terms of degree of success."[4] The New Left overlooked this aspect twice: first when they praised Castro for his rebelliousness, and now, when they criticize him for consenting to Soviet demands. Any analysis too specific and segmented of the relationship of influence can lead us to repeat the same mistake: to neglect that in the long run the inequality of resources increases the donor's probabilities to prevail upon the recipient. Expressions such as "Cuban dependence on the USSR seemed to have reached a point of no return in 1972,"[5] must be taken with serious reservations for the impression of conclusiveness that such a statement suggests. Not only in the long run, but most of the time, inequality of resources will place the recipient in a very disadvantageous position. Hence, he will have to invest his own resources very carefully. When ideological elements are involved in the relationship of influence, it would be wise for the recipient to emphasize the ideological component in his process of bargaining with the donor. This is the kind of resource that is less expensive, and which can be manipulated almost indefinitely.

Recently Peter Bachrach and Morton Baratz have identified two types of transactional behavior very similar to the one studied here. They have called them manipulative relationship and relationship of authority. The first one seems to me too broad and too frequent to be of any use. But the relationship of authority offers attractive possibilities for the explanation, at least, of one important aspect of Soviet-Cuban interactions. According to Bachrach and Baratz a relationship of authority is present when B complies not because he makes a choice of some lesser evil for the reason that he must, but rather "because he recognizes that the command is reasonable in terms of his own values. . . ."[6] One of the peculiarities of the Cuban situation is the existence of one political faction originated by the former affiliation of its members to the Socialist Popular Party (PSP), the legal name of Cuban Communists up to 1961. Regarding Cuban-Soviet relations this faction behaves in a way that strongly suggests it can be explained using the concept elaborated by Bachrach and Baratz. As will be seen later, despite the revolutionary process, the dissolution of the PSP, and the emergence of polycentrism in the international communist movement, the experience as militants for several decades in a Communist Party has internalized in the members of this faction a sense of loyalty to the decisions taken by the Soviet leaders that, it must be assumed, they find those decisions reasonable in terms of their own values.

The relationship of authority suggests other lines of speculation. For instance, once firmly established, a relationship of authority must be perceived by the donor as more stable and less costly than a relationship of influence. Of course, when authority is legitimized by one equalitarian ideology there will be serious tensions during the process of constituting the relationship. But once institutionalized, it seems reasonable to attribute to those in positions of authority a strong interest in submitting the greater number of international transactions to this less costly method of domination. It seems further that at variance with manipulative and influence relationships, the exercise of authority requires the presence of actors with the same values at both extremes of the interaction. Regarding the Cuban case, this will help to explain why the Soviet leaders are strongly interested in having members of the PSP faction participating in the decision-making process: they, and not others, are those who presumably have internalized the values legitimizing Soviet authority.

Finally, the ideology legitimizing Soviet authority is at variance with the present structure of international relations, based on national states. Therefore the recipient will always have some residual potentialities to nullify the donor's pretensions to get spontaneous compliance. Internal control, reinforcement of domestic unity, and nationalism are some of the most obvious means available to the recipient for achieving that purpose.

Michael Crozier calls descriptive hypotheses, those "which permit only an understanding, and in part a measurement, of the diverse systems of relations constituting the phenomenon under analysis in the particular case studied. "[7] The previous discussions suggest the formulation of the following "descriptive hypotheses":

1. In any influential relationship, disparities of resources will play a decisive role in the long run.

2. Relationships of authority are more stable and less costly for the donor than relationships of influence. Therefore, once that kind of relationship has been institutionalized, the "head" will tend to control the decision-making process of the "member" unit through domestic actors who have internalized such relationships.

3. The capabilities of the recipient's elite to maintain internal unity and control will increase the costs to the donor.

4. Once ideological affinity has been accepted by the donor, ideological manipulations will be preferentially used by the recipient in his bargaining process with the former.

5. An actor located near the prospective donor's principal opponent will be in a better position to increase the costs to its donor.

6. Distance and strategical considerations improve the potentialities of the recipient to increase the costs to the donor.

7. The less alternatives the recipient perceives, the more he is disposed to accommodate the donor's preferences.

8. The higher the costs the recipient can impose on the donor, the more cautious will the latter be to use its influence upon the former.

Cuban Factions

It is our contention that the study of Soviet influence in Cuba requires a close look at that element of communist politics known as factionalism. Growing dissatisfaction with the totalitarian model as a tool to explain Soviet developments since Stalin's death has brought about new analytical efforts, among which the so-called interest group model unquestionably underlines the Western aspects of the communist systems. Nevertheless, even the proponents of this model recognize that "at the top of the pyramid of power are the leadership groups or factions, which play a central and decisive role in policy-making. "[8] More recently William A. Odom has expressed some skepticism regarding the relevance of such factions, called by him cliques. "They cannot formalize themselves and thereby institutionalize the pursuit of an interest. " Further, "they probably do not extend beyond small face-to-face groups, " and their persistence capability is doubtful, since "they cannot openly pronounce their views and recruit new and younger members."9 It can be argued that these characteristics of factions do not prevent them from being significant for the study of communist politics, although they certainly impose upon the researcher a heavy burden. But we are not interested now in discussing communist politics in general. We argue that in the Cuban case there are at least three reasons why the fluidity and fugacity of factions are not so acute as in the model studied by Odom. First, Cuban factions are intimately related to Soviet influence. At least one faction had enjoyed a kind of external protection which is missing in the original model. Second, revolutionary struggle, the most propitious period for the flowering of factionalism, is yet fresh in the minds of the principal actors. Thirdly, factions are deeply rooted in that stage of the Cuban Revolution.

The present regime emerged in 1959 after the collapse of the Armed Forces, followed in a short period of time by all the other political and social structures. This is not the opportunity to elaborate on the previous weaknesses of these structures revealed by such an easy breakdown of a whole society. In retrospect it is possible to see that this sudden return to something like natural society, at the beginning more Rousseauian than Hobbesian, was the decisive factor for the transformation of the only victorious military leader in Cuban history into the head of a government where his will was the only visible center left for the future organization of the state.

Obviously the previous characterization simplifies, and therefore distorts, a very complex process which lasted from a few months to more than two years according to the criteria of each analyst.10 It especially neglects the polemics, rivalries, tensions, conspiracies, denunciations, persecutions, dismissals and new appointments through which the leader emerged in total control. It was from this turmoil that a significant cleavage began to appear between the two political forces allowed by the leader: the 26th of July Movement ("26th") and the PSP. The first one was the expression of a new generation called to political action by the coup of March 10, 1952. The "26th" was always weak in terms of organization, human resources and political sophistication. But its heroism in the struggle as well as fervid nationalism, and the fact that the victorious military leader was the founder of the movement, firmly established the "26th" as the embodiment of the hopes of the Cuban masses. On the other side the PSP was a typical Latin American Communist party, always stressing Marxism-Leninism and loyalty to the Soviet Union, lacking strong ties with the masses and poor in revolutionary elan. The PSP was under the leadership of veterans from the frustrated 1933 revolution, some of them participants in the first Batista government, and without any distinguished performance during the struggle from 1952 to 1958. As can be seen, the differences in ideology, generation, political experience and grass-roots basis between these two political forces were too deep for achieving any real fusion when the leader decided in 1962 to start the formalization of a one-party regime.

Such differences were intensified by the Soviet presence. As the head of the Socialist Commonwealth, the Soviets were vitally interested in the organization of a Cuban Communist Party (PCC). Because they were investing considerable prestige and resources in Cuba, they naturally wanted men known by them for a long time and who could be trusted at the highest levels of the decision-making process. Only the veterans of the PSP had both qualifications. But these Soviet preferences could not be shared by the leader, who would suffer a corresponding reduction of his powers; neither by the "26th," increasingly worried by this unexpected support of its rivals; nor by the masses which according to the present statements of revolutionary leaders[11] during these first years were not yet socialist, or even antiimperialist.

There were two outcomes from the initial confrontation which probably lasted from the Bay of Pigs' success to the unstable compromise disclosed by the founding of the Revolutionary Integrated Organizations (ORI) in February 1962.* On the one hand, the foreign image of the PSP as well as the cleavage between both factions was reinforced. On the other hand, although formally the powers of the leader were somewhat limited, Castro cleverly maneuvered to keep intact his capabilities to mobilize the masses against the "foreigners," which he certainly did a few days later, when Anibal Escalante was purged and exiled without a word of regret either by the Soviet Union or the PSP. The cleavage, officially admitted on March 26, 1962, has been again publicized on two other occasions: the trial against Marcos Rodriguez, March 1964 in which a top leader of the PSP, Joaquin Ordoqui, was a defendant, and the trial against the so-called "mini-fraction," January 1968. Since this latter date, open recognition of the conflict has been muffled. But this does not mean that factions have disappeared. For example, in 1973, nine years after Rodriguez' trial, and although "no evidence of definite juridical value" had turned up against Ordoqui, the Political Bureau resolved to change its former decision, definitively suspending the ex-PSP leader from all his positions in the Party and the Government, including his party membership. It seems then that factions are alive and well in Cuba.[12] Consequently we must know how to identify them, and their principal characteristics.

First, the use of labels such as "26th" and PSP does not imply that knowing the political origins of an actor is enough to identify him as a member of a faction. Things are not so simple. For example, Carlos Rafael Rodriguez, after being pro-Fidelist within the PSP for a long time, seems to have replaced the ex-secretary general of that party, Blas Roca, as the leader of the PSP faction, at least in Soviet

---

*A third organization, the Revolutionary Directorate, was also included in the intended fusion. The leaders of the R. D. will be neglected in this paper because they have not played an independent role in the later process.

eyes. Former political membership in the "26th" or the PSP gives us the initial clue for the ascription of the actor, but the real composition of the factions can only be ascertained by looking at the position taken by the actors on the important issues faced by the revolution, their abstention on such issues, the frequency in which they appear with the most conspicuous representatives of each faction, and so forth. This is indeed a tedious job, but rewarding since it corroborates both the permanence of the cleavage and the continuity of the factions.

Second, although the members of the factions are perceived by themselves as such, there will not be factions without these perceptions; and though factions are identified by those involved in the politics of the revolution, there is no indication that they possess the most rudimentary organization or even that members hold meetings to adopt common strategies. Militancy in terms of decades under the banners of the PSP has taught the membership to grasp the most subtle clues thrown by the old leaders or the Soviet Union. For the "26ths" their job is simpler. They have only to watch Fidel. This brings us to the third and final characteristic.

The capabilities for mass mobilization of both factions are extremely low. The nationalistic appeal of the "26th" has been personalized in Fidel. The PSP, lacking popular leaders and long alienated from the masses, only trusts mechanical devices, that is, impersonal organizations. This somehow explains why Fidel is so antagonistic to such devices, and also explains why the PSP is as dependent on the Soviet Union as the "26th" on Castro.

Politics is always a very complex affair, especially under revolutionary regimes. It would be easier to reduce Cuban factional politics to the two groups already known. But things are not so simple. Although Castro has promised the first Congress of the Communist Party for 1975, and in recent years there have been repeated indications of increasing formalization both at party and government levels, nevertheless up to the present time institutionalization has taken place only in the Army. Fidel is the Commander in Chief, but the Minister of the Armed Forces, who has the real administrative control of the apparatus, is his brother Raul. In addition, Raul is the First Deputy Prime Minister and Second Secretary of the Party. Raul, who was briefly a member of the PSP's Branch Youth, and commanded the Second Oriental Front during the war, has been more careful than his brother in the periods of tension with the Soviet Union; and Raul seems to have excellent ties with the Soviet High Staff. It is also apparent that the officers who fought under Raul have climbed to the highest positions not only in the Army but more recently even in the government.[13] Well-informed persons reject the possibility of any open conflict between the two brothers, and clues for quarrels between them are few as well as difficult to interpret. Nevertheless, such a formidable command of resources and so noticeable an amount of promotions suggest the advisability of not overlooking this emergence of a new kind of grouping. Its relevance to our present interest will be obvious. It would mean a split in the ranks of the "26th," consequently a threat to Fidel's maneuverability, and the potentiality for new coalitions.

Yet it is also clear that here we face a different type of grouping. Its roots are not in the rivalries generated by the struggle for power period; the boundaries between faction and the Army as interest group overlap, making any distinction difficult; and the configuration of this faction is extremely dependent upon the decisions of one leader, Raul Castro, who has always been very cautious. Nevertheless, we believe there are enough clues to postulate the presence of a "Raulist" group, and since its omission would impair our understanding of revolutionary dynamics, we conclude by adding a third faction to the other two already identified in this paper.

1966-68: Strains with Moscow

Observers agree that the Soviet influence in Cuba has substantially increased in the last few years, reaching levels without parallel in the course of these relationships. There is also complete accord that the present period was preceded by another one, roughly from 1966 to 1968, in which the donor's preferences were not only ignored but openly disputed by the Cubans.[14] The data below helps very little, if any, to explain the shift from one period to another.

The strategic umbrella remained without any appreciable change throughout the seven years. Military aid seems to have stopped at the end of 1966, to be resumed three years later.* Figures for Cuban trade with the Soviet Union in millions of rubles follow:

	1964	1965	1966	1967	1968	1969	1970	1971
Turnover	588.6	645.9	689.2	842.2	811.8	770.1	1,045	891
Import	329.4	337.9	431.9	506.7	561.8	561.6	580	602
Export	259.2	308	257.3	335.5	250	208.5	645	289
Cuban Deficit	70.2	29.9	174.6	171.2	411.8	353.1	105	313[15]

Unfortunately we know very little about aid for development. It seems that previous to 1970 the last loan was granted in 1964.[16] Oil supply apparently began to be reduced at the end of 1966. Military parades, for example, were set for alternative years since January 1967 "to save oil," and gasoline was rationed in January 1968. Finally, a new economic agreement was signed in December 1972, replacing the previous one, which expired in 1970-71.

---

* Castro mentioned a "new artillery missile unit" at the parade of the eighth anniversary. Havana Radio (January 2, 1967). References to new armaments are not found up to December 1969.

Obviously these data do not explain both switches in Cuban behavior in 1966 and 1968-70. The halt in arms supply follows, does not
precede, the Cuban shift in 1966; it then seems to be applied as a
sanction, without any success; and it was renewed two years later as
an inducement to the rectification already under way. Trade increased
from 1964 to 1968, especially during the two-year crisis; declined in
1969, when there were signs of rapprochement; achieved a new peak
in 1970; and decreased in 1971, the second year of full cooperation, to
more or less the same levels of 1967. Consequently, the question is
why were similar levels of largesse translated into such different
degrees of influence as those revealed by Cuban behavior?

In 1965 the Soviets and Castro seem to have reached a compromise:
the former continuing to offer the usual protection and aid as well as
recognizing Castro's domestic autonomy; the latter concentrating on
cleaning up the economic mess, building socialism, and supporting the
Soviet line in foreign relations. Before the year was over the strains
between both parties were apparent, later increasing so much that in
1968 there was not even one exchange of visits by high officials; and
the Cubans were complaining about Soviet pressures or denouncing
the intervention of Soviet minor officials in their internal affairs. We
have already seen that the quantitative data available do not explain
the rapid deterioration of Soviet-Cuban relations, and no one has given
a convincing answer to this problem. It is possible to speculate on
two alternatives. First, in his long discussions with Guevara, Castro
was persuaded by the Argentinian. According to Guevara, since the
Revolution faced mortal danger because imperialism had taken the
offensive, and the Soviet regime was going through a process of degen-
eration, it was the duty of every revolutionary "to create two, or more
Vietnams."* Second, aware of the growing Cuban indebtedness to the
Soviet Union, Castro rightly foresaw his impending dependency and
tried to strengthen his bargaining position by disseminating "Left
Revisionism." Once this attempt failed to impress the Soviets he had
no other way but to increase the stakes, launching the guerrilla band
headed by Guevara. It was always apparent that Guevara's operation
had all the shortcomings of a sudden improvisation. The last doubts
vanished after the recent interview between Norman Gall and the
Venezuelan guerrilla leader, Teodoro Petkoff. Previous to the Bolivian
adventure, the Venezuelans rejected a Havana proposal to infiltrate
Guevara into their country.17 After this denial the Argentinian hero was
left with only one place to die: Bolivia.

In any case, during the second part of 1966 Castro began to make
decisions contradicting the Soviet position. He not only preached but

---

* Castro asked "for four or five more Vietnams" in his speech of
December 18, 1966. Cuba Socialista, vol. 17, no. 65 (January 1967),
177. In this, he was not surpassed by Guevara in militancy.

fomented violent revolution in Latin America and Africa; stated that
Cuba was arriving at the stage of communism, preceding the Russians;
denounced material incentives and lauded the moral ones; disjointed
the administrative apparatus with the struggle against bureaucratism;
prevented rational decision-making in the economy, throwing the
accumulated data into the wastebasket;* wasted Soviet aid; and what
is even more striking for a member of the Socialist bloc, pretended that
he was the real revolutionary, not the Soviets.

There is no sign that Castro's policies found any strong opposition
in Cuba. In 1968 the government staged a trial of a small group called
"the mini-fraction," which was accused of discrediting the popular
trust in the leaders, having meetings for those purposes, and looking
for Soviet support. But a reading of the public record shows that the
mini-fraction was much more "mini" than "fraction," and the Soviets
in touch with the defendants were low-level officials. A careful
scrutiny of all the occurrences sourrounding this event discloses that
the real purpose of the trial was not to condemn a group of dangerous
conspirators, but to signal to the Soviets both the decision of the leader
and his control of the domestic scenario, as well as warning the higher
echelons of the PSP faction that from now on nonauthorized contacts
with Soviet officials were considered a crime.

A great majority of the defendants were members of the PSP faction.
This is not the only proof of its persistence. There are others. For
instance, the silence of PSP factionalists during this period or their
vocal support for the leader while avoiding any reference to his policies,
their total absence from the guerrillas, and their removal from the
party, the administration and the mass organizations to be seen later.
That they were not able to raise any meaningful opposition can be
explained by the already-known weakness of Cuban factions and,
probably, because the Soviets showed great restraint in responding to
Castro's challenge.

It is obvious that the Soviets had the means to prevent Castro
from competing with them in Latin America. A Soviet official told one
of the members of the mini-fraction that it would be enough to feign
some repairs at Baku Harbor, justifying a delay in oil supply, to put
Cuba very close to total paralysis.[18] Instead they tried a policy of
moderation, reducing the oil supply and stopping arms shipments.
Possibly they realized their constraints (the distance preventing any
drastic, rapid and effective imposition of sanctions), calculated their
costs in loss of revolutionary prestige as well as facilitating an

---

*In a recent speech President Dorticos has disclosed how "an
erroneous interpretation of the fight against bureaucratism" led to this
irreparable loss of economic data. Osvaldo Dorticos, "Economic
Control and Norms: First Priorities," Economia y Desarrollo, no. 11
(May-June 1972), 33.

imperialist success when the outcome in Vietnam was doubtful, and decided to wait. Probably there were also other factors advising postponement. After all, Castro's guerrilla war preempted the Chinese in Latin America. Furthermore, behind the curtain of radicalism and anti-Sovietism, Castro was sending signals difficult to decode. For example, the general disorganization characteristic of the period never touched the Army. On January 2, 1967, Fidel announced that Raul was leaving the Ministry of the Air Forces, "to study."[19] It is difficult to believe that Raul's educational improvement was so urgent as to step out from the government while his brother faced one of the most demanding challenges in revolutionary history; and the other triumvir, Guevara, was going through his ordeal and final death. There is no sign of a serious quarrel between the two brothers. It can be inferred then that Raul's leave had another purpose, such as to protect his communication lines with the Soviets. Raul stayed away until August 1968, a few days before Fidel gave his speech on Czechoslovakia, the first public indication of the change of line. The younger Castro was one of the accusers at the trial against the mini-fraction; but he took good care of exempting the Soviet military advisers of any wrongdoing. How would Brezhnev decipher these signals? We do not know. All we know is that he waited.

1968-73: Toward Entente

Castro's speech on the Czechoslovakian crisis is usually taken as the first indication of a change of policy oriented to improve relations with the Soviets. This interpretation can be criticized for several reasons. It overlooks Castro's silence during both the May movement in France and the Mexican student crisis, the trial against the mini-fraction already mentioned, the so-called March Offensive of 1968 (the final expropriation of the petite bourgeoisie), and the new goal of producing 10 million tons of sugar for 1970. Castro's silence could have been a signal to the Soviets to indicate the end of radicalism in foreign policy. The trial and the March Offensive showed not only his total internal control, but the resolution of the leader, as he once put it before, "to sink" in the Gulf, with the greater number of his fellow citizens of course, if he was not offered a viable alternative. Equally, the 10-million ton harvest signified his return to the tasks of economic construction and socialism.

This interpretation is also weak in the sense that it bestows on Castro contradictory qualifications. On the one hand, he is clever and powerful enough to manipulate the Soviets at will. On the other hand, he is so dumb as to be unable to anticipate his present critical situation.

It is more sophisticated, more congenial to the man, and fits the available data better, to argue that all the moves mentioned above are the components of only one strategy. Its goal would be to induce the Soviets to show some goodwill, otherwise threatening to increase even more their economic and political costs. Soviet acquiescence would help to overcome reservations in the minds of PSP factionalists on the feasibility of the 10-million ton harvest, ensuring in addition total tranquility for the massive mobilization of "voluntary workers." And the sugar goal, if fulfilled, would restore the charismatic image of the leader, somewhat blurred by the repeated failures suffered since the fall of 1962, giving him more room to face coming challenges, such as the negotiation of a new sugar treaty with the Soviets in 1970-71.

This interpretation fits the available data better. Castro's speech on Lenin's centennial, April 22, 1970, has repeatedly been mentioned both by Soviet and Cuban leaders as the policy guide for the new stage of the revolution. While Castro was giving the speech, his brother Raul visited Moscow, the first Cuban leader to do so since November 1966. He was followed a few days later by President Dorticos. On May 19, Castro publicly recognized the failure to achieve the Sugar Harvest Goal.[20]

Whichever interpretation would be preferred, the facts show that Castro's options had been dangerously restricted at the end of 1967. Guevara's death and the exhaustion of the Latin American guerrilla movement tragically revealed the serious miscalculations made by both leaders and pointed out the inviability of a policy oriented toward putting pressure on the Soviets from the left. Meanwhile, the Chinese remained disinterested in Cuba, ignored the apparent analogies between Cuban radical policies and the Cultural Proletarian Revolution, and even criticized Guevara after his death.[21] The Americans persisted in denying Castro any significant access to the Western markets.* Production decreased, trade deficits with the Soviets increased, rationing became total, and lines a way of life.

Fortunately for Castro, the military contacts with the Soviets had remained open. It seems that they played a crucial role in restoring Castro's good standing in the eyes of the Soviet leaders. From Kosygin's visit to Havana in June 1967 to the arrival of Grechko in November 1969, the only personal meeting held by significant Cuban and Soviet leaders took place when a military delegation headed by Pedro Miret, an old crony of Castro since the Moncada attack, visited Moscow for the anniversary of the Russian Revolution in November 1968. One of the first signs that relations were improving was the visit of a Soviet naval squadron to Cuba in July 1969. In November, Marshal

---

*The staggering effects of this policy in reducing Cuban leverage with the Soviet Union, without any visible advantage for the United States, at least since 1968, must be obvious. One example: In 1971 the U.S. government lifted the ban on the import of French products containing nickel, once France agreed to stop importing Cuban nickel. (Latin America, February 5, 1971). On August 10, 1973, Radio-Havana reported a Soviet-Cuban agreement to expand this domestic production.

Grechko arrived.* It was he who invited Raul Castro to visit the Soviet Union in April 1970. At the beginning of December, the Soviet press announced the resumption of military aid to Cuba, with "the newest weapons and military equipment."[22] The Soviet leaders played it cool during this new stage in Soviet-Cuban relations, opened by the Cubans, according to our interpretation, since the initial months of 1968. First came military aid. On April 22, 1970, Castro publicly accepted the Soviet credo.[23] This virtuoso performance was achieved without retracting one word of his former calls for guerrilla war, and using the new Military Peruvian Junta, which came to power by a coup in October 1968, and the Christian Left as examples of the new Latin American revolutionary wave.

In December 1970 a member of the Central Committee of the Soviet Communist Party was appointed ambassador to Cuba, and the Soviet-Cuban Commission for Economic, Scientific, and Technical Collaboration was established, presided on the Cuban side by a member of the PSP faction, Carlos Rafael Rodriguez. Two months later, the 1964 trade agreement was extended until 1975. There were no spectacular developments the following year. But in 1972, Cuba was admitted to the Council for Mutual Economic Assistance, represented by the same Rodriguez; and Castro twice visited the USSR, the second time to sign several economic agreements, after he had thoroughly reorganized his government one month before. In September 1973, at the Algiers Conference of Nonaligned Countries, Castro was effusive in his praise of the Soviet Union. Finally, in January 1974, Brezhnev arrived in Havana. He pointedly voiced his best wishes "for the 1st Congress of the glorious Communist Party of Cuba, to be held next year."[24]

Two features are most noticeable in this process. First, the long period of time spent to achieve the new accommodation: five years. In contrast, after the previous crisis in Cuban-Soviet relations, Castro needed only a few months to be invited to Moscow, and less than a year to sign a very favorable economic agreement. Second, the number and significance of Castro's concessions. The counterpart to these concessions, of course, is an increase in Soviet influence in Cuba. In the next section we will see how this growing Soviet influence is being reflected in the replacement of "26th" by PSP factionalists at the highest levels of the government, the Party, and mass organizations.

---

*There are many indications that Castro had to apply a final twist to the Soviets before making them willing to start serious discussions. For this interpretation, totally different from that usually given to Grechko's visit, see my paper: "How the Cuban System Works," delivered at the Southeastern Conference of Latin American Studies (Chapel Hill, North Carolina, April 1972).

Influence and Factions

Two sets of data are most frequently used in the literature on the growing dependency of Cuba on the Soviet Union: economic and military indicators, or parallels between Soviet and Cuban ideological pronouncements as well as economic and foreign policies. We already know that the former are not reliable. The latter seem more credible. But aside from the fact that they are difficult to measure, they present us with a problem. "What often seems to be influence," Professor Rubinstein has pointed out, "turns out instead to be joint interests of the two parties."[25] For example, when Castro woos the Peruvian Military Junta, is he under Soviet influence or behaving according to his own interests? Is the fact that material incentives are being reintroduced in the Cuban economy a sign of yielding to Soviet demands, or an indication that Fidel has learned from his disastrous experience with the moral ones? These problems have led us to look for new ways to ascertain, and possibly measure, the levels of Soviet influence in Cuba.

Hypothesis number three has alerted us to the significance of the recipient elite's capability to maintain internal unity and control; and hypothesis number two claims that "the head" in a relationship of authority — the Soviet leadership — will tend to control the decision-making process of the other unit through domestic actors who have internalized such a relationship — the PSP faction. Whatever Castro's motivations — pure power or the protection of national interest — there seems to be a conflict here that will be reflected in the removal of officials at the highest levels: ministers, party leaders, and heads of mass organizations.

The following analysis tries to describe the pattern of these changes of top officials from 1966 to 1973 (see Table 1). It is based on personal cards for each of the 100 members of the Central Committee, showing: (a) their records during the struggle against Batista; (b) positions in the government, the party and mass organizations since 1959; (c) selected pieces of information considered as significant cues to assess intragroup ties, and the positions taken by the top leaders concerning certain key issues in the course of the revolution. Military officers have been excluded, first, because maybe with only one or two exceptions PSP factionalists have never had access to the highest echelons of the Army, and second, the recent reorganization of the rank system in the Cuban Army possibly implies some changes in the military cadres which take at least months to appear in the public press, obviously the only source available to the present author.

In the 1965 compromise, Castro maintained the internal autonomy, since he dissolved, or atomized, every Cuban political organization. Consequently, from 1966 to 1968 personnel removals were not frequent, even though they were significant. PSP factionalists, such as the chairman of the Committee for the Defense of the Revolution (CDR), the Secretary General of the Confederation of Workers (CTC), the editor of

Table 1

Cuba: Factions in the Top Political Leadership
(Spring 1974)*

	"26"	"Raulist"	PSP	Unknown
Political Bureau, Central Committee, Communist Party of Cuba				
Fidel Castro	X			
Raul Castro		X		
Oswaldo Dorticos			X	
Ramiro Valdes				X
Guillermo Garcia	X			
Armando Hart	X			
Juan Almeida	X			
Sergio del Valle	X			
Secretariat				
Fidel Castro	X			
Raul Castro		X		
Oswaldo Dorticos			X	
Blas Roca			X	
Carlos Rafael Rodriguez			X	
Raul Chomon				X
Antonio Perez Herrero		X		
Jorge Risquet			X	
Isidoro Malmierca			X	
Raul Garcia Pelaez	X			
Pedro Miret	X			
Executive Committee of Council of Ministers				
Fidel Castro, Prime Minister	X			
Raul Castro, First Deputy Prime Minister		X		
Oswaldo Dorticos, President			X	
Ramiro Valdes, Deputy Prime Minister				X
Guillermo Garcia, "	X			
Joel Domenech "			X	
Flavio Bravo "			X	
Belarmino Castilla "		X		
Carlos Rafael Rodriguez "			X	
Diocles Torralba "		X		

*The occupants of formal positions are called top leaders. There
is no implication that all of them participate in the decision-making
process with the same weight, or even that all are participants.

Granma, official organ of the PCC, and the First Secretary of the Party in the Oriente Province, were all replaced, with one exception, by members of the other faction. The exception lacks important meaning: the substitute, Miguel Martin, was soon removed in favor of a "26th" man. Meanwhile in the government there were two changes, one of them of difficult interpretation: the access of Jorge Risquet to the Ministry of Labor. Risquet is one of the very few members of the PSP who moved to the rebel camp. He grew a beard, wore an olive green uniform, and climbed successfully after the victory. Recently he has been appointed to work in the Secretariat of the Party. My data classifies him as a "doubtful" who had returned to the PSP faction. The other change, the ambassadorship to the Soviet Union, went from the hands of a DR man to a "26th" one, and therefore for our purposes is not particularly significant.

In 1968 Castro began to innovate concerning the organization of the party. Personal representatives, officially called Political Bureau delegates, were appointed for the provinces. All of them were 26th factionalists. Finally, in the summer of 1968, one of the most intriguing and significant removals in the government took place. Ramiro Valdes stepped out from the Ministry of the Interior, as Raul Castro had two years before, on leave and "to study."[26] But while Raul returned to his Ministry, Ramiro never did. Valdes, a veteran of the Moncada attack and the Granma expedition, fought in the civil war; and up to August 1968, he was one of the most powerful among the leaders surrounding Castro. He was replaced by another loyal Fidelista. Nevertheless, it would be very helpful to have more information about his disguised demotion. As Minister of the Interior, he was the official responsible for the investigation and arrest of the members of the mini-fraction. There have been conflicting reports that Valdes objected to trespasses into his authority by members of the Soviet intelligence. After a while he reappeared as First Deputy Minister of the Revolutionary Armed Forces under Raul, in spite of the fact that he was a member of the Political Bureau like the younger Castro. In November 1972, he was appointed one of the Deputy Prime Ministers in the new Executive Committee of the Council of Ministers. He is in charge of the Construction Sector, which is far from the Ministry of the Interior as a source of power.

From 1969 to 1973 the shifts, or new appointments, were both more numerous and more significant. Besides, it was during this period that a pattern emerged from such changes in personnel which suggests the presence of the group called by us "Raulists." Consequently our data are organized in such a way as to make the presence of the new faction visible.

To fully understand the following data some background is needed. Strains within the "26th of July Movement" between the underground and the rebel army, the "llano" and the "sierra," appeared in the last months of the guerrilla war. After the triumph, the Rebel Army became the core around which the Revolutionary Armed Forces were organized; and up to 1961, when the revolution was declared socialist, the Armed Forces were supposed to be "apolitical." Therefore, the leaders of the Underground, the "politicos," were identified as the leaders of the "26th." Next to Fidel — Raul was never seen as a leader of the "26th" — among the most representative leaders of the Movement were Faustino Perez, Armando Hart, and Haydee Santamaria. In 1968 they held high positions in the government or the party. Today, Perez is the ambassador in Bulgaria; his former position in the government was cancelled. Hart lost his job as Secretary of Organization of the Party to be appointed recently First Secretary of the Party in the Oriente province. He was replaced by another "26th" man, lacking in the same symbolic qualities. Only Santamaria has kept the same position, but she has suffered a substantial reduction in her authority. Another important leader of the "26th," Llanusa, has also been demoted. His successor was a Raulist. This trend against the "26th" seems so consistent that in the new Executive Committee of the Council of Ministers, excluding Fidel, there is no one else who can be fully considered representative of the original movement and only one other member who can be clearly identified as a 26th factionalist.

While the "26th" vanishes from the government, PSP factionalists, and "Raulists," emerge. In the Executive Committee, a body created to supervise all governmental activities and departments, there are only two "26th" men, including Fidel; Raul plus two other "Raulists"; and four PSP factionalists. "Raulists" can also be identified in the Ministries of Education, Merchant Marine, and Transportation. And if rapid promotions by military men are accepted as indicators of "Raulism," which seems sensible, then the Ministries of Communications as well as Oil and Metallurgy also are "Raulists." Recently the PSP has captured another strategic position: the ambassadorship to the Soviet Union. He replaced a "26th" man. Since Carlos Rafael Rodriguez, today probably the top PSP man, has been charged in the Executive Committee with the supervision of all foreign agencies, this means that the lines of communication with Moscow have slipped away from the hands of the Maximum Leader.

There have not been such significant changes of personnel at the highest levels either of the party or the mass organizations. Nevertheless, the attendance by Raul, not Fidel, at the Annual Balance Meetings of the Provincial Committee of the Party, held for the first time in 1973, seems to indicate that the younger Castro is starting to make encroachments in this other former preserve of his brother. "Raulists" and PSP factionalists now also enjoy an easy majority in the Party Secretariat, where they can amass seven votes against Fidel, Miret, and possibly Chomon, if votes are counted in this body. Fidel, of course, continues to have a tight control on the Political Bureau.

The previous data show an unmistakable trend suggesting that at the governmental level the monopoly enjoyed by the leaders of the

"26th" up to 1968 is going through a serious process of erosion. The erosion is taking place because the PSP and new "Raulist" factions are both making substantial progress. The cleavage between the "26th" and the PSP was originated by the perception of a conflict between the national interest and the influencer, and it has strong roots in both the history and the imagery of the revolution. Therefore, "Raulists" seem to be in a better position to play a swing role, that is, to switch from one faction to the other in search for the coalitions more advantageous to their own interests.

Measuring influence, of course, continues to be an intractable problem. But our method can complement, at least, the other two mentioned above. Fidel can state, implement, and especially combine, his internal and foreign policies in such a way as to disconcert not only his adversaries but also the analysts — and he certainly does. But since 1970 he cannot prevent rival factions from sharing the decision-making process. Political reality offers new means to appraise the distribution of power: the demotion of highest level officials. Using these data it is possible to devise thresholds of significance for assessing Soviet influence in Cuba. For instance, aside from the charismatic leadership of Fidel Castro, there is, under the present regime, only one other potential source of legitimacy: the Party. As in every Communist party the control is in the Political Bureau. Therefore, we can expect the leader strongly to resist any increase of another faction's representatives in that body. Increasing participation, or attainment of a majority by the PSP faction could be considered a threshold of significance to the effects of measuring Soviet influence.

Conclusions

A final glance at our hypotheses will help to explain why similar levels of largesse have been translated into different degrees of Soviet influence in Cuba from 1966 to 1973. Having restored his total control of domestic politics in 1965, Castro started to perceive his options narrowing a few months later, and decided to launch an ideological challenge to the Soviets. Distance and strategic considerations advised the Soviets to answer this challenge with great restraint, but concede nothing. Once the attempt to strengthen the credibility of the Leftist orientation failed in Bolivia, the national economy began to show the scars inflicted by the radical drive, and the Americans denied to Cuba the advantage pointed out by Wriggins; Castro's political resources were almost exhausted, imposing an accommodation with the Soviets. The latter demanded the formalization of the Soviet model, that is, the participation in the national leadership of those who had internalized during long years of struggle their identification with democratic-centralism and proletarian internationalism, understood in the Soviet sense. As has been seen, Castro only yielded inch by inch. But relentless Soviet pressure forced him to accept a growing participation of bona fide Marxist-Leninists in the policy-making process.* The election of the new party organs, especially the Political Bureau, at the First Congress announced for 1975, will allow more rigorous evaluation of the real level of Soviet influence in Cuba. Meanwhile, a tentative effort in that direction appears as an appendix to the present paper.

The increasing institutionalization under Soviet prodding has brought to Cuba economic recovery and its correlates: growing modernization, bureaucratization, and differentiation. Interest groups begin to appear like those observed in communist societies: apparatchiki, technicians, army officers, managers, lawyers, judges, and so forth. Factions will have to deal with them in order to stay on the top. But it is highly improbable that they will disappear, since Cuban factions are rooted in those conditions which make the Cuban revolution a truly exceptional case.

Notes

1. Castro's speech, Granma, weekly review (February 10, 1974).

2. Howard A. Wriggins, "Political Outcomes of Foreign Assistance: Influence, Involvement or Intervention, " International Affairs, vol. 22, no. 2 (1968), 222.

3. David A. Baldwin, "Inter-nation Influence Revisited," Journal of Conflict Resolution, vol. 15, no. 4 (December 1971), p. 476. See also David Singer, "Internation Influence: A Formal Model, " American Political Science Review, vol. 57, no. 2 (June 1963).

4. Baldwin, op. cit.

5. Carmelo Mesa-Lago, "The Sovietization of the Cuban Revolution: Its Consequences for the Western Hemisphere, " World Affairs, vol. 136, no. 1 (Summer 1973), p. 10.

6. Peter Bachrach and Morton S. Baratz, "Decisions and Non-Decisions: An Analytical Framework, " American Political Science Review, vol. 57, no. 3 (September 1963), 632-42.

7. Michael Crozier, The Bureaucratic Phenomenon (Chicago: The University of Chicago Press, 1967), p. 5.

8. H. Gordon Skilling, "Group Conflict and Political Change, " in Chalmers Johnson (ed.), Change in Communist Systems (Stanford: Stanford University Press, 1970), p. 216. See also H. Gordon Skilling

---

*A thorough reconstruction of the Party was started in 1972, including the reorganization of the apparat of the Central Committee, the regulation of the relationships between the party and the administration, and the formulation of Provisional By-rules, to be applied until the First Congress. See speeches by Raul Castro, Granma, weekly edition, January 13, and Isidoro Malmierca, Radio Havana, April 2, 1974.

and Franklyn Griffiths, Interest Groups in Soviet Politics (Princeton: Princeton University Press, 1971); Andrew C. Janos, "Group Politics in Communist Society: A Second Look to the Pluralist Model, " in Samuel P. Huntington and Clement H. Moore (eds.), Authoritarian Politics in Modern Society (New York: Basic Books, 1970).

9. William E. Odom, "The Party Connection, " Problems of Communism, vol. 22, no. 5 (September-October 1973), 24-25.

10. See my own interpretation of this period in Andres Suarez, Cuba: Castroism and Communism, 1959-1966 (Cambridge, Mass.: MIT Press, 1967).

11. See, for example, President Dorticos' speech in Granma, daily (January 4, 1968), and Castro's speech in Granma, weekly review (July 2, 1972), p. 8.

12. Political Bureau's decision in case of Joaquin Ordoqui Mesa. Granma, weekly review (April 22, 1973), p. 3.

13. See Table 1.

14. For Soviet-Cuban relationships since 1966, see among others: Kevin Devlin, "The Castroist Challenge to Communism, " in J. Gregory Oswald and Anthony J. Strovel (eds.), The Soviet Union and Latin America (New York: Praeger Publishers, 1970); Bruce D. Jackson, Castro, the Kremlin and Communism in Latin America (Baltimore: Johns Hopkins Press, 1969); Robert F. Lamberg, "La formacion de la linea Castrista desde la Conferencia Tricontinental, " Foro Internacional (Enero-Marzo, 1968); Edward Gonzalez, "Relationships with the Soviet Union, " in C. Mesa Lago (ed.), Revolutionary Change in Cuba (Pittsburgh: University of Pittsburgh Press, 1971); Herbert S. Dinerstein, "Soviet and Cuban Conceptions of Revolution, " Studies in Comparative Communism (January 1971); and Leon Goure and Julian Weinkle, "Soviet Cuban Relations: The Growing Integration, " in Jaime Suchlicki (ed.), Cuba, Castro, and Revolution (Miami: University of Miami Press, 1972).

15. For the sources, see Leon Goure and Julian Weinkle, "Soviet-Cuban Relations: The Growing Integration, " in Suchlicki, ibid., p. 159.

16. Eric N. Baklanof, "International Economic Relations, " in C. Mesa Lago (ed.), Revolutionary Change in Cuba (Pittsburgh: University of Pittsburgh Press, 1971), p. 158.

17. Norman Gall, "Teodoro Petkoff: The Crisis of the Professional Revolutionary, Part II: A New Party, " American Universities Field Staff, South America, vol. 17, no. 9 (1972), 3.

18. See the minutes of the trial of the mini-fraction in Granma, weekly review (February 11, 1968), pp. 2, 4, 5, 7-12.

19. Castro's speech in Cuba Socialista, vol. 17, no. 65 (January 1967), p. 33.

20. Granma, weekly review (May 31, 1970), pp. 2-5.

21. Cecil Johnson, Communist China and Latin America, 1959-1967 (New York: Columbia University Press, 1970), pp. 128, 172-73, 228-29.

22. Quotation from the Soviet press in The New York Times, December 3, 1969.

23. Granma, weekly review (May 3, 1970), pp. 2-5.

24. Granma, weekly review (February 10, 1974), p. 4

25. See Chapter 1 of this volume, p. 32.

26. Resolution of Political Bureau, Granma, weekly review (August 4, 1968), p. 1.

9

THE SOVIET VIEW OF CHINESE INFLUENCE IN AFRICA AND LATIN AMERICA
George Ginsburgs

Ever since Sino-Soviet polemics have become a matter of public record, Moscow's spokesmen have accused Peking of following a self-serving line that seeks solely to exploit the nations of Africa and Latin America for its private ends, subordinating their real interests to its own big-power chauvinist aspirations to attain global hegemony. In light of the fact that the USSR and its allies represent a key obstacle to the consummation of these schemes, the main thrust of Chinese exertions in the countries of the so-called Third World has therefore been directed at trying to discredit the performance of the socialist states in the eyes of the local people and steal the spotlight itself. To quote a Soviet source:

> All forms of relations of the present Chinese Government
> with the young national states (economic and military aid,
> propaganda, displomatic ties and agreements, contacts
> with ruling parties and public organizations) are designed
> specifically to arouse in them mistrust of, and hostility
> towards, the USSR, the other socialist states, and the
> working class of Western Europe and the United States.
> All this is being done in order to put into power in these
> countries such men who would obediently follow Peking's
> policies. Those states which rebuff the interference of
> Peking in their internal affairs and stop the activities of
> its agents and the dissemination of its propaganda
> material are subjected to malicious attacks.[1]

These objectives, according to the Russians, are pursued by various means.

Doctrinal Revisionism

The charge of doctrinal revisionism heads the Soviet indictment sheet. For many years now, the Kremlin claims, the Communist Chinese leaders have been busy formulating and promoting a series of theoretical blueprints calculated both to "legitimize" their ambitions in these quarters and facilitate the achievement of their particular goals in the area. All these efforts have one thing in common: they strive to inculcate the notion that the nations of Africa, Asia and Latin America constitute an entity sui generis in which prevails a set of economic, social, and political conditions fundamentally different from those encountered in Europe and North America and where novel solutions must be devised to handle their special problems. Treating the Third World as a unique phenomenon means, of course, isolating it from the mainstream of socialist experience in the USSR and East Europe, driving a wedge between it and the Communist parties of the industrialized countries, and fostering in its midst a sense of insularity and ethnocentrism which would leave it vulnerable to the machinations of its largest and most powerful member, to wit, Communist China. Or so says the Kremlin.

While the spirit and tenor of the script have remained the same throughout, the language and tone have fluctuated widely in step with the tactical needs of the moment. As far back as 1946, we are reminded, Mao had already toyed with the concept of "intermediary zones, " dividing the world into three parts which comprised, respectively, American imperialism, the USSR and the other socialist states, and the countries of Asia, Africa and Latin America.[2] Coinciding with Mao's advocacy of a distinctive "Oriental" or "Asian" road to socialism inspired by the lessons of the history of the Communist movement in China, the thesis naturally operated to strengthen the Chinese Communist Party's candidacy for the role of intellectual mentor of the smaller and weaker sister-parties of the East.[3] By 1956, in a conversation with an Italian communist delegation, Mao was reportedly telling his listeners: "The communist parties of the old continent had better neither deal with nor comment on the revolutionary movement in Asia and Africa but leave it to the Chinese to work out for them the ideology, methods and objectives of the political struggle. "[4]

Then, as the two former friends drifted farther apart, the Chinese began to act more boldly. Thus, in the late 1950s, they launched the slogan, "The East Wind Prevails over the West Wind, " intended to demonstrate China's revolutionary primacy and its total commitment to the worldwide battle against the forces of imperialism. The pitch was correctly perceived by Moscow as a maneuver to wrest the initiative from the USSR, push the latter's massive campaign to advertise the virtues of peaceful coexistence into the background, and wreck it by provoking, if possible, a clash between the USSR and the United States; and today Soviet spokesmen assert that "this nationalist password, belittling the role of the world socialist system, the international working class, substituted for the class approach to the phenomena of social development a geographical and even a racial one. " Next, the Chinese put into circulation the thesis of Asia, Africa, and Latin America as the epicenter of the revolutionary storms of modern times, with Peking anticipating that inasmuch as the People's Republic of China personified the interests of the peoples of the states located within these regions, it would "determine the direction of the various types of 'winds' and 'storms'."[5] Again, the Soviets could not but bridle at the Chinese bid to portray the Third World as the chief foe of contemporary imperialism in contrast with their own interpretation which ascribed that function to the socialist camp, to exclude the USSR and its allies from the primary picture and relegate them to the humble position of furnishing a support base for the national-liberation forces waging the real war against imperialism.

The stake on the ultra-leftist elements did not pay off; so after a while the Peking regime decided to adopt a more moderate front, without, however, entirely swearing off its earlier addiction to the oratory of violence. The years 1963-65 saw a series of visits to the African continent by top Chinese dignitaries and return trips by sundry African leaders to China. Sensitive to the feelings of their African hosts and guests, hoping to win their confidence, the Chinese muted their revolutionary rhetoric (permitting themselves just occasional references to the "superb revolutionary situation" which presumably marked the current scene) and stressed instead their sincere desire to cooperate with the established governments and forge between them ties of close friendship, reciprocal benefit, and mutual respect. To further its goal, Peking also trotted out a refurbished version of its theory of "intermediary zones," which lumped the countries of Asia, Africa, and Latin America ("first intermediary zone") together with certain developed capitalist countries allegedly opposed to the United States ("second intermediary zone") into a "common antiimperialist front." The scheme, we are assured, was deliberately aimed at replacing the struggle between socialism and capitalism with the struggle of the Third World headed by China against both the USSR and the United States. The great advantage of the latest formula resided in the fact that it skillfully avoided the issue of shared political coloration as a precondition for intimate collaboration between China and the governments it viewed as prospective associates in its crusading venture. Assignment of membership in either "intermediary zone" by the application of mysterious criteria known to Peking alone seemed reason enough to guarantee that those so favored would be looked upon by the leaders of Communist China with due sympathy and understanding. The experiment in smiling diplomacy reaped handsome rewards: as a result, the PRC received official recognition from several African states and concluded its first economic agreements in the region.

The partial moratorium on vociferous professions of faith in the universal validity of the radical creed lasted only a short spell; and by 1965, China once more sallied forth to the strains of Lin Piao's call for the "world countryside" to surround and defeat the "world city," a motto which drew the sharpest dichotomy yet between the Third World to the "spiritual" leadership of which China persistently laid claim and the "imperialist" clan within whose framework the USSR and its fellow travellers were bracketed with the United States and its confederates. As the Cultural Revolution gained momentum on the mainland, the tone of Peking's foreign policy pronouncements likewise increased in stridency. The Chinese authorities now openly glorified resort to "people's war," ascribed global relevancy to the thought of Mao Tse-tung, and urged its immediate adoption as a universal model and guideline, attempted to export Red Guard tactics to other countries, crudely interfered in their internal affairs in the name of spreading the Maoist gospel, and generally, according to the Russians, sought to turn the planet into a vast battlefield between the vision of "progress" of which they were the self-appointed prophets and the forces of "darkness" represented by all whom Peking happened at the moment to count among its enemies. Simultaneously, the Chinese leadership denounced the Soviet-sponsored concept of the "noncapitalist path of development" because it postulated a tight partnership between the proletariat of the technically advanced socialist countries and the laboring classes of the less developed nations to help the latter build up the sinews of a socialist structure at home by skipping the capitalist stage and, by contrast, sang the praises of self-reliance.[6]

In short, the Russians contend, despairing of their ability to compete with the USSR in constructive terms, the Chinese switched to championing a philosophy of nihilism and mindless extremism; and, lacking positive remedies for the ills afflicting the Third World, the Chinese were constrained to fall back on extolling the superiority of a national life-style that set a premium on asceticism, discipline, introversion and sacrifice.[7] In the end, Maoist excesses managed to alienate a considerable portion of African public opinion, and compelled several African states to rupture diplomatic relations with the PRC in protest against recurrent incidents of intervention into their domestic matters and gross breaches of the accepted norms of interstate conduct. Equally disenchanted with the failure of the African regimes to rally behind China and follow in Mao's footsteps, Peking drastically reduced the scope of its local operations and concentrated on cultivating contacts with just a few countries which it found congenial because of their ostensibly "socialist" orientation — at first, Mali, Guinea, Congo (Brazzaville), and Tanzania; subsequently, Guinea, Congo (Brazzaville), Tanzania, and Zambia.[8]

By the time the Cultural Revolution had run its course, Communist China's isolation was virtually complete. Ever since, the current crop of Chinese leaders has worked hard to put China back on the diplomatic map, heal the wounds left by the earlier convulsions and reknit and expand China's ties with the rest of the family of nations. They have posted some remarkable successes on that score.[9] With the gradual reversion to normalcy and especially after admission of the People's Republic of China into the United Nations, Peking had to outfit itself with a suitable new image. To the Russians, only the words changed;

but the message remains identical. Today's match pits a loose coalition of medium and small countries, spearheaded by China, against the two "superpowers," the USSR and the United States. Peking misses no occasion to dramatize its role of staunch defender of the lesser states from the evil designs of Moscow and Washington, the communality of interests uniting the junior members of the global community to resist the encroachments of the Soviet-American axis, China's spotless record in that connection, and its vital contribution to the job of keeping the "beasts of prey" at bay.

China's appeal is not confined to national-liberation movements. Rather, in its drive to broaden its clientele and enroll fresh recruits under its banner on the pretext of combatting the pervasive danger posed by the Soviet and American "superpowers," Peking scorns no source of possible assistance and has not hesitated to align itself with reactionary regimes of the worst stripe even at the expense of betraying detachments of the native national-liberation movement in the process, whenever it felt it could extract a profit from the association. Indeed, China's recent shift in emphasis from the slogan "national liberation" to the theme of the "Third World" is presumably motivated by appreciation of the fact that "the 'Third World' is heterogeneous and, therefore, could also include China." Besides, the switch meant that Peking would no longer have to explain the curious discrepancy between its own canon of behavior (notably vis-a-vis Hongkong and Macao) and the credo of the national-liberation movement,[10] or account for its overt flirtation with the un-Marxist, retrograde, nationalistic and class-blind features of such phenomena as pan-Arabism, pan-Africanism, and negritude.[11] In a word, every imaginable topic and forum is pressed into the service of political gamesmanship, the Soviets bitterly complain, even purely technical issues: For example, international cooperation in outer space, the protection of the natural environment, maritime law, and kindred questions, are seized upon by the Chinese in their endeavors to promote dissension, fan antagonism between the less developed countries and their wealthier cousins, and aggravate existing difficulties in order to polarize political allegiances and capture control of those elements that for various reasons are dissatisfied with their present lot, altogether regardless of the intrinsic merits of the respective case.[12]

Thus, to the Russians, the conclusion is inescapable that over the years the Chinese have systematically engaged in concocting a potpourri of pseudotheories in essence designed to persuade the governments and peoples of the African, Asian, and Latin American belt that: the experience of the Soviet Union and its acolytes is either irrelevant to the needs of these nations or actually injurious to their real interests; this group of countries stands apart from the rest of the world in terms of its unique historical, political, economic, cultural, social and racial heritage which China also shares; for that reason and because of the proven success of Mao's revolutionary program in China proper, all those desirous of ridding themselves of Soviet and American tutelage and exploitation and building a socialist life must solidarize with China and learn from its example.[13] However couched at any given moment (and the Chinese regime has indeed shown itself quite adept at tampering with the lyrics of the score to suit the circumstances), whether espoused singly or in different combinations, these dicta never deviated from their set goal of engineering an incurable estrangement between the countries of Africa, Asia, and Latin America and the socialist camp presided over by the USSR, drawing the former into China's orbit and harnessing them to the exigencies of China's master plan to rule the world, and using them as testing grounds or expendable pawns in its private struggle against both the United States and the Soviet Union for global dominion.

Party Factionalism

The second item in the Soviet bill of particulars criticizing China's record in this area revolves around the issue of alleged Chinese activities aimed at stirring up Party factionalism in the countries concerned. According to the Russians, the first major Chinese efforts to create pro-Maoist groups abroad date back to the early sixties when, unhappy with the "tameness" of the more important national-liberation movements in Black Africa and pursuing its "bogus revolutionary" strategy of manufacturing "several Vietnams" in the Congo (Kinshasa), Mozambique, Angola, and other places, Peking encouraged its local sympathizers to secede from the parent fronts and form competing splinter organizations purporting to operate from "far left" positions. A similar pattern emerged in some of the independent states of Africa and much of Latin America where by 1965 pro-Maoist wings had crystallized in the Communist parties of, among others, Algeria, Sudan, Cameroon, Niger, Madascar, Peru, Bolivia, Brazil, Colombia, Equador, and Paraguay. Up till 1963, for instance, having no official diplomatic relations with the capitalist governments of Latin America, the Maoists had counted on gaining a foothold on the continent by capturing the existing native Communist parties and seizing control of the whole Latin American Communist movement. In this connection, Peking supposedly staked its hopes on the close ties established between these Communist parties and the CCP in the fifties and on the Latin American Communists who visited China, studied in the Chinese Party schools, and were posted by the Party to work in Sino-Latin American friendship societies. When these expectations did not pan out and the bid of Peking's allies to take over the leadership of the respective parties failed, the Chinese ordered them to set up a rival machinery and introduce their product to the masses as "genuine Marxist-Leninist parties."[14]

The affair accomplished nothing more, the Kremlin insists, than to sap the strength of the existing revolutionary forces, play into the hands of the imperialists, and leave the pro-Maoist "splitters" isolated and ineffectual. Instead of contributing to the tasks of national-liberation, many of these fringe elements soon ended up with an agenda that consisted exclusively of spreading anti-Soviet propaganda and indulging in provocations against and even terroristic attacks on "true revolutionaries."[15] Thus, for all their revolutionary bombast, when the chips were down, the pro-Maoist fragments carefully disassociated themselves in 1963-66 from the antiimperialist armed struggle being waged in a number of Latin American countries — Guatemala, Venezuela, Bolivia: they recklessly engaged in incendiary oratory and then preferred to watch the unfolding contest from the sidelines, conserving their resources until an opportunity arose to increase their own sectarian influence and power.[16]

As the Cultural Revolution mounted to fever pitch, Peking abandoned its last remaining inhibitions. Soviet sources paint a lurid tableau of what ensued:

> They [the Chinese] turned China's diplomatic, trade and technical missions and Chinese minorities living in Afro-Asian states into propaganda media for "Mao's ideas."
>
> Crude attempts to influence public figures in the newly independent countries, bribery of reactionary dissident groups and circulation of inflammatory and plainly anti-government leaflets, "red books" containing Mao's writings, badges and buttons with Mao's picture — all this has become routine practice of Maoists abroad.[17]

The Chinese no longer bothered to disguise their subversive activities. They consorted with and supported individuals and factions plainly dedicated to the overthrow of the established authorities and violently denounced any government which moved to suppress the extremist segments as a capitalist stooge. No wonder then that the situation quickly came to a head. In Kenya, for example, the Chinese were charged with having tried to "influence that country's foreign policies." Reportedly,

> . . . a document had been discovered in Nairobi signed by "Kenyan friends of China" in which all the leading members of the government are called "imperialist puppets." That the Maoists had a hand in the document soon became known. In late June [1967] the Kenyan government declared China's charge d'affaires in Kenya "persona non grata" and demanded that he leave the country. The Kenyan government noted at the same time that it was studying the question of severing diplomatic relations with the CPR in connection with criticism by the Chinese embassy personnel of the state bodies in Kenya.[18]

A second such episode involved Tunisia. Here, "as a result of unceasing attacks on the Tunisian Government, insults and threats from Peking and gross violations of Tunisia's laws by the Chinese embassy, the whole embassy staff was expelled from the country."[19] Diplomatic relations were likewise severed in 1965 with Burundi, the Central African Republic, and Dahomey on grounds of constant Chinese interference in their domestic matters; and in 1966 Ghana followed suit.[20] Serious tension also marked Peking's dealings with the UAR, Tanzania and Sudan due, the Russians assert, to ill-advised Chinese attempts in the heat of the Cultural Revolution to spark separatist movements in these and other countries. Soviet observers further point out that during that period of upheaval, Maoist elements often gravitated toward the local Trotskyite organizations, a development that was especially pronounced in Latin America.[21]

In the end, according to the Kremlin, the Chinese offensive met with total defeat. The ruling circles and the overwhelming majority of the population in the countries that had been the target of Peking's assault rejected the latter's pretensions to exercise leadership of the Third World and Communist China's hierarchy was in short order compelled to take a different tack if it wanted to retain any shred of credibility in these lands and regain its former political status. This time, however, the Chinese expanded the scope of their diplomatic quest and, the Russians now charge, from the extreme of radical exclusiveness swung to the opposite pole of indiscriminately mixing with all sorts of ideologically dubious, not to say utterly disreputable, regimes. In any event, in the next two years (1970-72), China managed to mend fences with a number of African and Asian countries, including Burma, Mali, and Kenya, once again exchanged ambassadors with Ghana and Tunisia, and added 17 countries of Asia, Africa, and Latin America to the roster of states with whom it maintained diplomatic relations.

Yet, the Russians claim, none of this really altered the substance of Chinese policies in this domain; for, while at this stage Peking is bent on displaying a proper public visage, it has not in fact given up its commitment to violence as a stock political instrument. True, Communist Chinese authorities have modified their style somewhat, generally adopting a lower profile, exhibiting greater caution in advertising their divisive concepts, and have even made a few concrete concessions on token issues, such as divorcing themselves from various pro-Maoist cliques in South Africa, as well as in Cameroon and Zaire. On balance, though, if one chooses to believe the Russians, the Chinese continue to conspire with extremist elements in most of the Third World, except that they do it in secrecy rather than out in the open as in the past. Today, we are told, the Chinese leadership veils its real intentions, feigns condemnation of pro-Maoist groups in some countries for those very "putschist adventurist tendencies" that it had urged upon them and strives to cover its tracks, particularly in Latin America, by directing its native sympathizers (for example, in

Argentina, Brazil, Bolivia, and Colombia) to reorganize and publish new programs expressing Maoist views transplanted to national soil.

The chief purpose of the latest maneuver, as explained by Soviet spokesmen, is to fit the current situation (with top priority assigned to the business of winning diplomatic recognition from the governments in power, irrespective of their philosophical complexion), "attract to its [that is, Peking's] side and exploit politically inexperienced youth, the student body and other circles."[22] Pursuant to these instructions, "legitimate"-sounding Maoist committees and factions have recently sprung up in Mexico, Guyana, Rwanda, Jamaica; whereas Chile, Brazil, Venezuela and Colombia saw the proliferation of clubs for the study of the "works" of Mao Tse-tung designed to appeal and cater primarily to students and intellectuals.[23] On the African scene, too, Peking has allegedly followed a "dual revolutionary" tactic: where the local pro-Maoist groups have stood in the way of China's drive to normalize relations with the host countries, Peking has not hesitated to cast them adrift; on the other hand, in the dependent territories, Peking has shown the utmost reluctance to terminate its association with the radical fringes of the major national-liberation fronts and back the dominant coalitions, "in the hope apparently of preserving them [that is, the pro-Maoist contingents] for subsequent use in its hegemonistic policy."[24]

China's recent rapprochement with the capitalist powers, principally the United States, has spelled fresh difficulties for China's already ambivalent performance on the African and Latin American arena. To the Russians, the evidence indicates that the anti-imperialist forces on both continents fear a possible betrayal by Peking of their interests for the sake of ingratiating itself with the Western capitals; the PRC, they say, has irrevocably compromised its image as the implacable foe of the United States; and this dramatic reversal of the traditional roles has, in turn, plunged pro-Chinese cells everywhere into a deep moral crisis which Peking's lieutenants are vainly trying to exorcise by vague promises of imminent revolutionary prospects.[25]

In this case also, it is the Kremlin's contention that the Chinese deliberately sought to promote strife within the ranks of the African and Latin American national-liberation movements and the native Communist parties in order to divert them from a pro-Moscow orientation, wreck their faith in the wisdom of relying on the Soviet Union's friendship and support, convert them into embracing Peking's doctrinal positions, array them solidly behind China, and parlay the investment into a personal bid for global supremacy. Hence, in the Kremlin's opinion, there is no mystery about what motivated the Chinese leadership's current venture in gentility: still, rabid anti-Sovietism, on the one hand, and unbridled chauvinist ambitions, on the other. Presumably, the ploy has proved just as futile on all counts as the companion experiment at doctrinal revisionism.[26]

Leadership of "International Democratic Organizations"

Party warfare coincided with a carefully orchestrated Chinese campaign to seize control of various so-called international democratic organizations, through the technique, among others, of resorting to nakedly racist arguments based on the theme of a coalition of "colored" and "poor" peoples against their "rich" and "white" neighbors, with the Soviet Union and the European "socialist" states assigned to the latter category. In that vein, in December 1961, at the session of the Executive Committee of the Organization of Solidarity of the Peoples of Asia and Africa, the Chinese representative insisted that the initiative for planning and convening the conference must rest solely with "the anti-imperialist people's organizations of Asia, Africa and Latin America, and not the organizations of other regions." He then demanded that the USSR not send a delegation to the conference. Next, at the preparatory meeting of the Conference of Journalists of the countries of Asia and Africa in Djakarta, the Chinese delegation objected against full participation in the work of the session by representatives of the Soviet Asian republics. "At the third Afro-Asian solidarity conference held in February 1963 in Moshi (Tanzania) the Chinese for the first time clearly stated Peking's intention (in conversation between the Chinese delegation and Soviet representatives) of trying to exclude the USSR from the Afro-Asian solidarity movement."[27] The Maoists took the same line at subsequent international conferences, in particular in Nicosia at the session of the Executive Committee of the Organization of Afro-Asian Solidarity (September 1963) and at the Ninth World Conference for the Prohibition of Atomic and Hydrogen Weapons in Hiroshima (August 1963).

Such incidents continued to multiply. At the fourth session of the Organization for Economic Cooperation of the Countries of Asia and Africa (Karachi, December 1963), Chinese spokesmen opposed granting membership to Uzbekistan. At the following session, in May of 1966, in Rabat, the Chinese called for the expulsion of representatives of the Soviet Asian republics who were attending as observers. When in April 1964, the representatives of 22 states of Asia and Africa met in Djakarta to discuss preparations for the Second Afro-Asian Conference, several states advocated issuing an invitation to the Soviet Union, reportedly in recognition of its record as consistent purveyor of huge amounts of aid to the Afro-Asian nations; the Chinese delegation attacked the proposal and threatened to quit if the suggestion were not withdrawn by its sponsors. The Russians further claim that Chou En-lai's and Chen Yi's subsequent trips to Africa were in large part designed to convince the governments concerned of the correctness of China's position and that when the Chinese leaders perceived that the majority of these countries did not share their view, they decided to scuttle the conference and indeed did so. Concurrently, Peking demonstrated its "chauvinist policy" by its attitude toward the summit conclaves of the nonaligned countries, doing everything in its power to torpedo the second conference arranged for October 1964. When, despite these exertions, the conference opened in Cairo, Peking spared no effort "to hamper the adoption of resolutions, sow suspicion and mistrust with respect to some states and cast doubt on the goals which the countries attending the conference had set out to achieve."

Again, at the fourth conference of Afro-Asian solidarity held in Winneba (Ghana) in May 1965, the Chinese diplomatists directed their main fire not against imperialism and colonialism but against the foreign policies of the USSR and other socialist states, determined to belittle the importance of Soviet support for the national liberation movement on the African continent.[28] The Chinese emissaries at the First Conference of Solidarity of the Peoples of Asia, Africa and Latin America, staged in Havana in January 1966, behaved in similar fashion. When they realized that they could not impose their will in that forum, they tried to hamstring the proceedings and voted against the resolution which endorsed unity of action against imperialism. Peking's bid to subvert the movement of solidarity of the peoples of Asia and Africa from within soon forced the other members to take the necessary steps to safeguard their own interests. Resistance grew to the projected scheduling of the Conference of Solidarity of the Peoples of Asia and Africa in Peking and the Secretariat included the item on the agenda of the Council's pending session in Nicosia. Realizing that they might find themselves badly isolated on this occasion, the Chinese sought to prevent the meeting from taking place, were rebuffed, but nevertheless sent a contingent of observers who used every kind of trick to disrupt the work of the collective until the presiding officer was compelled to have them removed from the premises. The meeting approved transferring the site of the forthcoming conference from Peking to Algiers.

China bitterly denounced the ruling and retaliated by setting up rival institutions operating under its auspices[29] and staffed by emigre elements living on the mainland and political fellow-travellers from splinter groups of national parties in some countries. In flagrant violation of the decision reached in Nicosia, the creation of a Chinese committee to plan the fifth conference in Peking was announced. Along parallel lines, the Maoists captured the Secretariat of the Association of Journalists of the countries of Asia and Africa, although, the Russians say, this left them without any journalists, and in 1966 managed to split the Afro-Asian Writers' Organization and form a Peking bureau.[30] Meanwhile

. . . they continued to denounce participants in anti-imperialist meetings organized by progressive forces from the "outside." Thus, for example, Peking did not take part in the international conference, held in Khartoum in January 1969 in support of the peoples of the Portuguese colonies and South Africa, but sent to Khartoum a large group of "reporters" who, together with the Chinese

embassy staff, distributed leaflets put out by a non-
existent "solidarity committee" and did their utmost to
undermine Africa's trust in the USSR and other socialist
countries and discredit outstanding fighters for peace
among nations.[31]

In the final analysis, the Kremlin contends, the Chinese push
registered no significant gains: the status and prestige enjoyed by
the USSR and its loyal allies in the Third World was not to any measurable degree adversely affected by Peking's activities on this front; the
Chinese side posted no victories of note and, in fact, over the long
haul lost much ground since the Afro-Asian audience soon saw through
the duplicity of the Chinese stratagem, correctly understood the selfish-
ly nationalistic impulses motivating the scheme, and henceforth successfully resisted Chinese attempts to manipulate their interests and
precipitate a crisis between them and the socialist camp.

Use of Aid and Trade

Finally, we have the heated controversy over the role of aid and
trade in foreign affairs and the uses to which China has supposedly
put this item in pursuit of its political goals in Africa and Latin America.
Even in conceptual terms, the protagonists stand miles apart on this
issue. The Soviets, able to deliver impressive quantities of foreign aid
and eager to capitalize on the advantage they have over the Chinese in
this respect, have, as already mentioned, pressed the formula of the
"noncapitalist path of development" to solve the problems of the Third
World countries, a blueprint which couples the maxim of intimate
cooperation with the socialist states with the dogma of the priority of
consummation of a thorough socio-economic revolution in conjunction
with the task of erecting the foundations of a socialist community.
Both propositions clearly favor Russia over China. To compensate for
the apparent handicap, the Chinese have riposted by stressing the
theme of the centrality of the factor of political power in the equation
and relegating the other ingredients, including the economic component,
to an ancillary position.
Not only does this approach help provide a doctrinal rationale for
China's abstention from engaging in a contest with the USSR to match
the volume of the latter's foreign aid traffic; but it has also allowed
Peking to justify structuring its program differently, since presumably
its objectives in this domain are not identical to Moscow's. Hence,
the Russians emphasize the scale and tenor of their economic assistance
operations in the Third World, accentuating their physical scope and
functional thrust that cumulatively are calculated to transform the very
fabric of the recipient countries. The Chinese instead have preached
the superiority of political weapons in achieving the desired meta-
morphosis, plus the inherent virtues of self-reliance, and treated

economics as a subsidiary sphere in which they would contribute what they can afford but need not invest heavily or concentrate in the classical Marxist pattern on specific types of projects falling within the so-called key industrial sectors in the expectation that progress here would shape the final denouement.[32]

It is interesting to note in this connection that, unlike most Western analysts who see at least some evidence of a direct correlation between the magnitude of foreign aid disbursements and the quantum of influence wielded by the donor power as a result, Soviet commentators outwardly attach no importance to size as such and have no compunctions at all about drawing invidious comparisons between how much economic assistance the USSR has furnished the Third World countries and the little that the Chinese have thus far dispensed. Whether motivated by sincere conviction or sheer expediency (since the pitch happens to fit practice so neatly), the Kremlin's mouthpieces persist in contrasting the gross amount of Soviet foreign aid with the limited dimensions of the corresponding Chinese effort without once feeling called upon to alibi Moscow's performance from the charge that at a sufficiently high level of intensity the device might become a potent political lever nor, of course, do they give credit to the Chinese regime for perhaps wanting to eschew the danger of such an imputation by keeping its outlay within modest proportions.

The Russians also jibe at several other aspects of the Chinese record in this realm. For one, they accuse the Chinese of willfully slandering Soviet aid policy by equating it with the "help" extended by the capitalist nations and describing both as crassly egotistical and viciously exploitative. According to Moscow, Peking is guilty of "distorting the nature of Soviet assistance to developing countries, belittling its significance and discrediting its noble internationalism" in order to malign "the Soviet Union and isolate the national-liberation movement from it and then to play up China's importance for the destinies of the developing countries and make it easier for the Mao group to achieve its hegemonic aims."[33] To believe the Soviet accounts, the Chinese did not even flinch at resorting to racial arguments to accomplish their ends: in their zealous courtship of the Japanese and blind hatred for the USSR, China's officials on their visits to Africa reportedly let no occasion slip by to lecture their hosts that "if you need technical aid, it is best to apply to Japan, for it is an Asian country."[34]

Next, logically enough, they pillory the Chinese leaders for the kind of aid China has been granting, pointing out that in most cases the Chinese have built only small industrial enterprises and a few schools, bridges and motor roads. Under these circumstances, the Russians claim, the African countries derived no benefit from Peking's assistance in seeking to create their own industrial capacity and escape from economic bondage to "monopoly capitalism."[35] Indeed, the reverse is said to be true: Peking's attempt "to prevent the developing countries from utilizing international experiences in building the new society [that is, Soviet emphasis on the primacy of industrial growth]" operates to doom "them to dependence on advanced capitalist countries, and, in view of the current scientific and technical revolution, to maintaining and even widening the gap separating them from the advanced states and retaining poverty and backwardness in the 'Third World'."[36] We are told, however, that the Chinese are not unduly disturbed by this prospect; for their chief concern lies in identifying themselves in the public eye with the popular appetite for consumer goods and in this way gaining maximum visibility in return for a limited cash investment. Hence, the intrinsic viability of the African states is furthest from their mind as they address themselves instead to egregious political considerations and concentrate on trying to please the crowds and sway their sentiments by forging a widespread image of China as a provider of the items they require in daily life and associate with a better standard of existence and increased creature comforts for the average man, thereby acquiring a potential friend in every household.

Yet, major Chinese technical projects have not proved immune from harsh criticism either. The Tanzam railroad is a prime example. The Russians cite African scepticism about how sound the whole scheme is, unhappiness with the schedule of repayment of the loan, and uneasiness over the implications of the Chinese declaration that African laborers could not be used for construction work but that 100,000 Chinese had to be brought in from the mainland for that purpose, a clausula which, Moscow asserts, now has the Africans guessing as to whether China's real plans envisage building a railroad or occupying the two countries involved.[37]

Another feature of the Chinese foreign aid program in Africa has also come under fire. Earlier, the Chinese government had announced eight principles which it would apply in extending economic assistance to developing countries, among them the rule that Chinese specialists posted abroad would receive the same wages as local personnel of comparable skill. In the West, observers of the scene concluded that the Chinese attitude won them considerable sympathy in native circles. The Russians, though, look at the matter quite differently. In their estimation:

> The given principle has no practical economic significance for the developing countries. On the contrary, by idealizing a low standard of living, it has a disrupting effect on their economy, for it causes an outflow of highly qualified cadres from the country. The main aim of this "principle" lies in the desire to slander the work, the way of life of the specialists from the USSR and the other socialist countries, and undermine the economic cooperation between the developing countries and the socialist commonwealth in general.[38]

Finally, the Russians assail the Chinese for blatant use of foreign aid for political purposes. The list of charges is long: employing the mechanism of economic assistance to exert political pressure; rendering economic aid with the sole aim of putting the countries of Africa and Asia under China's influence; making the implementation of such help conditional on the attitude and behavior of the recipient governments; creating — by building roads and industrial enterprises, supplying arms and sending in Chinese specialists — strongpoints for themselves in African countries; tying offers of aid to demands that the prospective beneficiary publicly denounce "Soviet revisionism," as in the case of the Zimbabwe African People's Union.[39]

Soviet sources document the indictment with concrete illustrations. For example, it is clear to Moscow that when in 1964 Peking loudly publicized its decision to furnish credits to various African states, it was counting on gaining their support in connection with the current preparations for holding the Second Afro-Asian Conference in Algiers. Relatively large loans were promised to Algeria, Guinea, the UAR, Somalia, the Central African Republic and Congo (Brazzaville); but, says the Kremlin, the Chinese authorities then proceeded to execute these agreements selectively — depending on whether or not the leadership of the particular country endorsed the Chinese plans and the basic Maoist formulations. Presumably, that is the reason why, among others, the credit to the UAR in the amount of $80 million in practice was never applied, and the industrial objectives which it was intended to finance remained undefined. Similarly, in June 1967, China offered the UAR a free gift of $10 million in hard currency and shipment of 100,000 tons of wheat to demonstrate Chinese sympathy for the Arab peoples who had been the "victims of an aggression." As it turned out, the gesture in no sense stemmed from "internationalist motivations," since Peking subsequently cancelled the offer because, reportedly, the position adopted and maintained thereafter by the UAR at the Khartoum meeting of Arab heads of governments did not suit the Chinese hierarchy.[40] Kenya shared a like fate. Again, China ostensibly did not keep her promise to grant Kenya a $3 million loan and stayed silent on the subject of the $15 million interest-free loan she had pledged: "The Chinese have withheld credits on the pretext that the Kenyan Government has forbidden the Chinese to pursue their activities in Kenya. . . . Instead of sending text-books and technical literature, the Chinese persisted in dispatching Mao's works."[41]

At the height of the Cultural Revolution, the political character of China's economic presence in Africa became even more pronounced. Peking zeroed in on a few countries identified by their "socialist orientation" (Tanzania, Zambia, Guinea, Congo [Brazzaville], Mali and some others) and lavished attention on them in the hope, we are told, of transforming these "elite" units into strategically located springboards for the expansion of its operations on the African continent, for example, continuing its penetration of the local national-liberation movements, prevailing on the states concerned to change their policy toward the events in Nigeria and back Biafra's secession, and so forth. In 1969-71, China signed a new series of economic agreements with its African socialist partners, plus Mauritania, so that by 1971 approximately 60 percent of Chinese aid to the Third World was earmarked for the latter's socialist contingent in Asia and Africa. The bulk of the industrial installations completed by the Chinese also fell to their lot. According to the Russians, the Tanzam railroad was no accident or altruistic venture either: Peking was well aware of Tanzania's geographic accessibility to China, its value as a corridor for infiltrating Africa's heartland, its importance in light of the closure of the Suez Canal, and its potential advantages as a stepping-stone for establishing a foothold in Zambia and thence spreading out into Central and South Africa. With so much at stake, it is no wonder that the project ranks near the top of China's diplomatic agenda.[42]

In the aftermath of the Cultural Revolution, Peking adapted its style to the requirements of the latest drive to normalize relations with the rest of the world; but trade and economic aid were still slated to fulfill a subservient function to the political exigencies, except that this time rather than dramatizing China's ideological radicalism, they were expected to whitewash China's tarnished reputation and convey an impression of benevolence and decorum. In Latin America, for instance, where Peking today sets itself the task of securing official recognition by the existing governments, a Chinese trade delegation toured Chile and Peru in April-May 1971, and negotiated a commercial agreement and protocol, the first such arrangements in the history of Sino-Latin American relations, not counting Cuba. In June 1971, a Peruvian trade delegation and Peru's Minister of Fisheries visited China. The parties concluded a trade protocol and consented to exchange trade missions. Commercial contacts are also developing with Ecuador and Mexico, and there have been press reports of negotiations with Guyana reflecting China's interest in purchasing bauxite and aluminum. Moscow attributes the sudden surge to the impact of the Sino-American rapprochement which encouraged the capitalist circles of Latin America to hasten to assure themselves of a slice of the Chinese market and exuberantly welcome Chinese business since China was no longer persona non grata in Washington.[43]

In South Africa, too, the Russians accuse the Chinese of mixing politics and economics: the alleged price of large-scale Chinese military cooperation with the South African Republic and the Portuguese colonial authorities is a vigorous, albeit surreptitious, trade flow funneled, respectively, through Hong Kong and Macao.[44] Peking's vehement denials regarding the whole affair are shrugged off or branded a routine propaganda trick.

One last form of economic aid deserves to be mentioned at this point — the crude, direct, but time-honored and often effective medium of recourse to private bribery. The Soviets claim that the Chinese have tried to avail themselves of this technique on at least two occasions. At the Nicosia session of the Council of the Conference of Solidarity of the peoples of Asia and Africa, so the story goes, Peking's emissaries unceremoniously attempted to suborn some delegates.[45] In a second episode, one of the participants in the 6th session of the Council of Afro-Asian solidarity (Algiers, March 1964) has apparently revealed that the Chinese delegation offered him a large sum of money if he would vote with it. When he asked on what issue he was expected to share its point of view, the answer was: "You do not have to know that, just vote along with us. "[46]

At any rate, whatever the stratagem employed, the Russians insist that all Peking's efforts to further its political designs through resort to economic indulgences ended in failure, whether the Chinese had sought to win positive concessions for themselves or merely tried to alienate the countries concerned from the socialist camp headed by the USSR, or endeavored to promote their own theories and practices in these regions or simply essayed to induce the local regimes not to follow in the Kremlin's tracks or put their trust in the Soviet prospectus.

Conclusions

Now that we have taken stock of the inventory, what does all this data mean and what light, if any, does it shed on the subject of how at least one great power perceives and appreciates the techniques of acquiring and wielding international influence associated with the behavior of a competitor state and the degree of success chalked up for this experiment, in the process unwittingly betraying its own set of assumptions and biases in that connection. Or, as often happens in such situations and, I am afraid, is also true in this instance, is the scenario too ambiguous to lend itself to a neat and positive interpretation? Indeed, the latter problem is particularly troublesome in the present case, when one realizes that Soviet spokesmen throughout prudently avoid either defining influence or spelling out the mechanics of winning and exerting influence as a regular utensil of diplomatic strategy or tactics. Rather, the approach always boils down to the staple, common-sensical proposition that "everybody knows what constitutes influence [on the principle that if nailing the phenomenon down may be a ticklish task in the abstract, recognizing the article in daily life poses no challenge to a person of even average intelligence] and can tell when influence is being applied to achieve certain desired ends." Under the circumstances, systematic evaluation of the record runs into considerable difficulty in that the relevant evidence turns evasive and ambivalent, and the attendant reasoning sorely lacks the requisite quality of consistency and sustained coherence in the use of the operative concepts and syntax.

One can, of course, look at the stylistic side of the script and, noting the intensity and persistence of Soviet criticism of Peking's performance on this score, arrive at the conclusion that Moscow was indeed gravely worried about the concrete effects of the Peking regime's activities in Africa and Latin America in terms of ability to translate these inroads into a practical capacity to exercise influence and control over the local decision-making process. While the approach would hardly qualify as scientific analysis and, in fact, would owe nearly everything to instinctive impression, this sort of artful criterion is common enough to the field of Sovietology and can sometimes help clarify the picture when more routinized methods are useless, because the store of available data is sparse or the testimony is contradictory. Judged by these standards, the above verdict would not be unreasonable and has much to recommend it, provided, I repeat, that the investigation concentrate on what may be called the atmospherics of the case.

The alternative is to focus on substantive issues, and then a quite different perspective emerges. Here, the overwhelming illusion is that the Soviets deal only in trivialities, generalities, and abstractions. They postulate that the Chinese are pursuing sundry strategic objectives without bothering to prove the veracity of the assertion — and proceed to enumerate a host of random incidents which are intended to demonstrate that Peking is energetically working to achieve these grandiose goals — again, without elucidating how the individual steps will accomplish the designated ends. In other words, Soviet spokesmen never address themselves to the salient problem of tracing the operational linkage between a specific tactical initiative and the overall blueprint hinging on the key question of what a given move may be expected to contribute toward fulfilling the desideratum of increasing the quantum of influence/control that China can mobilize in these countries. Between vague attributions of visionary aspirations and scattered references to occasional samples of ad hoc behavior and absent a middle range of staple political fare, the whole story sounds like a wild goose chase — intangible, artificial and implausible — so that perusing the script leaves one with the curious feeling of having just witnessed a magnified tempest in a teapot, a spectacular verbal hurricane, or a strenuous bout of shadow boxing, experiences with remarkable little solid texture or content.

Perhaps that is where the true answer resides after all. Consider for a moment the implications of this statement by a Soviet author:

Many peculiarities of Peking's current tactics on the international arena are accounted for by the following circumstances. The far-reaching plans and ambitions of the leaders of present-day China in the province of international politics are in manifest contradiction with the real possibilities of their realization. This concerns in the first place the economic potential of the country, to say nothing of factors of a moral-political character, which impose definite limitations on Peking's hegemonial inclinations. It would seem that this is precisely what impels the Chinese leaders to search for some other techniques by means of which they count on accelerating already at the present stage the execution (even if not on a full scale) of their Big Power designs.

Peking's foremost strategic conception rests on the notion of transforming China, by means of various types of political combinations and alignments, primarily with the imperialist circles, into a separate, independent power center and pole of attraction, capable of exerting if not a decisive, at least a rather considerable influence on the international situation. In the name of what purpose then? As long as China's position is still relatively weak, it is imperative to freeze, so to speak, the present international situation, prevent the positive resolution of pending world problems — such, apparently, is the calculation of the Maoists which casts some light on their current foreign policy tactics. The Peking leaders assume that, in the future, in step with the consolidation of China's position, they will acquire greater real possibilities to steer the settlement of these problems into channels more propitious to themselves.[47]

Another Soviet commentator echoes the theme, with a slight, but significant, twist aimed at driving home the point that the mere "fact that Peking, by exploiting the 'theory of intermediary zones,' hopes to occupy a leading position in the 'Third World,' causes the Western powers little worry," for reasons that, "taking into account China's inadequate economic potential, they simply do not believe in such a contingency."[48]

Accepting this assessment at face value (and I see no grounds for acting differently), the inferences are fairly obvious. If among Western statesmen the imminent prospect of China seizing control of the Third World galaxy enjoys no credibility whatever, why should the men in the Kremlin embrace the opposite view, especially since their own spokesmen put so much stress throughout on the gaping disparity between the goals the Chinese seemed to pursue in Africa and Latin America and the resources they could afford to plow into the venture, between the size of the Chinese investment and the meager dividends which accrued to them in spite of the sustained effort, between the vigor with which the Chinese pushed the project and the long string of defeats and setbacks which crowned their labors. My personal feeling is that the Soviet hierarchy in fact does not consider that China poses an immediate threat to its interests in Africa and Latin America in the sense of possessing the capability to wield preemptive influence or absolute control vis-a-vis a significant segment of the states concerned, notwithstanding its impassioned oratory on the subject. The motives for

engaging in fierce competition with China on this front must therefore
lie elsewhere — in the shadowy realm of the psychology of one-upmanship,
ideological intolerance, status or stardom complex, and sundry other
incorporeal impulses. These are easy enough to imagine, even if they
are difficult to quantify or rationalize.

At any rate, the mystique that attaches to the rank of a superpower, for example, almost automatically spells an urge to get involved
in every political contest that may arise, irrespective of its intrinsic
merits or relevance or the prize at stake in the game. The incident
alone of China immixing itself in the affairs of Africa, Latin America,
or any other corner of the globe, no matter how marginal the bid in scope
or impact, would be likely to prompt a countervailing response if for no
other reason than to keep a live finger in the pie. Fear of losing by
default, obsession with the virtues of minimal prophylaxis, commitment
to the frivolous logic of the zero-sum equation, and kindred stimuli,
play an analogous role. Chinese operations in Africa or Latin America
may have no visible connection with the Soviet Union's welfare, but
one can safely anticipate an appropriate Soviet reflex on the principle
of the old cliche that an ounce of prevention is worth a pound of cure,
that since every eventuality cannot be foreseen, it is better to take
advance measures than be sorry later, that any gain for the foe (whether
China proper or, by a process of universal fallout, the imperialist camp)
in itself entails a commensurate disadvantage to the USSR. However
specious these propositions may strike us, the fact remains that they
do palpably affect the shape of human conduct; and this episode, in
my opinion, illustrates the phenomenon in singularly graphic fashion.

The preceding survey has focused on the dynamics of the Soviet-
Chinese interplay in Africa and Latin America. In some respects, though,
the moral of the story may have and, I think, does have a wider application, at least as far as the USSR is concerned, in also determining the
Soviet attitude towards, say, the United States when deciding upon the
style, format, and content of the policies that the Kremlin has, to date,
been prepared to pursue on both continents. The situation may yet
change drastically; but, I would argue, up till now, Moscow has shown
no evidence that it would greet even a major adverse shift in the center
of gravity in either place as a critical development, or rush to redress
the balance thus compromised unless the rescue expedition incurred
not the slightest risk. Admittedly, vindicating the contention is a different matter altogether.

Notes

1. Roots of Chinese Developments (Moscow: Novosti Press
Agency Publishing House, n. d.), p. 67.

2. See M. S. Kapitsa, Levee zdravogo smysla (o vneshnei
politike gruppy Mao), (Left of Common Sense, On the Foreign Policy of
the Mao Group) (Moscow: Politlitizdat, 1968), p. 96.

3. G. V. Astaf'ev, M. V. Fomicheva, "Izvrashchenie Maoistami leninskoi teorii natsionalno-osvoboditelnogo dvizheniya" (Distortion by the Maoists of the Leninist Theory of National-Liberation Movement), in Lenin i problemy sovremennogo Kitaya, sbornik statei (Lenin and the Problems of Contemporary China, Collection of Articles) (Moscow: Politlitizdat, 1971), p. 234. Interestingly enough, the authors now assign (pp. 234-35) to the Chinese the responsibility for the ultra-leftist course pursued in the colonial and ex-colonial territories in Asia in the immediate postwar years:

In 1945-49, with the aid of the Chinese minority, the Maoists dogmatically pressed the specific Chinese experience of revolutionary action on the peoples of Malaya, Burma, and the Philippines, risen in struggle against British and American imperialism. Despite the fact that the Chinese experience was not validated and the insurrectionary movements in Malaya and the Philippines suffered defeat, the Maoist leadership of the CCP in 1949 declared at a series of congresses in Peking that the Chinese path in the national-liberation revolution constitutes the model for many colonial and semi-colonial countries.

In 1950, the Chinese revolution was already proclaimed the "classical type" of revolution for all colonial and dependent countries and contraposed in this sense to the Great October socialist revolution. The latter, in the opinion of the Maoists, could serve as an example only for revolutions in imperialist countries.

4. O. Leonidov, Peking Diversionists (Moscow: Novosti Press Agency Publishing House, 1971), p. 89, citing Rabotnichesko delo (Sofia), August 24, 1970.

5. G. Apalin, "Nesostoyatelnost maoistskoi teorii o 'sverkhderzhavakh'"(Insolvency of the Maoist Theory of "Superpowers"), Politicheskoe samoobrazovanie, 1972, no. 2; antirevolyutsionnom, velikoderzhavnom kurse Maoistov (Dangerous Course, On the Anti-revolutionary, Great Power Course of the Maoists), (Moscow: Politlitizdat, 1972), vyp. 3, p. 114.

6. For example, G. Apalin, op. cit., p. 115; N. Simoniya, Peking and the National Liberation Struggle (Moscow: Novosti Press Agency Publishing House, 1970), pp. 38-39; G. Apalin, "Ideological Bases of Maoist Foreign Policy," International Affairs, no. 6 (June 1968), p. 52; N. Kapchenko, "The 'Cultural Revolution' and the Mao Group's Foreign Policy," ibid., no. 2 (February 1968), pp. 19-20; G. V. Astaf'ev, M. V. Fomicheva, op. cit., p. 255; Vneshnyaya politika KNR, O sushchnosti vneshnepoliticheskogo kursa sovremennogo kitaiskogo rukovodstva (The Foreign Policy of the PRC, On the Essence of the Foreign Policy Course of the Contemporary Chinese Leadership) (Moscow: "Mezhdunarodnye otnosheniya," 1971), p. 99.

7. M. S. Kapitsa, op. cit., p. 96; O. Leonidov, op. cit., p. 98.

8. M. S. Kapitsa, op. cit., p. 90; "Politika gruppy Mao Tsze-duna na mezhdunarodnoi arene" (The Policy of the Mao Tse-tung Group on the International Arena), Kommunist, no. 5 (1969), p. 110, and Opasnyi kurs, Po povodu sobytii v Kitae (Dangerous Course, Concerning the Events in China) (Moscow: Politlitizdat, 1969), vyp. 1, p. 212; G. Apalin, "Peking and the 'Third World'," International Affairs, no. 12 (December 1972), p. 28; D. Vostokov, "Vneshnyaya politika KNR posle IX s'ezda KPK" (Foreign Policy of the PRC after the IXth Congress of the CPC), Mezhdunarodnaya zhizn', no. 12 (December 1971); and Opasnyi kurs, O politike Pekinskikh rukovoditelei (Dangerous Course, On the Policy of the Peking Leaders) (Moscow: Politlitizdat, 1971), vyp. 2, p. 287; M. S. Kapitsa, KNR: dva desyatiletiya-dve politiki (PRC: Two Decades — Two Policies) (Moscow: Politlitizdat, 1969), p. 253.

9. G. Apalin, op. cit. (note 8 supra), p. 28.

10. Ibid., p. 30.

11. M. S. Kapitsa, op. cit. (note 2 supra), p. 109; D. Vostokov, op. cit., pp. 284-85.

12. G. Apalin, op. cit. (note 8 supra), p. 32; V. Rybakov, "China in the United Nations: A Barren Policy," International Affairs, no. 3 (March 1973), p. 52; "Hungweiping View of International Law," ibid., no. 6 (June 1973), pp. 89-90.

13. Compare, V. Rybakov, "Behind the Scenes of Peking's 'Peace Strategy'," International Affairs, no. 11 (November 1972), p. 18; O. Ivanov, "With Whom, Against Whom? A Look at Certain Modifications of Peking Policy," New Times, no. 35 (1972), p. 4; B. Gafurov, "Fifty Years that Changed Asia," International Affairs, no. 12 (December 1967), p. 20; N. Aleksandrov, "O nekotorykh takticheskikh osobennostyakh nyneishnei politiki pekinskogo rukovodstva" (Concerning Certain Tactical Peculiarities of the Current Policy of the Peking Leadership), Pravda, September 5, 1972, pp. 4-5.

14. E. Tarabrin, "Manevry Pekina v Afrike" (Peking's Maneuvers in Africa), Novoe vremya, no. 6 (1972), and Opasnyi kurs, vyp. 3, pp. 228-30; Vneshnyaya politika KNR, pp. 78, 82-84, 86; O. Leonidov, op. cit., pp. 91-95.

15. G. V. Astaf'ev, M. V. Fomicheva, op. cit., pp. 256-57. Also, O. Leonidov, op. cit., pp. 96-97.

16. Vneshnyay politika KNR, pp. 89-90. And, O. Leonidov, op. cit., pp. 97-98.

17. N. Simoniya, op. cit., p. 38.

18. Ibid., pp. 38-39.

19. N. Kapchenko, op. cit. (note 6 supra), pp. 20-21.

20. M. S. Kapitsa, op. cit. (note 8 supra), p. 253.

21. Opasnyi kurs, vyp. 1, p. 216.

22. G. V. Astaf'ev, M. V. Fomicheva, op. cit., p. 259. Compare D. Vostokov, op. cit., pp. 278, 286.

23. Vneshnyaya politika KNR, p. 107.

24. D. Vostokov, op. cit., p. 288.

25. L. Trofimenko, "Peking and Washington, " New Times, no. 31 (1971), p. 10.

26. N. Kapchenko, "Whence the C.P.C. Leadership's Political Line?", International Affairs, no. 3 (March 1967), p. 20.

27. N. Simoniya, op. cit., pp. 43-44. See, too, E. Yu. Bogush, Maoizm i politika raskola v natsionalno-osvoboditelnom dvizhenii (Maoism and the Policy of Splittism in the National-Liberation Movement) (Moscow: "Mysl, " 1969), pp. 77-78.

28. N. Simoniya, op. cit., pp. 44, 47-48.

29. Roots of Chinese Developments, p. 65; Political Profile of Chinese Splitters (Moscow: Novosti Press Agency Publishing House, 1968), p. 39.

30. For example, M. S. Kapitsa, op. cit. (note 2 supra), pp. 87, 99-102; E. Yu. Bogush, op. cit., p. 92; M. S. Kapitsa, "National Liberation and the Mao Group's Splitting Activity, " International Affairs, no. 7 (July 1968), pp. 13-14.

31. N. Simoniya, op. cit., p. 45.

32. For example, see L. S. Kyuzadzhyan, Proletarskii internatsionalizm i melkoburzhuaznyi natsionalizm (Proletarian Internationalism and Petty Bourgeois Nationalism) (Moscow: Politlitizdat, 1968), pp. 38-40, 42-43; Vneshnyaya politika KNR, p. 91.

33. M. S. Kapitsa, op. cit. (note 30 supra), p. 12. In similar vein, O. Leonidov, op. cit., p. 90, and A. G. Kruchinin, "Antisovetskaya liniya gruppy Mao Tsze-duna i antikommunizm" (The Anti-Soviet Line of the Mao Tse-tung Group and Anti-Communism), in Antimarksistskaya sushchnost vzglyadov i politiki Mao Tsze-duna (sbornik statei), (Anti-Marxist Essence of the Views and Policy of Mao Tse-tung: Collection of Articles) (Moscow: Politlitizdat, 1969), pp. 255-56. Compare, L. Kirichenko, "Peking's Diplomatic Game, " New Times, no. 17 (1971), p. 4: "One could only welcome Chinese aid to Third World countries if it were internationalist aid. The fact is, however, that it is aimed at driving a wedge between the recipients and the socialist community to isolate them and turn them into Peking's tools. This is something that runs counter above all to the interests of the developing countries. "

34. N. Simoniya, op. cit., p. 52.

35. For example, M. S. Kapitsa, op. cit. (note 8 supra), p. 169; Vneshnyaya politika KNR, op. cit., pp. 93-94.

36. G. Apalin, op. cit. (note 8 supra), p. 31. Also, O. Vladimirov, M. Kuranin, "Teaming Up with the Reaction, Notes on Peking's Foreign Policy, " New Times, no. 46 (1972), p. 5.

37. M. S. Kapitsa, op. cit. (note 8 supra), p. 269.

38. Vneshnyaya politika KNR, op. cit., p. 94.

39. L. Kirichenko, op. cit., p. 4; E. Tarabrin, op. cit., p. 231; O. Leonidov, op. cit., pp. 91-92; M. S. Kapitsa, op. cit. (note 30 supra), p. 13; Roots of Chinese Developments, p. 68; O. Vladimirov, M. Kuranin, op. cit., p. 5.

40. Vneshnyaya politika KNR, pp. 96-97.

41. M. S. Kapitsa, op. cit. (note 8 supra), p. 269; idem, (note 30 supra), p. 13.

42. Vneshnyaya politika KNR, op. cit., pp. 97, 106-7; D. Vostokov, op. cit., p. 287.

43. D. Vostokov, op. cit., pp. 288-89. See, too, G. Ginsburgs, A. Stahnke, "Communist China's Trade Relations with Latin America," Asian Survey, no. 9 (September 1970), pp. 803-19.

44. N. Simoniya, op. cit., pp. 60-61.

45. M. S. Kapitsa, op. cit. (note 2 supra), p. 101.

46. Idem, (note 8 supra), p. 261.

47. N. Kapchenko, "Vneshnepoliticheskaya platforma Maoizma" (Foreign Policy Platform of Maoism), Mezhdunarodnaya zhizn', no. 1 (January 1972), and Opasnyi kurs, vyp. 3, p. 103.

48. E. Tarabrin, op. cit., p. 227.

10

The preceding essays analyze Soviet and Chinese influence relationships with key Third World countries and regions, and bring into
focus the problems and challenges relating to the study of this important
aspect of Soviet and Chinese international behavior, and of foreign
policy studies in general. These assessments of Soviet and Chinese
efforts at influence-building over the past two decades lay bare the
uncertainties and ambiguities inherent in the nature of relationships
between Communist powers and Third World countries. Differentials in
power are clearly not the appropriate standards for gauging the actual
character of interstate relations; neither are studies of direct interactions, defined in economic, military, political, or cultural terms,
sufficient for making accurate evaluations. The soundness of these
preliminary conclusions needs further testing to ensure their correctness; for, if true — as the contributors here believe them to be — they
have far-reaching implications for the way in which the foreign policy
between a great power and a Third World country should be studied.

A number of observations emerge from the essays. First, the
influence of the Soviet Union and China on the actual domestic and
foreign policy behavior of courted Third World countries has been
modest. There is a substantial consensus on this point, notwithstanding
lack of unanimity on the criteria to be used in determining the existence
of influence. As the essays make clear, the amount and kind of aid does
not appear to make much difference when it comes to exercising influence; the donor can seldom dictate policy to the recipient. In case
after case — Ghana, Cuba, Indonesia, Iraq, and Egypt — Soviet/Chinese
inputs produced gains that were marginal at best and in areas that were
of little consequence to the Third World country. For example, the
massive Soviet military and economic inputs into Egypt during the
1967-72 period did not result in the Soviets acquiring any significant
influence over their disposition. During this period of maximum
Egyptian weakness and vulnerability, Cairo accepted Soviet advice on
how best to use the new weaponry, but it did not look to Moscow to

develop a foreign policy for its new strategic position; nor, despite much fanfare in the press, did Nasser or Sadat really shake up Egyptian economic ministries, practices, or priorities, in line with Soviet suggestions.

Yet the Soviet Union and the People's Republic of China did not give without reason or expectation. The advantages, as the donor perceived them, can be described more in terms of broad strategic-political aims than in terms of tangible increments in the ability to manipulate or manage developments in the recipient country: the great power gives to provide the recipient with options that it believes will redound to its own general regional political aims. By enabling the Third World country to do what it prefers, the great power expects consequences congenial to its own overall interests.

Second, the interpretations in these essays raise serious questions concerning the validity or value of an approach that explains Soviet-Chinese successes in Third World countries in terms of a grand design or Manichean manipulations; and they contravene conspiratorial theories of USSR and PRC policies. The essays reveal that neither of the Communist powers conducts its diplomacy in the Third World according to any preprogrammed track. Rather, they react to opportunities, in pursuit of limited objectives, conscious (especially in recent years) of the constraints inherent in the situation and of the need to adapt means to circumstances. The ad hoc responses do not mean that Moscow or Peking lack a strategic rationale for a "forward policy," but only that the particular response is a function of the specifics of the situation and that pragmatism acts as a restraint on ambition. The tendency of Western analyses to attribute more influence than is warranted to the Soviet Union or China as a result of their inputs derives from a past propensity to minimize the real political independence of new nations and to exaggerate the ability of great powers to bend weaker nations to their will, as in the heyday of European colonialism. To many Western analysts the process was the same; only the source of power had changed. This egregious misreading of the evolving international system is a fundamental shortcoming of Western writings on the Third World.

There is no gainsaying the importance of trying to evaluate the intentions of the Communist powers. To this end, Soviet or Chinese purposes may be inferred from behavior — in default of any more precise or practicable method of actually knowing what their aims are — with due consideration being given to discernible accomplishments. These, in turn, need to be judged on the basis of what is manifested in the behavior of the target country. The focus on influence imposes on the analyst the necessity of basing his judgments fairly stringently on demonstrable causal connections, on linkages between inputs and outputs that require a detailed knowledge of the process of interactions between the great power and the Third World country. It means that contentions about the spread of Soviet or Chinese influence must be proven, not postulated.

Third, there is a premium on linking external behavior to domestic politics and vice versa. The essays show that to evaluate the extent and character of a great power's influence, one must know as much about the domestic politics of the Third World country as about its foreign policy. It is important for the analyst to have expertise both on the policy and behavior of the Communist power under study and on the developing country and region that is the target of Soviet or Chinese attention. Unless this integration of knowledge is achieved, there is a danger of mistaking a presence for influence. Furthermore, the patterns of interactions need to be studied on as microcosmic a scale as possible, the better to discern the signs of influence within the political system of the developing country.

Soviet and Chinese policies seem to have made adjustments to the needs of Third World countries more often than the latters' decisions have yielded to the preferences of the Communist courters. Third World countries followed the lead of the Soviet Union, for example, on Czechoslovakia, disarmament, and the German question, but only because these issues were of no consequence to them. Soviet leverage on issues of importance to the leaderships of countries such as India, Indonesia, Ghana, and Egypt was marginal at best. This strongly suggests that the gratitude of these Third World countries does not convert to any willingness to tolerate Soviet interference in domestic decision-making on key issues. It is as easy to overestimate the extent to which Soviet or Chinese inputs into Third World countries bring influence as it is to underestimate the profound constraints on this influence inherent in the institutions, practices, and political climate of Third World countries. Only through a thorough grasp of day-to-day interactions can we be assured of an accurate chart of the total picture of Soviet/Chinese-Third World relationships that will allow for a proper assessment of the actual influence relationship.

Fourth, Soviet/Chinese-Third World influence relationships are asymmetrical both as to aims and accomplishments; but they do involve a two-way flow. The donor is not unaffected by the courtship. In its quest for influence, the great power accepts limits that are systemic and self-imposed: in an age of near universality of sovereign nations and an international balance of power among the great powers that is kept in stable equilibrium by the threat of nuclear war, there is greater tolerance by the strong of irritating local fractiousness and unpredictability on the part of the weak; and the great powers no longer seek physical possession of areas lying outside their essential security system, thus unintentionally enhancing the flexibility and underlying self-assurance of Third World countries. In situations where a great power invests heavily in a Third World country — for whatever combinations of military, political, economic, and psychological reasons — it seems unwilling to employ its power directly to compel the recipient to do something it does not wish to, in part because of possible global complications with the principal great power adversaries, and in part because of fear of jeopardizing its overall position in the Third World country itself.

Paradoxically, though the capabilities of great powers were never greater, their options in the Third World are fewer and less predictable in outcome than heretofore. For example, on a number of occasions, in Indonesia in 1965-66, in the Sudan in July 1971, in India in December 1971, and in Egypt in October 1973, Third World countries acted in ways that went contrary to what the great power patron optimally preferred and that forced it to accept a new status quo, whose features were not in every respect as attractive as the situation that existed previously.

Fifth, the determination of what data are useful and practical for identifying the existence of influence is still a goal to be achieved. This may have to await the availability of more detailed studies of individual countries, after which we can decide whether certain kinds of data are salient cross-nationally or whether salience is ideographic and has to be established for each country or sets of countries. Also, the essays make clear the need to refine the criteria for assessing influence. In all probability these may turn out to be establishable only within a range of probability. Certitude is no more likely here than anywhere else in the social sciences, but there is certainly room for improvement over present methods and criteria.

Finally, the study of Soviet and Chinese influence in the Third World is in its infancy also because detailed in-depth analyses of Soviet/Chinese-Third World interactions, so crucial to making judgments on the basis of what is actually occurring, are pitifully few in number. To reverse the present trend of an increase in the number of academically-generated works on Soviet and Chinese foreign policy and yet a decreased interest in them on the part of government officials, a trend that must be viewed with concern by all who are interested in foreign policy analysis, a two-pronged approach is called for: first, we need to clarify assumptions, establish the relevance or nonrelevance of data that are available for studying the Soviet/Chinese influence relationship with particular countries, agree on more precise criteria for assessing influence, and formulate hypotheses that are both testable and pertinent to illumining such influence relationships; and second, we must encourage in-depth case studies of Soviet and Chinese relations with Third World countries. Just as a journey of a thousand miles begins with a single step, so, too, do these essays constitute an advance toward a more accurate understanding of Soviet/Chinese influence in Third World countries.

WILLIAM J. BARNDS is a Senior Research Fellow at the Council on Foreign Relations. From 1952 to 1966 he was employed by the Central Intelligence Agency, chiefly in the Office of National Estimates. He is the author of India, Pakistan and the Great Powers and The Foreign Affairs Kaleidoscope, and he has written articles on U.S., Asian, and Soviet affairs for many journals, including Foreign Affairs, Problems of Communism, and International Affairs.

GEORGE GINSBURGS is Professor of Foreign and Comparative Law, School of Law, Rutgers University, Camden, specializing in Marxist Legal Systems and International Law. He is the author of Soviet Citizenship Law and Soviet Literature on Korea, 1945-1970. He has coauthored several other books and has published extensively on Soviet foreign and domestic affairs, Communist international law doctrines and practices, and Sino-Soviet relations.

MALCOLM H. KERR is Dean of the Division of Social Sciences and Professor of Political Science at the University of California at Los Angeles. He is the author of The Arab Cold War: Gamal 'Abd al Nasir and His Rivals, 1958-1970 and Islamic Reform: The Political and Legal Theories of Muhammad 'Abduh and Rashid Rida. Dr. Kerr is a former president of the Middle East Studies Association of North America. He has taught at the American University in Beirut and has studied under various research fellowships in England, Egypt, and Tunisia.

ROBERT LEGVOLD is Associate Professor of Political Science at Tufts University. He is the author of Soviet Policy in West Africa and several articles on Soviet policy in Black Africa. In 1974-75 he is a Research Fellow at the Russian Research Center, Harvard University, and is completing a major study of Soviet-French relations.

MOSHE MA'OZ is Professor of History in the Institute of Asian and African Studies of The Hebrew University of Jerusalem. He is the author of Ottoman Reform in Syria and Palestine and State and Society in Modern Syria.

ALVIN Z. RUBINSTEIN is Professor of Political Science at the University of Pennsylvania. He is the author of a number of books, including The Foreign Policy of the Soviet Union, Yugoslavia and the Nonaligned World, and The Soviets in International Organizations. During the 1974-75 academic year, he is the recipient of research grants from the Earhart Foundation and the Joint Committee on Soviet

Studies of the American Council of Learned Societies and the Social Science Research Council, and he will be a Visiting Fellow at Clare Hall, Cambridge University.

BETTIE M. SMOLANSKY is Assistant Professor of Sociology at Moravian College, and has collaborated with Oles M. Smolansky on a number of research projects relating to Middle Eastern affairs.

OLES M. SMOLANSKY is Professor of International Relations at Lehigh University and author of The Soviet Union and the Arab East Under Khrushchev. He has written extensively on Soviet foreign policy and the international relations of the Middle East.

ANDRES SUAREZ is Professor of Political Science and Director of the Center for Latin American Studies at the University of Florida (Gainesville). He is the author of Cuba: Castroism and Communism, 1959-1966 and many articles on Latin American affairs.

JUSTUS M. van der KROEF is Charles Dana Professor of Political Science and Chairman of the Department at the University of Bridgeport. He has written a number of books on Southeast Asia, including The Communist Party of Indonesia: Its History, Program and Tactics and Indonesia After Sukarno. In 1965-66 he was a Senior Fellow in the Research Institute on Communist Affairs of Columbia University, and in 1968-69, a Research Fellow at the University of Queensland in Brisbane, Australia.

RELATED TITLES
Published by
Praeger Special Studies

CHINA'S AFRICAN POLICY: A Study of Tanzania
George T. Yu

CHINA AND THE GREAT POWERS: Relations with
the United States, the Soviet Union, and Japan
edited by Francis O. Wilcox

CHINESE AND SOVIET AID TO AFRICA
Warren Weinstein

SINO-AMERICAN DETENTE AND ITS POLICY
IMPLICATIONS*
edited by Gene T. Hsiao

SINO-SOVIET TERRITORIAL DISPUTE
George Ginsburgs

———————————

*Also available in paperback as a Student Edition.